Bureaucracy, Aristocracy, and Autocracy

The Prussian Experience
1660-1815

Bureaucracy, Aristocracy and Autocracy
The Prussian Experience
1660 – 1815

By
HANS ROSENBERG

BEACON PRESS : BOSTON

First published as a Beacon Paperback in 1966
by arrangement with the Harvard University Press
Beacon Press books are published under the auspices
of the Unitarian Universalist Association

Printed in the United States of America

International Standard Book Number: 0–8070–5689–8

9 8 7 6 5

TO LENI

Preface

This slender volume is concerned with the emergence of the modern state bureaucracy and with its impact upon social stratification and political power under the *ancien régime*. The inquiry focuses on three coalescing lines of development. Its purpose is to piece together a triangular historical process which ran its course in a society dominated by aristocratic standards and authoritarian government.

I have studied, first of all, the formation and the personnel structure of the new elite of bureaucratic government executives and its character as a professional group. This rising force of powerful officials in an increasingly powerful state made possible the building of the absolute monarchy and the enduring triumph of political and administrative centralization on a large scale.

Secondly, I have explored the relations of bureaucratized state service to status and class and, thus, the nexus between occupation and social mobility. This aspect of my theme deals with the evolution of a professional class into an aristocratic status group. Accordingly, I have attempted to show how the upper grades of the governmental career service, in their quest for privilege, high social standing, economic gain, and public influence, advanced to a position akin to that derived from lineage, landed property, and patrimonial rights of government. Limited amalgamation with the old ruling nobility—the landed aristocracy—consolidated the transformation of the bureaucracy into a social elite.

In the third place, I have sought to clarify the status, outlook, and primary function of the bureaucracy as an authoritarian political group. As such, it came into being to serve the monarchical state and to curb or take away the powers of the old established oligarchies. But in the course of its political career during the era of absolutism, the bureaucracy acquired an *esprit de corps* and developed into a force formidable enough to recast the system of government in its own image. It restrained the autocratic authority of the monarch. It ceased to be responsible to the dynastic interest. It captured control of the central administration and of public policy. At the same time it also prevented the imposition of legal and political checks from below. It governed in authoritarian fashion although, in terms of effective power, its mastery over both the public and the Crown was limited by the resurgent political influence of the landed aristocracy.

In the introduction and in the postscript, I have briefly indicated some of the long-range political consequences of this development. In the case of Germany, with her long tradition of obedience to authority, centralized power in the hands of self-interested groups unwilling to learn the rules of democratic coöperation was particularly tragic. The conservative heirs of the absolute monarchy share the responsibility for the rise and victory of mass dictatorships and twentieth-century totalitarianism.

Even if focused on a single country, a scrutiny of the historic ancestors of contemporary bureaucracy and an inquiry into the regrouping of the governing classes in a predemocratic and pre-industrial order touches on problems which are important for all modern society and especially for students of history, political science, and sociology. The present book is addressed to scholarly readers interested in the study of the bureaucratization of the modern world.

I have concentrated my effort on a specific regional investigation. This is a modest but also a manageable undertaking. I offer an empirical study, limited in time and space. It deals with a concrete situation, Prussia under the Old Regime, and aims at an intensive rather than an extensive treatment. It approaches political, institutional, and ideological changes in terms of social history, and it does not reduce social history to an appendix of economic history. In singling out the Prussian bureaucracy for special attention, I do not describe its activities and remarkable accomplishments as a technical instrument of professional public administration (*Berufsbeamtentum*). Instead, I attempt to trace its grow as a peculiar social and political status group (*Beamtenstand*) and to determine its relations to the Junker squirearchy and to the Hohenzollern monarchs.

To set forth the general problems relevant to my central purpose, it might have been equally profitable to select as an historic medium some other country, such as Turkey, Russia, France, Spain, Italy, Japan, or Argentina. I have chosen Prussia because of my background and training.

The Prussian experience in bureaucratic, aristocratic, and autocratic rulership was exceptional in some respects. On the whole, however, it was representative of general European trends. In consequence, the experience of "the Sparta of the North," as Frederick II called his dominion, throws light upon issues of more universal concern.

For the sake of proper balance and perspective it has been necessary, therefore, to look beyond the Prussian borders in occasional references to different but cognate polities as well as in generalized comments which seek to place the particular within the general and to appraise its significance from a supranational point of view. Thus I have tried to demonstrate the broad implications of area research and, at the same time, to arrive at a better understanding of Prussian-German history itself.

In presenting the results of my labor and in making my points, I have been economical, perhaps stingy, in the supply of factual details and concrete illustrations. Readers who prefer fat to lean meat should follow up the hints and references in the appended notes.

At various stages of my work I have been aided by a grant from the Social Science Research Council and by a fellowship awarded to me by the John Simon Guggenheim Memorial Foundation. I am deeply grateful for this indispensable assistance.

Due to circumstances beyond my control, the publication of this study has been long delayed. Four years ago, a draft of the whole manuscript was read by Samuel Hurwitz, esteemed colleague, devoted friend, and discerning critic. From his comments and advice I have derived great benefit. My obligations to Oscar Handlin are equally extensive. His penetrating observations and excellent editorial suggestions proved most valuable for the task of final revision. It goes without saying that I am to blame for all the weaknesses that remain.

H. R.

Contents

Bureaucracy, Aristocracy, and Autocracy

The Prussian Experience
1660-1815

Introduction

I

All the states of the contemporary world, despite enormous differences in the moral, legal, and material basis of their authority and in the function, efficiency, control, and responsibility of governmental action, form part of a single political order. Everywhere government has developed into a big business because of the growing complexity of social life and the multiplying effect of the extension of the state's regulative functions. Everywhere government engages in service-extracting and service-rendering activities on a large scale. Everywhere the supreme power to restrain or to aid individuals and groups has become concentrated in huge and vulnerable organizations. For good or for evil, an essential part of the present structure of governance consists of its far-flung system of professionalized administration and its hierarchy of appointed officials upon whom society is thoroughly dependent. Whether we live under the most totalitarian despotism or in the most liberal democracy, we are governed to a considerable extent by a bureaucracy of some kind.[1] This condition represents the convergence of a great number of social movements.

Bureaucratic public administration in the modern sense is based on general rules and prescribed routines of organized behavior: on a methodical division of the integrated activities of continuously operating offices, on clearly defined spheres of competence, and a precise enumeration of official responsibilities and prerogatives. Thus, in principle, nothing is left to chance and personal caprice. Everybody in the hierarchy has his allotted place, and no one is irreplaceable. In the past two centuries, this impersonal method of minutely calcu-

[1] Arnold Brecht, "How Bureaucracies Develop and Function," *The Annals of The American Academy of Political and Social Science*, CCXCII (1954), 2.

lated government management by a standing army of accountable salaried employees has acquired world-wide significance.

In the free societies of our time, nonbureaucratic forms of administration remain important. Even the totalitarian dictatorships make substantial use of nonprofessional agents for policy enforcement, although here bureaucracy is the intolerant and vindictive master of the government. Under fully developed totalitarianism all social activity, including the private life of the individual itself, is the object of public administration. As summed up by Mussolini: "All in the State; nothing outside the State; nothing against the State."

The totalitarian system has produced two novel kinds of professional "public service": the ruling party bureaucracy and the permanent secret police force. They are postdemocratic because they presuppose the ascent of the democratic ideal, officially proclaim its superiority over all competing creeds, and masquerade as the vanguard of "real democracy," of a progressive "people's democracy." They become barbarous when they make organized lawlessness, brute force, and irrationality parts of "normal" government.

II

The modern bureaucratic state is a social invention of Western Europe, China's early civil service notwithstanding.[2] Aside from its administrative system, nothing so clearly differentiates the modern state from its predecessor as the legitimate monopoly of physical coercion, the vast extent of the central power, and the distinction between public and private pursuits, interests, rights, and obligations.

Incipient, though largely ephemeral, features of this new type

[2] See E. A. Kracke, Jr., *Civil Service in Early Sung China 960–1067* (Cambridge, 1953). Max Weber still offers the most penetrating generalized discussion of the major problems of the evolution of the modern bureaucratic state. See *From Max Weber: Essays in Sociology* (New York, 1946), 196–244; and his *Staatssoziologie*, ed. Johannes Winckelmann (Berlin, 1956). See also Robert K. Merton *et al., Reader in Bureaucracy* (Glencoe, 1952), 11–47, 114–135; Joseph A. Schumpeter, *Aufsätze zur Soziologie* (Tübingen, 1953), 6–22, 111–118; William E. Mosher and J. Donald Kingsley, *Public Personnel Administration* (New York, 1941), 3–13; Reinhard Bendix, *Higher Civil Servants in American Society* (Boulder, 1949), 1–12, 69–88.

of state evolved during the half millennium of inconclusive struggle which marked the transition from feudal to bureaucratic forms of political organization. Genuine bureaucratic elements and some seemingly "modern" characteristics of governmental administration crystallized within the Occidental feudal monarchies, after they had appeared and receded in the Byzantine and Saracen polities.[3]

The emergence of nuclei of a literate class of appointed professional administrators accompanied the rise of centralized institutions. Most notable was the reorganization of royal household government, as carried out in the kingdom of Sicily under Roger II (1101–1154) and Frederick II (1208–1250), in the English monarchy after the Norman Conquest, and in the French royal demesne during the thirteenth and fourteenth centuries. Social experimentation was instigated to increase the personal power and profit of forceful and imaginative rulers.

These reforms entailed the establishment of new, central, bureaucratic bodies in finance, administration, and justice such as the famous Exchequer and Chancery in England and the *parlement, chambre des comptes* and *cour des aides* in France. These innovations were associated with the employment of more efficient methods in the management of the king's estate and the introduction of improved techniques in revenue administration. On the local level, the growth of the effective power of the reconstructed royal court (*curia regis*), insofar as it was exercised through centrally controlled professional personnel, was symbolized by the royal itinerant justices in England and by the *baillis* and *sénéchaux* of the French king.

As the new administrative departments and field offices were nothing but special parts of the king's personal organization, so no

[3] For what follows, see Erich Caspar, *Roger II (1101–1154) und die Gründung der normannisch-sicilischen Monarchie* (Innsbruck, 1904), 288–327; Heinrich Mitteis, *Der Staat des Hohen Mittelalters*, 3rd ed. (Weimar, 1948), 422–426, 430–460, 499–512; Marc Bloch, *La société féodale. Les classes et le gouvernement des hommes* (Paris, 1949), 214–222; Thomas Frederick Tout, "The English Civil Service in the Fourteenth Century," in his *Collected Papers* (Manchester, 1934), III, 194–221; S. B. Chrimes, *An Introduction to the Administrative History of Medieval England* (Oxford, 1952), 33ff., 150ff., 221–22; G. R. Elton, *The Tudor Revolution in Government* (Cambridge, England, 1953), 1–40, 370ff., 424–25.

distinction was made between household and other officials. The dynastic court remained the center of initiative and decision. Management of the ruler's affairs meant administration in and through his household. In consequence, the rising bureaucrats belonged to the same category of servitors as the domestic servants. Originally, like the king's cooks, scullions, grooms, and valets, they were amenable to their master's will and dependent upon the pleasure of their employer. In fact, however, they formed a special group within the household staff, distinguished by their education, special skills, and superior functions.

These clerks, accountants, secretaries, judges, and councilors were in charge of delegated executive tasks. Whether they sprang from the ecclesiastical order or from the secular bourgeois, they were men who had studied in the schools. Through this permanent body of trained professionals, learning became important for large-scale government. In contrast to their deceptive legal status as dynastic underlings, these technicians enjoyed a good deal of discretion in their work and, as a rule, permanent tenure. Living mainly on fees and other perquisites of office and securing their jobs through patronage and open or disguised purchase, they were quick to develop a strong proprietary claim to their positions.

The reformed system of rulership through personal servants made the exercise of dynastic authority more effective. But it did not substantially add to the very limited tasks of medieval government. Nor did it signify, prior to the revival of the late Roman-Byzantine principles of *ius publicum*, a departure from medieval concepts of government.

Some kings and princes grew stronger by effecting a redistribution of existing authority, by compelling the contending magnates to relinquish some of their traditional powers and jurisdictions. But the consequent shift in the relations of might and right affected the location and qualitative utilization rather than the nature and functional extent of governmental power.

The medieval central executive concerned itself only with two major administrative activities. Aside from the dispensation of justice, that is, the income-yielding protection of established rights and privileges in the realm, practical government was preoccupied with securing the prince's claims as a proprietor in accordance with the feudal principle of dynastic ownership in countries.[4] The public role of the rulers was incidental to the employment of their power in the service of personal enrichment and dynastic advantage. And since the proprietary principle centered in land and in legal rights over people living on the land, the drive for greater effectiveness in "public" administration was directed toward tightening the prince's authority in his demesne. To be master in his household; to be free in the selection, promotion, and removal of his officials; and to obtain through them bigger revenues from his estate—these were the dominant objectives of the successful princely reformers.

In their deliberate advancement of dynastic jurisdictions, the progressive princely polities of the twelfth and thirteenth centuries were the precursors of the absolute monarchies. But in all other vital matters the pre-absolutist states retained their medieval character and base. The extent of the central authority in "the State" remained highly limited. The personal qualities of the feudal ruler continued to be of cardinal importance for the effective operation of the government. The modern distinction between private and public life was nonexistent.

The proprietary conception of rulership created an inextricable confusion of public and private affairs. Rights of government were a form of private ownership. "Crown lands" and "the king's estate" were synonymous.[5] There was no differentiation between the king in his private and public capacities. A kingdom, like any estate endowed with elements of governmental authority, was the private concern of its owner.[6] Since "state" and "estate" were identical, "the

---

[4] Fritz Kern, *Kingship and Law in the Middle Ages* (Oxford, 1939), 185–86, and *passim*; Joseph R. Strayer, *The Administration of Normandy under Saint Louis* (Cambridge, 1932), 12.

[5] W. C. Richardson, *The Tudor Chamber Administration 1485–1547* (Baton Rouge, 1952), 10.

[6] In the early nineteenth century, the last prominent theoretical defender of this conception was the Swiss patrician von Haller. Incidentally, his doctrines, as expounded in his *Restauration der Staatswissenschaften*, exerted a strong influence on the early ideology of Prussian Junker conservatism.

State" was indistinguishable from the prince and his hereditary personal "patrimony."

It is therefore misleading and lacking in historical perspective to classify the patrimonial bureaucrats of the feudal age and their immediate successors as "public servants" and embryonic "civil servants" in the modern sense. Although they were appointed, professional government executives, it was not their business to act in behalf of the public interest, let alone to equate the public with the general interest. Instead, they were employed to make their master the richest and most powerful man in the country by means of peaceful, routinized exploitation of his private resources and personal prerogatives. This was true even of the Anglo-Norman monarchy, despite England's early centralization of judicial administration on a national scale and her development of a common law.

A number of factors combined to give considerable public significance to the newly created administrative departments and their permanent staffs. Their lucrative activities grew wider in geographic scope. Procedural norms were gradually worked out. Eventually they detached themselves from the court in the narrow sense and partially emancipated themselves from their ruler's personal intervention. Increasingly, too, they tended to employ for their personal ends the authority delegated to them. All these incidents of change were, of course, important to the common weal. The deeds and misdeeds of the practitioners of effective princely government affected the security and welfare of the community at large. These men acquired public power by wielding power over the public. However, this alone was not enough to make them public servants.

In medieval times, the later notion of a public trust, given for a public purpose, gained practical significance and found, to some extent, formal recognition not in the larger principalities and kingdoms but in numerous cities, established as legal associations under a corporate authority and vested with varying rights of self-government. These bodies, acting through the creative leadership of their wealthy patrician governors, devised the rudiments of a modern system of public administration, public taxation, public finance, public credit, public works, and public utilities.[7] Here a managerial personnel arose which, as a group, served the collective ends of their little commonwealths.

Aside from some full-time clerks, accountants, notaries, and the like who formed the tiny body of the permanent municipal bureaucracy, the great bulk of a city's administrative officials consisted of part-time employees, appointed or, now and then, elected, for a definite period of time. Being only semiprofessionals, they were, at the most, semibureaucrats. These men, like the directing and hiring city fathers, did not keep official activity neatly apart from private life. They did not perform impersonal public functions, for, as a rule, they collected and appropriated, in part or in whole, a fee for their personalized services. Their relationship to their local clients was quite similar to the cash nexus that existed between a handicraftsman and his customers. As the artisan was paid for his labor or the product of his labor, so the town functionary was entitled to charge a "just price" for his exertions. But while the management of urban administration remained semiprivate in character, its ownership and control had become public.[8]

Abuse and corruption notwithstanding, a reasonably clear line was drawn between private and public property, private and public buildings, private assets and public funds. The separation of public from private affairs and the disentanglement of governmental authority from patrimonial property found particularly noteworthy expression in the pattern of municipal taxation. The proceeds of direct and indirect taxes, unlike princely exactions, were devoted to objects of general utility. They were employed for the construction of town halls, market places, warehouses, wharves, locks, bridges,

---

[7] Aside from Henri Pirenne's well-known studies, see Richard Ehrenberg, *Capital and Finance in the Age of the Renaissance* (London, 1928), 44–48; and W. Lotz, "Zur Geschichte des öffentlichen Kredits im italienischen Mittelalter," *Sitzungsberichte der Bayerischen Akademie der Wissenschaften, Phil.-histor. Abteilung*, V (1932), 1–7.

[8] For a penetrating and detailed analysis of some of the points touched upon in this paragraph, see Karl Bücher's local study, confined to the city of Frankfurt on the Main, in his *Beiträge zur Wirtschaftsgeschichte* (Tübingen, 1922), 332–344, 359–371.

canals, fortifications; for the purchase of land and forests by the town; for the pavement of streets and for assuring the city's water supply.

All this stimulated civic sentiment: loyalty was attached not to a personal lord, but to a communal entity, founded on association and voluntary coöperation from below rather than on coercion from above. Concomitantly, there developed a new set of civic obligations, as epitomized by the collective liability of all burgesses for the debts of their local *patrie*.

The larger polities of the later Middle Ages were not rebuilt in the image of the pioneering municipalities. Nonetheless, these town governments produced some of the tools and, unwittingly, adumbrated some of the modern ideas of public need and public service which the thoroughly bureaucratized absolute monarchies applied in their practice of public administration at a later period and in perverted form.

The extension of real royal power was not a continuous process in western Europe and southern Italy. It was followed by a secular trend of retrogression. The impetus to renewed and, this time, more decisive growth came a few centuries later, under the aegis of dynastic absolutism. Meanwhile, the Magna Charta, the great palladium of the "feudal reaction," indicated at an early date how evanescent were many of the princely gains. A massive resistance movement against royal encroachments checked the stabilization of an independent monarchical authority which had been sustained by the formation of a civil bureaucracy. But the "feudal reaction" was progressive as well as reactionary. It made possible the triumph of medieval constitutionalism. Thus came into being a new, transitional type of state, in which the Estates (*Stände*) were the cobearers of the central power.[9] This *Ständestaat*, as the Germans call it, was no longer really feudal and not yet really bureaucratic, but betwixt and between.

[9] For a fine summary, though mainly focused on England, see C. H. McIlwain, "Medieval Estates," in *The Cambridge Medieval History*, VII (1932), 665–715. For an account emphasizing the bewildering developments in Germany and central Europe, see Hans Spangenberg, *Vom Lehnstaat zum Ständestaat* (Munich, 1912).

After the thirteenth century, the course of administrative bureaucratization did not halt. There were marked increases in the number and variety of administrative tasks. These were undertaken either by professionals or by "gentlemen" amateurs. For instance, the status and mobility of the labor force and the fixing of maximum wages on a vast territorial scale became objects of central government regulation and supervision. In the English and French monarchies this expansion of state activity was precipitated by the Black Death of the mid-fourteenth century. Similar policies, likewise attendant to the sharp decline of population and the sudden rise of acute labor shortage, were adopted in the Prussian state of the Order of the Teutonic Knights during the fifteenth century.

Bureaucratic officialdom itself continued to increase in numbers, especially in France, but at the same time its political and social position changed. Its members ceased to function as mere instruments of the ruler's will. Slowly and imperceptibly, government by the king in person had begun to shade into government under the king exercised in his name. In fact, "royal household servants," capitalizing on the procedures and strong traditions of corporate action which they had evolved, were the first effectively to limit princely caprice. The bureaucratic "routine, devised to restrain the aristocracy, grew into a check on the arbitrary power of the Crown."[10]

Quite often, and mainly because of the heavy influx of incompetents, this transformation was associated with a lowering of the bureaucracy's professional quality. Most of its members developed, in law or in fact, into owners of government offices. They regarded the authority delegated to them as their heritable freehold. They replenished their ranks, in accordance with the ancient practices of all privileged groups, largely by coöptation, which in practice meant by nepotism and favoritism. Such patronage kept in active government a string of self-perpetuating family dynasties, assuring managerial continuity. Though this official oligarchy developed rules and habits of professional conduct upon its own terms, it exerted its

[10] T. F. Tout, *Collected Papers*, III, 226. See also S. B. Chrimes, *Administrative History of Medieval England*, 151.

energies, above all, to affirm the time-honored rights and customs of the aristocratic power elites, to which it belonged.

Many of the patrimonial dignitaries were noble dilettantes who had snatched up valuable posts as profits arising out of their superior social status. Others, not blessed with high-born ancestors, had found it worth their while to exchange a bag of money for a leisurely place of public distinction. Frequently, these noble placemen and plutocratic social climbers served as members of advisory councils, administrative boards, or collegiate courts of law. If so, they shared their responsibilities with colleagues who, whatever the modes of their appointment, possessed specialized skills, and who did the actual work.[11] The experts were chiefly "hired Doctors" and trained jurists. They took charge of the day-to-day business of central and regional government as a running concern.

Concurrently, the notables, comprising the ecclesiastical magnates, the seignioral lay aristocracy and the patrician governors of the chartered towns, pressed forward their interests and views in defense of their special liberties and immunities. They managed to impose restraints upon both the prince and his councilors and executives. The organizational result of this extremely complicated, unresolved contest for supremacy was the gradual reconstruction of the central government on the basis of institutions, representative of the ruling groups, which were identical with the most affluent and most privileged elements of society. Thus, a sort of coregency developed among the prince, the government bureaucrats, and the notables. Politically, the latter were constituted as the Estates of the realm. Since these associations of local rulers were often divided by intergroup as well as intragroup quarrels, they held only an unstable share in the exercise of the central authority. In numerous instances, however, they succeeded in formally restricting the freedom of the prince to choose "his" servants as he wished. Time and again, they wavered between

[11] By far the best comparative account of the coexistent nonbureaucratic, semibureaucratic, and bureaucratic patterns of public administration from the later Middle Ages to the early eighteenth century is to be found in Gustav Schmoller, "Über Behördenorganisation, Amtswesen und Beamtentum im allgemeinen und speziell in Deutschland und Preussen bis zum Jahre 1713," in *Acta Borussica. Behördenorganisation*, I (Berlin, 1894), 15–143.

organized coöperation and passive or active resistance. Their chief weapons were the techniques of political barter and contract which had developed within the feudal system. But when confronted with acute crises and sharp conflicts over the interpretation of customary law, the estates did not shun the use of violence.

In essence, then, the *Ständestaat* was a corporate-aristocratic form of superficially centralized territorial rulership in which the elite of the patrimonial bureaucracy and the notables were the decisive forces. Both central and local government management were the preserve of a hereditary, pluralistic oligarchy which did not have, however, the character of a rigorously closed corporation. The princely ruler, himself regarded as a superior estate, was a *primus inter pares*. Such a federative government of ill-defined though constitutionally limited and divided powers was the typical basis of statehood throughout Europe from the thirteenth to the fifteenth centuries. Only the political tyrannies of the Italian Renaissance stood apart. Against this background monarchical absolutism arose during the period from the late fifteenth to the late seventeenth centuries.

III

The whittling away of the powers of the assemblies of estates ushered in a new era in the history of the ownership, control, and management of the means of political domination. The emergence of centralizing authoritarianism found conspicuous expression in the partial or total eclipse, as organs of government, of the Spanish *cortes*, the French *états*, the south Italian *parliamenti*, the German and Austrian *Stände*, and the Russian *zemskii sobor*. Their decline was both the cause and the effect of the establishment of a princely monopoly over the central power in the state.

Through this momentous usurpation of preponderant influence, backed up by superior military force, the *Ständestaat* gave way to an absolute state in the sense that the legal authority of the prince was released from the restraints which natural law, rivaling juris-dictions, old-standing customs, and the special liberties of the ruling groups had imposed upon him. In real life, unchecked authority did not mean unlimited power, and the claim to omnipotence was scarcely more than wishful thinking. But despite its pretentious legal façade, at the prime of its development the absolute monarchy was an exacting fiscal and military police state. In accord with the revised ideas of Roman imperial absolutism, the exclusive right to make policy and law and to direct enforcement at will was concentrated in a single individual. The newly proclaimed "sovereignty" of the state was embodied in the person of the monarch.

In politics and governmental administration the abandonment of the proprietary conception of rulership was extremely slow. The differentiation between kingship as a public trust and a personal status advanced faster in theory than in practice. Wherever princely despotism did become the legitimate government, the identification of the dynastic interest with *raison d'état* and *salus publica* was the official mainspring of political integration. In consequence, obedience to the monarch and his appointed designees supplanted, in principle, voluntary coöperation by the old co-owners of public jurisdictions. Even the hitherto independent few—the hopes and desires of the many hardly mattered—were now expected to bow their heads and to take orders.

The rise of centralized domination under the leadership of autocrats, whether kings, princes, prime ministers, or political cardinals, wrought profound changes in the functions of the central government; in the methods of political and administrative management; in the recruitment and behavior of men in authority; and in the conception of the rights and duties of officeholding.

Absolutism also altered the nature of political power. The new state rulers were not content to add to their "patrimony" the traditional jurisdictions of the estates and to absorb most of their functions. They also built a new bureaucratic empire. They raised sizable permanent armies, imposed ever larger taxes, multiplied fiscal exactions. They extended and intensified the regulative and administrative intervention of the dynastic government into the sphere of private rights and local home rule. And they made a place for the Crown as a strong commercial competitor and monopolist in production and distribution.

Thus, the makers of the absolute monarchy did not merely learn to handle old institutions in a new way. They also invented novel and more effective instruments of compulsion. By constructing a large-scale apparatus of finance, administration, and military might operated by a class of appointed career executives accountable to them, they became the founders of a thoroughly bureaucratized state with many strikingly "modern" features. The great political entrepreneurs had the wit to realize that "a bureaucratized autocracy is a perfected autocracy."[12]

An aggressive, methodical, and often oppressive machine of hierarchical state management by dictation and subordination came to prevail over the less elaborate, more slovenly, and infinitely more personal medieval contrivances. Dynastic absolutism itself was only a passing historic phenomenon. But it gave birth to an administrative system which survived to enter the common heritage of contemporary civilization.

The growth of the power of the central authority meant the growth of the power of the executive bureaucracy. Everywhere throughout the formative stage, new, removable bureaucrats and not the "old" patrimonial officials and notables were in the lead. The *nouveaux arrivés* challenged the diehard notion that the privileged should continue to derive the right to govern by inheritance or purchase without special training and without devoting their energies to it exclusively. The power of the monarch to nominate officers at his discretion, unconfirmed by the estates and in violation of ancient usage, and to regulate the functions and status of the incumbents as he saw fit, deeply affected both the practice and theory of government.[13]

The crown's arrogated power to appoint and to remove at will made possible the resurgence and rapid expansion of autocratic personnel administration. The rise of absolutism furnished an important basis for gaining authority, income, wealth, external dignity,

---

[12] Gaetano Mosca, *The Ruling Class* (New York, 1939), 406.
[13] See M. P. Gilmore, *Argument from Roman Law in Political Thought 1200-1600* (Cambridge, 1941), 105ff.; Paul Koschaker, *Europa und das Römische Recht* (Munich, 1947), 167ff.

social honors, and for the extraction of deference from the lower orders. It raised a dependent parvenu elite of commissioned government managers to a position of functional superiority in the polity.

Henceforth, centrally directed executive government was far more ramified than in medieval times. Impersonal relations were to prevail over personal ties, since administrative *étatisme* was growing into a big business. Its operators originated as "dynastic servants." But unlike the professional officials in the feudal states, they were, a few relics of the past notwithstanding, clearly separated from the princely household.

The new bureaucrats were not modern civil servants, but their forerunners. They were dynastic rather than public servants. They served the welfare of the government of the autocratic prince, not that of the governed. The well-being of the subjects was not an end in itself but a means to bolster the position of the government. Nowhere in Europe did the conversion of dynastic bureaucrats into public agents present itself as a serious issue before the end of the eighteenth century. Only thereafter did allegiance to the king-employer as a person or to the crown as the institutional embodiment of authority or to the aristocratic few begin to merge into loyalty to the abstract ideas of the State or of popular sovereignty.

Government bureaucracy and civil service are not synonymous terms or identical concepts. The modern civil service is a special type of responsible bureaucracy. It deserves its name only if it equates the public interest with the general welfare. In reality, during the nineteenth century the evolving civil service elites of the European world showed a strong propensity toward attaching themselves to the interests and ideals of limited groups rather than to "the people" and egalitarian conceptions of civic right and political liberty. The tardy adjustment demonstrated how great was the vitality of the ancient aristocratic societies.

IV

The New Monarchy, as it is sometimes called, modified but did not destroy the confused mass of jurisdictions which had been transmitted from the past. It merely made a start in disengaging public prerogatives from the law of private property, from vested family interests, and from the grip of the possessors of legal, social, and political privilege.[14] The new bureaucrats epitomized this trend which in medieval times had been noticeable only in the cities.

France, the most populous political unit of Europe in the sixteenth and seventeenth centuries, was then the chief model of the absolute monarchy. Here law and political theory drew a sharp distinction between the numerous patrimonial officials, the strongly entrenched *officiers*, and the rising small body of absolutist bureaucrats, the *commissaires*.[15] All the modernized states of Europe, in their own peculiar and fleeting ways, developed striking analogies to this dual personnel pattern which reflected two antagonistic principles of officeholding and the coëxistence of two distinct managerial hierarchies.

The *officiers*, as defined and protected by French law, gave concrete expression to the close association of public authority with rights of private ownership, which the feudal state had passed on to its successors. The *officiers* were holders of administrative and judicial jobs whose appointment had legally to be approved by the crown. Actually, in the course of the fourteenth and fifteenth centuries, when the French *Ständestaat* was built, the purchase of offices was common enough to reduce royal confirmation to a formality. Through this practice the buyer gained a personal proprietary title to a particular *charge* or *fonction*.

[14] See Ernest Barker, *The Development of Public Services in Western Europe 1660–1930,* 2nd ed. (New York, 1945), 4–6.

[15] See Roland Mousnier, *La vénalité des offices sous Henri IV et Louis XIII* (Rouen, [1946]), XXVII–XXIX, 1–71, 495–541, 622–624; Martin Göhring, *Die Aemterkäuflichkeit im Ancien Régime* (Berlin, 1938), 7 ff., and *passim*; Gaston Zeller, *Les institutions de la France au XVIe siècle* (Paris, 1948), 129–145; R. Doucet, *Les institutions de la France au XVIe siècle*, I (Paris, 1948), 403–436; Philippe Sagnac, *La formation de la société française moderne,* I (Paris, 1945), 59–63; J. Ricommard, "Les subdélégués des intendants," in Georges Pagès, ed., *Etudes sur l'histoire administrative et sociale de l'Ancien Régime* (Paris, 1938), 54ff., 96ff. See also Otto Hintze's brilliant article, "Der Commissarius und seine Bedeutung in der allgemeinen Verfassungsgeschichte," in his *Staat und Verfassung. Gesammelte Abhandlungen zur allgemeinen Verfassungsgeschichte* (Leipzig, 1942), 232–264.

Sale of offices on a large scale was peculiar to France. There it grew rapidly during the dislocating price revolution of the sixteenth and early seventeenth centuries. Fiscal expediency accounted for this further growth which was to prove a blight to the public and disastrous to the long-term interests of the "sovereign" monarch striving for supreme mastery. The financial straits of the crown coincided with a strong craving for public distinction. This demand came not from the increasingly impoverished class of noble landed *rentiers*, but from socially ambitious families who had made fortunes in trade, in finance, or in the legal profession. As in the immediately preceding centuries, officeholding was one of the chief means by which men from the middle ranks of society entered the old upper class.[16] All over Europe, the expansion of acquisitive business enterprise gave a fresh impetus to social mobility and to the amalgamation of private and public activity.

The *Paulette* of 1604, named after the secretary of state Paulet, provided a firm legal foundation for the perpetuation of venal authority and the sanctity of commercialized government administration in France. The office was made transferable at the will of the incumbent who in return for this right was obligated to pay an annual fee to the crown. In theory and practice, the office was recognized as a regularly established public function as well as an object of private ownership. It was distinct from an "ordinary" capital investment, since it was a springboard of legal privilege, a secure base of personal power, and often also a means of acquiring prestige titles and noble status. The income derived from it was not so much in wages and allowances as in fees and perquisites. The *officier* owned his post and appendant rights almost like a piece of real estate which he had either bought with hard cash or inherited or acquired as a dowry. He was the "old" bureaucrat and hence a

---

[16] See Jean Richard Bloch, *L'anoblissement en France au temps de François Ier* (Paris, 1934), 74ff., 212–213; Henri Pirenne, "Stages in the Social History of Capitalism," in Reinhard Bendix and Seymour Martin Lipset, *Class, Status and Power A Reader in Social Stratification* (Glencoe, 1953), 514ff.; Frederic C. Lane, *Andrea Barbarigo Merchant of Venice 1418–1449* (Baltimore, 1944), 11ff.

semi-autonomous, virtually irremovable and largely unaccountable functionary with strong regional and local attachments.

The *commissaire* appeared in the sixteenth century as an irregular and more carefully selected representative of the king. He differed fundamentally from the *officier*, with regard to both legal status and political function. The *commissaire* was the new bureaucrat, the official champion of monarchical centralization, and a salaried subordinate, although his emoluments were seldom confined to a fixed stipend. He was a "permanent probationer," subservient to the wishes of his ruler. Entrusted with a revocable *commission*, he was subject to specific instructions regulating his functions and duties, to disciplinary controls, to sudden transfer or dismissal. He was the creature but also the maker and chief direct beneficiary of the absolute form of government.

The concept of the *commissaire* was distinct from that of the *officier*. Historic reality, however, was less precise and more perplexing. Actually the two categories shaded into each other, and sometimes the lines of demarcation became hopelessly blurred. Everywhere a more or less substantial percentage of the rising *commissaires* was originally recruited from the ranks of the old official hierarchy. They were then, literally speaking, "commissioned officers."

From the outset, the power elite of "commissars" was built up, like their age-old competitors, on gradations of rank and permeated with hierarchical conceptions.[17] Their initial political status was that of a mere transmission belt. They were commissioned by the monarch to ensure his sovereignty by curbing or destroying the powers of the traditional leadership groups in general and by working out a *modus vivendi* with the corporate organizations of the *officiers* in particular. They had to make a place for themselves in a neatly stratified and predominantly noncompetitive society, founded on status, unequal rights, class privileges, and the persistent aristo-

---

[17] Throughout this study, save for a few explicitly stated exceptions, the term "elite," designating the holders of high positions in a given society, is used in a purely descriptive sense without normative connotations. See in this connection Harold D. Lasswell *et al.*, *The Comparative Study of Elites* (Stanford, 1952), 6–7, 13.

cratic conviction "that the inequalities which distinguish one body of men from another are of essential and permanent importance.[18] In such a social order, the commissars, loosely scraped together from heterogeneous strata, could not relax until they, too, had arrived.

The long and bitter struggle of these interlopers for dominance in the management of public administration, for political leadership, and for recognition as a superior status group was concentrated on two fronts. They could not attain their ends without putting into their place the old political and executive elites and without effecting their own emancipation from monarchical autocracy.

Nowhere in Europe under the absolutist Old Regime were the new administrative bureaucracy and the time-honored bodies of aristocratic rulership implacable enemies. The upper brackets of the commissar class found their social identity in close interaction with those very forces who as independent *seigneurs* or as semi-independent *officiers* had heretofore owned the means of government and administration. The commissars gained an assured social position and extended their power by infiltration and limited amalgamation, chiefly through holding interlocking positions. Thus they developed into a social elite which was not merely a self-perpetuating official aristocracy but also a highly prominent segment of the nobility and of the plutocracy. Thus they fortified themselves as a political hierarchy. As a group, they grew almost independent of effective royal control in the exercise of delegated administrative and judicial tasks. But in addition, and whether or not they came from the new or the old bureaucracies, the top executives, and sometimes even strategically placed subaltern officials, eventually managed to capture the lion's share in the central power of political decision.

This whole process was accompanied by the regrouping of all the competing governing elites. The principal political result was the subtle conversion of bureaucratized monarchical autocracy into government by an oligarchical bureaucracy, self-willed, yet representative of the refashioned privileged classes. Everywhere, earlier or later, dynastic absolutism was superseded by bureaucratic

[18] A. V. Dicey, *Lectures on the Relations between Law and Public Opinion in England* (London, 1905), 50.

absolutism before the absolute state itself was seriously challenged by modern liberalism.

The transition to the more advanced stage in the evolution of the Old Regime began to be quite conspicuous in France in the late days of Louis XIV, in Russia under the successors of Peter I, and in the monarchy of the Austrian Habsburgs during the reign of Maria Theresa. In Prussia this development did not become clearly discernable before the latter part of the eighteenth century. The main reason for this delay was not so much the fact that the Hohenzollerns were relative latecomers in practicing political integration by coercion, but rather the accident that here princely leadership was nominal only from 1688 to 1713. At the helm of the Prussian absolute state, prior to the French Revolution, stood three men who for long periods ruled autocratically in person: the Elector Frederick William, later called the Great Elector (1640–1688), King Frederick William I (1713–1740), and Frederick II, better known as Frederick the Great (1740–1786).

In substance, but on a grander scale and with the aid of perfected methods, the commissars played a social and political role which closely resembled that of their far distant professional forebears. The bureaucratic managers of the reformed feudal monarchies had supplied the initial kernel of the growing body of patrimonial officials. And the elite of this old hierarchy had succeeded in trimming the discretionary powers of the prince, but had been forced to share the spoils of victory with the large landowners and the urban patricians.

So enormous was the influence of the historic heritage that the absolute dynastic state turned out to be merely another phase in the history of the inveterate struggle for the abridgment of royal prerogatives. As for the social forces in the state, the "modern Old Regimes" were indeed not more than a variation of the aristocratic monarchy, a monarchy dominated by aristocratic power groups of bureaucrats and notables. Related by direct descent to the *Ständestaaten* and the feudal polities, the absolute monarchies retained certain traits of their predecessors. At the same time, however, they were far more centralized and bureaucratized, more active and more strictly utilitarian, more machine-like, more authoritarian, and more efficient in the use of material resources and in the direction and coördination of human energy.

V

The present study deals only with the period from the emergence of irresponsible central authority in the Hohenzollern lands until the triumph of bureaucratic absolutism under Stein and Hardenberg. A new stage in the history of the Prussian polity, its executive hierarchy, its governing classes, and the German people in general began with this remaking of the authoritarian state in constructive response to the triple challenge arising from the appearance of liberal tendencies in German society, the advent of democratic doctrines and aspirations, and the Bonapartist experiment in plebiscitary dictatorship.

For the purposes of this investigation, a basic knowledge of the course of Prussian history and of the social and political institutions of the Hohenzollern monarchy is taken for granted.[19] The technical, legal aspects, the organizational details, and the functional tasks and routines of the Prussian system of public administration have been exhaustively explored under the tireless leadership of two great scholars: Gustav Schmoller and Otto Hintze. Along this line of approach nothing of consequence, except for an interpretative reëvaluation, could be added to the vast literature which already exists on the subject.[20]

[19] For a very elementary introduction in English language, see S. B. Fay, *The Rise of Brandenburg-Prussia to 1786* (New York, 1937). For a more detailed survey, though decidedly inferior to earlier German works, of the complicated organizational structure of the administrative state under Frederick William I and his immediate predecessors, see Reinhold August Dorwart, *The Administrative Reforms of Frederick William I of Prussia* (Cambridge, 1953).

[20] This literature is listed in Dahlmann-Waitz, *Quellenkunde der deutschen Geschichte*, 9th ed. (Leipzig, 1931), and in the 55 volumes of the *Forschungen zur Brandenburgischen und Preussischen Geschichte* (1888–1943). The most outstanding of the older contributions are Gustav Schmoller, *Acta Borussica. Behördenorganisation*, I; *idem, Umrisse und Untersuchungen zur Ver-*

The realistic assessment of Prussian government as a going concern, the analysis of the course of action adopted by its leaders and executives, and the critical appraisal of the historical significance of these policies for society at large still call for further research and thought. Fortunately, a good deal of solid work which squarely meets the still modest standards of the applied social sciences has already been accomplished.

Only in a roundabout way does this inquiry touch on the problems as to how the government was organized, what it did, and why it succeeded in elevating Prussia to the rank of a Great Power. What matters here are the human beings, grouped into social forces, who as components of the upper class gave coherence to the dynastic

fassungs-, Verwaltungs- und Wirtschaftsgeschichte (Leipzig, 1898); Otto Hintze, "Behördenorganisation and allgemeine Verwaltung in Preussen beim Regierungsantritt Friedrichs II," in *Acta Borussica. Behördenorganisation*, vol. VI, part I (Berlin, 1901), 3-614; *idem, Staat und Verfassung* (Leipzig, 1941), 176-348; *idem, Geist und Epochen der preussischen Geschichte. Gesammelte Abhandlungen* (Leipzig, 1943). Particularly relevant for the problems dealt with in the present study are Karl Twesten, "Der preussische Beamtenstaat," *Preussische Jahrbücher*, XVIII (1866), 1-39, 109-148; G. Schmoller, "Der preussische Beamtenstand unter Friedrich Wilhelm I," *ibid.*, XXVI (1870), 148-172, 253-270, 538-555; Walter Dorn, "The Prussian Bureaucracy in the Eighteenth Century," *Political Science Quarterly*, XLVI (1931), 403-423; XLVII (1932), 75-94, 259-273; Herman Finer, *The Theory and Practice of Modern Government* (New York, 1949), 724-740, 794-810; Fritz Hartung, *Studien zur Geschichte der preussischen Verwaltung*; Erster Teil: *Vom 16. Jahrhundert bis zum Zusammenbruch des alten Staates im Jahre 1806* (Berlin, 1941); Zweiter Teil: *Der Oberpräsident* (Berlin, 1943); Dritter Teil: *Zur Geschichte des Beamtentums im 19. und 20. Jahrhundert* (Berlin, 1948); Herbert von Borch, *Obrigkeit und Widerstand. Zur Politischen Soziologie des Beamtentums* (Tübingen, 1954), 118-156.

Next to Hintze, I am particularly indebted to Dorn's study, although his major emphasis is on the functional, administrative aspects of the Prussian bureaucracy rather than on its evolution as a socio-political group. Chronologically, Dorn is primarily concerned with the reign of Frederick II. In consequence, he virtually ignores the preceding rift between the old and the new state bureaucracy. Though Dorn is more critical than his predecessors in this field of study, except for the cautious and restrained Hintze, the lonely and unromantic Johannes Ziekursch, and the naughty but refreshing amateurhistorian Franz Mehring, even he has paid his tribute to the extremely powerful influence of the Prussian myth in German historiography. For a more qualified analysis, see Dorn's *Competition for Empire, 1740-1763* (New York, 1940), 52-62.

entity called Prussia, with its queer and constantly changing shape on the map of Europe. Only one of these elites, the civil government bureaucracy, is the "hero" of the collective "biography" that follows. It should be borne in mind that this book focuses neither on the history of an institution, nor the history of an idea, let alone a chronological narrative of surface events, but on the formation and transformation of a social and political group, as such.

The Hohenzollern monarchy, by virtue of its geographic location and social fabric, was linked both to western and eastern Europe. The culture which previously had evolved in northern Germany was firmly rooted in the Western tradition. There is much, therefore, in Prussian history, including political, administrative, military, and legal developments, which belongs to the common bases of European civilization.

Some influences, such as the role of peasant serfdom, the caste system in the ownership of land, and the stiffening of seignorial lordship in the seventeenth and eighteenth centuries, set Prussia off from western Europe. In these respects, most of the principalities which the Hohenzollerns added to their heartland Brandenburg had already become typical representatives of the central and eastern European societies in the age of the *Ständestaat*.

In the course of her growth as an absolute state Prussia acquired certain traits which, by entering into a peculiar synthesis, gave her a rather singular complexion. The rigorously autocratic practice of "cabinet government," as worked out by Frederick William I and Frederick II; the blending of civil and military administration and personnel; the excessive militarization of social life; and the emergence of "Prussian Puritanism," allied with the political docility and social quietism of orthodox Lutheranism, were deviations from general European trends. They prefigured the far graver detachment from the West, as it developed in the nineteenth century: the alienation from the Western ways of public life and the prevailing frame of values of Western social and political thought. This separation was symbolized, above all, by the prolonged concentration of political leadership in the irresponsible central executive, the adoration of state power, and the far-reaching political and intellectual influence of the irrational teachings of German Romanticism.

Yet, in the basic direction of development under the Old Regime, Hohenzollern Prussia moved in harmony with the other absolute polities of Europe. Perhaps its most distinguishing characteristic was the fact that here, as in Petrine Russia, many political innovations, administrative reforms, and fiscal measures were carried to extremes by overzealous leaders. In "the Sparta of the North" this single-minded extremism was more methodical and more efficient than in Russia. But it also was put to the test over a longer period of time, and as a matter of principle, and moreover, with what came to be proverbial German thoroughness.

The historian benefits from "Prussian radicalism" under the Old Regime. It enables him to point up sharply some major consequences and social perils of bureaucratized monarchical autocracy in aristocratic ages. For, without losing sight of the peculiarities of the Prussian experience, it is reasonable to expect that a study of the manager class of this particular state will throw light upon the evolution of the modern government bureaucracy in general.

VI

At the dawn of the nineteenth century the harshness and soulless-ness of the Prussian system began to give way to a softer and more benignant pattern of authoritarian rule. The administrative servants of the crown finally succeeded in curtailing the arbitrary powers of the king and in making him the political prisoner of the ruling class. In helping themselves, they also helped, to some extent, the Prussian people. But in the midst of this freedom-loving revulsion of "ideal-istic" bureaucrats moving against the moribund state of Frederick II, there appeared an ominous new trend: the flight into a world of dangerous illusions and misconceptions and the immoderate use of high-sounding words.

In practicing the vices of self-glorification and group arrogance, the Prussian bureaucracy was not unique in the nineteenth century. To be sure, its pretensions and its extravagant hierarchism were often harmless and simply amusing. But in posing as the practical incarnation of the social and political teachings of German Idealism; in operating behind a metaphysical smoke screen; in persuading many that public administration was "the" government, bureaucracy "the" State, authority liberty, and privilege equality of opportunity, the Prusso-German bureaucracy made indeed a special place for itself among the governmental services of the European world.[21]

Because of their aristocratic-oligarchic traditions and of their strong vested interests everywhere, it has not been easy, in more recent generations, to turn the bureaucratic manipulators of unaccountable upper class government into public servants, representative of the freely expressed will of "the people" who make up the State. No nation can rightfully claim that it has completed this transformation of masters into agents. In the large European states, the failure to effect this change and the bleak impact of this failure have been greatest in modern Germany, aside from Russia.[22]

The Hohenzollerns and their partners in the seventeenth and eighteenth centuries unintentionally laid the groundwork for the later conquest of Germany by Prussia. Bismarck, a conservative squire and a statesman of moderation and reasonableness, accomplished this feat by developing into a *Herrenmensch* with democratic gloves and by posing as a German nationalist. His bold, dynamic

[21] See Alfred Weber, *Ideen zur Staats- und Kultursoziologie* (Karlsruhe, 1927), 93ff. The emerging pattern of thought, here alluded to, did not become important before the nineteenth century, when it served as a defense mechanism against liberal and democratic movements. Heavy reliance on "bureaucratic metaphysics," beclouding many issues, became a striking attribute of the Prusso-German government bureaucracy. In the Scandinavian countries, where the influence of German philosophy was strong, a similar trend of thought developed among bureaucrats and their admirers. See B. J. Hovde, *The Scandinavian Countries, 1720–1865* (Boston, 1943), I, 206ff., 328; II, 512ff.

[22] As for the Civil Service since 1945, within the boundaries of the German Federal Republic, see Alfred Weber, "Beamtendämmerung?" *Die Wandlung,* IV (1949), 332–339; Ernst Kern, "Berufsbeamtentum und Politik," *Archiv des öffentlichen Rechts,* LXXVII (1951), 107–110; Taylor Cole, "The Democratization of the German Civil Service," *The Journal of Politics,* XIV (1952), 3–18; Theodor Eschenburg, *Der Beamte in Partei und Parlament* (Frankfurt on the Main, 1952), 59–77; Arnold Brecht, "Personnel Management," in Edward H. Litchfield, ed., *Governing Post-War Germany* (Ithaca, 1953), 263–293.

leadership helped to release forces beyond his control. But, typically enough, Bismarck was also, as were almost all Prussian ministers and imperial chancellors, a select bureaucrat promoted to high political office. From its inception until 1918, except for a few months in 1848, the Prussian state was governed by "impartial" career bureaucrats, "nonpolitical" army officers, and landed Junkers. Though members of self-assertive groups, they held the honest conviction that men of their kind were destined to be for all time the natural guardians of the general interest.

In the course of the development of German conservatism from the war dictator Ludendorff to Hugenberg, these habits of mind, deeply rooted, as they were, in the Old Regime, had catastrophical repercussions. The increasingly frantic determination to assure against all odds the subjection of the governed to the will of a privileged minority accelerated not only the transformation of "aristocratic" into "plebeian conservatism," it also made many members of the old authoritarian leadership groups lose their heads. Thus, toward the bitter end and at a colossal cost to themselves and to millions of innocent people, they set out to salvage their political fortune and traditional social position in alliance with the totalitarian Nazi movement.

Clearly, a study of the bureaucratic elite in absolutist Prussia is not a matter of barren antiquarianism. It is concerned with problems which are a significant part of the prehistory of contemporary society.

Chapter One

The Emergence of Dynastic Absolutism

I

During the turbulent first half of the seventeenth century the Hohenzollerns of the small Electorate of Brandenburg rose from obscurity to potential eminence among the princes of Germany by greatly enlarging their patrimony. They became the rulers of a string of heterogeneous principalities scattered across the northern parts of Germany from Poland to the Netherlands. In reality, this merely meant that they possessed the legal title to the dynastic domain in these territories and held also certain customary rights of limited government over polities which until then had been organized as independent *Ständestaaten*. The Elector of Brandenburg had acquired these intermixed, private and public claims almost without military effort and mainly in consequence of dynastic family agreements.

After the middle of the seventeenth century the Hohenzollern autocracy converted a legitimate title to the discretionary management of the princely estate and to restricted powers of territorial government into an illegitimate absolute monarchical authority. The revolutionary break with the old forms and concepts of government gave rise to modern Prussia and thus to a large new state so artificial and so rootless that, long after its adventitious establishment, it remained without a name.

As late as the mid-eighteenth century, it was only in the language of international diplomacy that "Prussia" (*la Prusse*) denoted all the

27

territorial possessions of the Hohenzollerns. In domestic parlance the formula "His Royal Majesty's States and Provinces" was then still in general use. In the official technical jargon, the Prussian "kingdom" was confined to the province of East Prussia only. The "King in Prussia" (since 1701) was at the same time "Elector" of Brandenburg, "Duke" of Pomerania, Magdeburg, Cleves, and Silesia (since 1740), "Prince" of Halberstadt and Minden, "Count" of Mark and Ravensberg, etc. Not before the First Partition of Poland did the "King *in* Prussia" become "King *of* Prussia" by acquiring the western parts of the territory of the ancient Prussians, "the Prussians before the Prussians." These lands had been conquered by the Teutonic Order who, in 1466, had been forced to cede them to Poland. When Frederick II, in 1772, adopted the title "King of Prussia," this did not mean that he was now the ruler of a unitary monarchy. Significantly, in 1794, the General Legal Code (*Allgemeines Landrecht*) was imposed not upon "Prussia" but upon "the Prussian states." Not before 1807 did "Prussia" become the official name of the Hohenzollern monarchy as a whole. Similarly, the agglomeration of territories held by the Austrian Habsburgs had no common name until 1804, when "the lands of the House of Habsburg" became the "Austrian Empire."

Political integration by centralized dictation, on a broad territorial basis, was then a novelty in northern Germany, for the centralized, knightly-monastic state of Prussia, as built by the Teutonic Order in the thirteenth and fourteenth centuries, had been torn asunder in the fifteenth century. Yet, the extensive growth of small-scale autocracy had thoroughly prepared the ground for the advance of despotic statecraft. In "East Elbia," in Germany east of the Elbe-Saale line, local tyranny had been the backbone of the social order since the fifteenth century. The absolute monarchy was built on this foundation. Servile land tenure and peasant bondage by legal status, an impoverished burgher class, crippled municipal liberties, and Junker dominance, therefore, were from the start fundamental characteristics of the modern Prussian system, as cemented by the "three great Hohenzollerns."

This dismal historic inheritance was of recent origin. Prior to the agrarian crisis of the fifteenth century, personal liberty, economic independence, and opportunities for all had been typical of the life of the common people in German frontier society. The "manorial reaction" shattered the free institutions of East Elbia and wrought a radical shift in class relationships. In eastern Germany, as in most parts of eastern Europe, the progressive degradation of the peasantry started in the fifteenth century. Simultaneously, the process of the disintegration of the seignorial system developed further in western Europe, including German "West Elbia." Here the commutation of servile labor obligations into money payments and produce rents approached its final stage as did, except for sixteenth-century England and parts of Spain and southern Italy, the break-up of manorial demesnes into free peasant tenancies or even freeholds.

In East Elbia, the manorial reaction restricted all the desirable opportunities to the privileged few. This entailed a drastic redistribution of the land and a reorganization of estate management which fostered the expansion of old and of newly created demesne farms. The debasement of the status of the peasantry, rural poverty, the contraction of the urban economy and of political burgher strength, and the unrestrained manipulation of village government by the squires were intimately associated with the decline of small-scale cultivation and the ascendancy of commercialized production, based on large and middle-sized units. These trends helped to consolidate the institution of *Gutsherrschaft*, henceforth the great citadel of seignorial coercion.

The Junkers, the reconstituted landed nobility of eastern Germany, profited most from this economic, social, and legal upheaval.[1] Radically changed in personnel and way of life, this reforming class of owners of "knight's estates" (*Rittergüter*) functioned as a highly productive economic leadership group but also as a selfish oligarchy, after having gained control of the agrarian economy as well as of the government. Among the forebears of this aristocratic working

[1] See Hans Rosenberg, "The Rise of the Junkers in Brandenburg-Prussia, 1410–1653," *The American Historical Review*, XLIX (1943–44), 1–22, 228–242; F. L. Carsten, *The Origins of Prussia* (Oxford, 1954), 101–116, 149–164. For a neat delimitation of the term *Gutsherrschaft*, see Friedrich Lütge, *Die mitteldeutsche Grundherrschaft* (Jena, 1934), 195ff.

class were long-established knightly landlords, professional promoters of frontier settlements (*locatores*), and numerous noble *condottieri* immigrants. A few others, who in the pioneering days managed to enter the ranks of the "superior people," had been horse and cattle thieves, dealers in stolen goods, smugglers, usurers, forgers of legal documents, oppressors of the poor and helpless, and appropriators of gifts made over to the Church.

The mainspring of Junker strength was the combination of large-scale landownership with the patrimonial possession of autocratic rights of local government. Local dominance was complete, for, in course of time, the Junker had become not only an exacting landlord, hereditary serf master, vigorous entrepreneur, assiduous estate manager, and nonprofessional trader, but also the local church patron, police chief, prosecutor, and judge. Given to peaceful pursuits since the late fifteenth century, many of these men, in constructive response to the changes in prices, labor supply, costs, and demand during the sixteenth century, had learned to devote their energies to their profitable business affairs. Agricultural commodity production for foreign markets was their chief source of cash income. Their wealth came from western Europe which, throughout the era of the Price Revolution, was a large consumer of east German grain and timber.

The manorial entrepreneurs of East Elbia expanded and grew richer until the Thirty Years' War. Their prosperity was the great exception to the adverse trend in German economic development after the great international financial crash of the late 1550's. For the next two generations, except for Danzig, Hamburg, Leipzig, and some towns in central Germany, commercial stagnation was followed by decline. The uninterrupted success of the Junkers, as an economic group, accounts, in part, for the momentous fact that in the latter sixteenth century the whole center of gravity in German economic and political history shifted more decisively than ever before from the west and south to the east and north, where it remained until the middle of the nineteenth century.

The emergence of the large farmers as the economic masters of East Elbia was an essential cause as well as an effect of important changes in the nature of territorial government and in the forms of political and administrative organization.[2] The age of the manorial reaction coincided with the building of the *Ständestaat* in the east German principalities. Step by step, representatives of the local squires captured the decisive positions. In the course of the Price Revolution Junkerdom reached the peak of its influence in the shaping of territorial state policies, in the control of state administration, and in developing a comprehensive system of exclusive class privileges. Thus, political triumph in its home territories was the counterpart to the consolidation of the squirearchy's economic position as the elite of large-scale owner-producers in German society as a whole.

In the sixteenth and early seventeenth centuries, then, government of, by, and for the landed aristocracy was the preponderant pattern of rulership in the east German principalities. Political status, rights, and freedom were functions of landowning. As in England under the Old Regime, so here, on a more modest regional and economic scale, the body politic was what Blackstone had called a "great corporation," in which the larger landed proprietors were the principal shareholders. As for the various territories gathered by the Hohenzollerns during the seventeenth century, only in the small duchy of Cleves in the Lower Rhineland and in the county of Mark in the valley of the Ruhr were the privileged burghers of the corporate towns the dominant social force in the political as well as in the economic community.

Prior to the rise of Hohenzollern despotism and an "all-Prussian" bureaucracy, the "ruler" of an east German principality was scarcely more than a super-Junker. The authority of the prince as head of a territorial polity was greater than the authority of his fellow squires because it was wider than theirs, but not because it was higher in

---

[2] See *The American Historical Review*, XLIX (1943), 15ff. In addition to the literature listed there, see Friedrich Julius Stahl, *Die Philosophie des Rechts*, 3rd ed., II, 2 (Heidelberg, 1856), 338ff.; Carl Schmitt, *Verfassungslehre* (Munich, 1928), 44f.; Otto Brunner, *Land und Herrschaft. Grundfragen der territorialen Verfassungsgeschichte im Mittelalter*, 3rd ed. (Brunn, 1943), 473–506.

kind.[3] His legal status was indeed superior, although not supreme. Actually, however, he was often the debtor and political prisoner of his aristocratic inferiors. For, in the course of time, the dynastic patrimony, because of princely extravagance, shady financial transactions, or plain peculation, had largely been alienated by the resolute practitioners of government of, by, and for the wellborn.

In the polities of East Elbia, as in all typical *Ständestaaten*, the central government was a government of limited powers. Moreover, its authority was divided between the prince and the territorial estates (*Landstände*), politically assembled, at irregular intervals, in the diets (*Landtage*). These parliamentary bodies, representing the privileged classes, were effective units of power. Legislation and taxation required their assent, and they also possessed independent legal competence. Hence they exercised through their delegates and appointed agents diverse fiscal, judicial, and administrative functions over which the prince had little or no control.

In the east German principalities the will of the landed nobility prevailed. Except for Brandenburg after 1604, when the electoral privy council was founded, the aristocratically controlled legislatures were closely affiliated with the standing executive state governments, the collegial *Regierungen*. The Junkers thus functioned as coregents of territorial government and the more select also as the chief administrators of the dynastic domains and regalian rights. By the early seventeenth century, the squirearchy was on the verge of holding a virtual monopoly of political power.

During the sixteenth century the owners of *Gutsherrschaften* had entrenched themselves as the masters of eastern Germany by occupying interlocking positions of economic, political, and social dominance. In law, they were the most privileged group of the hierarchical and corporative society, as it had evolved since the fifteenth century. Since the Protestant Reformation, the redistribution of the church lands, and the disappearance of an ecclesiastical estate in the territorial diets, they made up the First Estate, the "Upper Estates," in the terminology of the time. Economically, the

---

[3] C. H. McIlwain, *Constitutionalism and the Changing World* (New York, 1939), 50.

landed nobility constituted the plutocracy of the country. As such, it was not a parasitical class, for it supplied entrepreneurial leadership in agriculture, trade, and finance. Politically, the squires "owned" the seats of real power. They were the unquestioned elite and almost identical with the governing class. Socially, they enjoyed the enormous advantage of preëminence, since they formed the hereditary aristocracy which guarded itself against intruders. In short, at the price of keeping the bulk of the population in a state of poverty and servility they had become the rulers of East Elbia. The Junkers were not only the chief holders of power in the economy and body politic; they also possessed the highest social status in terms of prestige, deference, esteem and honor.

This position was rudely challenged when the German borderlands in the northeast became a battle area for the great powers in consequence of the widening conflict over control of the Baltic. Until the great social commotion of the Thirty Years' War, eastern Germany had been free from the scourge of war for more than a whole century, and the military arts and martial ways of living had fallen into oblivion. But invasion, occupation, and exploitation by the imperial and Swedish armies created a host of thorny new problems for the self-assured squirearchies of "Prussia."

The great depression from 1618 to 1650 terminated the era of profitable economic expansion for the Junkers. Not until the closing decades of the eighteenth century were they to experience another big business boom. The dislocation of organized economic life, the chronic political instability, the general confusion of material and nonmaterial values wrought by a ferocious war and by its ugly aftermath weakened the position of the old masters. They were threatened by alien forces which most of them did not understand and which they were unprepared to view within the unfamiliar context of international affairs. Set in their old ways, the vast majority were reluctant to discard time-honored habits and cherished ways of thinking. The more fortunate managed to hold on to their landed estates. But the Junkers as a class gradually lost control over the tottering institutions of the territorial *Ständestaat*. In a society suddenly plunged into a state of flux and exposed to severe shocks from without and within, they passionately yearned, as their East Prussian spokesmen put it, as late as 1678, for the restoration of their "still unforgotten blissfulness, liberty, and peaceful tranquillity. . . . Why should they let themselves be exploited to death since the Roman Empire is, after all, not of the slightest concern to them?"[4] In the meantime, the initiative, in matters of domestic political reorganization, had been snatched up by their prince, no longer content with his modest role as a magnified squire. His adoption of an ambitious, aggressive, and costly foreign policy marked the beginning of "all-Prussian" life.

There followed basic alterations in the forms of government, in the distribution and character of public authority, and in the composition, mentality, and behavior of the managerial and political elites.

II

To ride with the treacherous currents of his time; to make political capital out of international conflict, domestic disorder, and economic calamity; to turn to his own personal ends the pressing common need for leadership—this became the historic "mission" of Frederick William of Brandenburg, the "Great Elector."

This Dutch-trained, impetuous climber was a highly talented and imaginative political entrepreneur who developed into an importer of novel instruments of domination, and a daring improviser of institutional reforms. Unlike his Junker antagonists, he was unencumbered by antiquated attitudes and old-fashioned conceptions of political morality. His accomplishments were extraordinary. By catching up with Western models of absolutist statecraft, Frederick William converted the disjointed depressed area which had come to him into a centrally directed though as yet only superficially united state. Although he continued to regard this state as a collection of huge private estates, "Prussia," by the end of his reign, was the

---

[4] *Urkunden und Aktenstücke zur Geschichte des Kurfürsten Friedrich Wilhelm von Brandenburg*, XVI (1899), 850.

largest German polity next to "the lands of the House of Habsburg" and a power to be reckoned with in Europe.

Relative to the far more advanced drive for royal sovereignty in western Europe and even in the German-Slav dominions of the Austrian Habsburgs, the concentration of autocratic authority in the monarch and the concomitant evolution of a bureaucratic service class of "commissars" had a late start in the political complex assembled by the Hohenzollerns. Here, after fumbling and inconclusive beginnings in the 1620's and 1630's, the process of eliminating division of authority at the top got under way not at the outset, but near the middle of Frederick William's public career.

In 1640, when he became prince of the Hohenzollern territories, he was only twenty years of age. An immature youngster then, he needed twenty years of practice before he was ready to seize such a favourable opportunity as the Swedish-Polish War of 1655-60 provided for him. During the 1650's, Frederick William, avoiding a showdown, began to test seriously the strength of his domestic contenders, the Estates, through fitful acts of illegality, such as the unauthorized maintenance of troops and the collection of unauthorized taxes by armed force. The destruction of the *Ständestaat* system proceeded in spurts and without any preconceived long-term plan. The decisive turning point was the illegitimate establishment of three dynastic political monopolies: the making of foreign policy without consent, the introduction of permanent taxation, and the maintenance of a standing army.

Dynastic absolutism in the Hohenzollern states arose in typical fashion. The initial impetus came from the ascendancy of princely power over the Estates. The past had known only occasional negotiated tax burdens. Such state levies, imposed upon peasants and townsmen only, were based on grants, voted by the territorial diets in response to a special emergency and only for its duration. Whatever their own self-seeking designs, the Upper Estates usually exercised commendable restraint in giving away other people's money. As a rule, an agreement between the prince and his corporate coregents was preceded by the ventilation of grievances and by collective bargaining, resulting in reciprocal give and take.

To the political tastes of Frederick William such a cumbersome procedure had become repugnant. After the end of the Thirty Years' War, he began to base his shifty policy on the flimsy fiction of a permanent state of war, on the "necessity" for perpetual military mobilization. By 1660, his political reëducation was completed. Thereafter he treated constitutional laws of long standing as scraps of paper. Frederick William usurped coercive fiscal powers by brushing aside the *Landtage* and by gradually crushing even the nobility's right to organized opposition. By degrees the Estates of the various territories were stripped of their policy and law-making powers and of their ancient privilege to vote public taxes, let alone to assess, collect, administer, and audit them through agents of their own. Only in the outlying Rhenish-Westphalian provinces were the parliamentary bodies allowed to linger on, after their resistance had been whittled down to the honorific function of periodically applying a rubber stamp. Dynastic taxes were made permanent throughout "Prussia"; and they were substantially increased, regardless of the effect upon human welfare.

The standing army of the Hohenzollerns originated, in accord with the pattern established by western European rulers, from the simple omission to disband upon the coming of peace, in this case the Peace of Oliva terminating the Swedish-Polish War.[5] Everywhere these armies were "at once the expression of the authority of the central government and the instrument for increasing its power."[6] Prior to the Thirty Years' War, in the politically self-contained and secluded regions of eastern Germany, regular military forces had been unknown, except for palace guards and small detachments of garrison troops. The *Ständestaat* politicians regarded regular regi-

[5] See Curt Jany, "Der Anfang des stehenden Heeres in Brandenburg," *Forschungen zur Brandenburgischen und Preussischen Geschichte* (referred to hereafter as *Forschungen*), LI (1938), 178ff.; Fritz Kaphahn, "1648 und 1919. Ein historischer Vergleich," *Vierteljahrsschrift für Sozial- und Wirtschaftsgeschichte*, XV (1917), 252–267; Carl Hinrichs, *Friedrich Wilhelm I. König in Preussen* (Hamburg, 1941), 442ff. For the corresponding developments in Austria after 1650, see Thomas Fellner and Heinrich Kretschmayr, *Die Oesterreichische Zentralverwaltung*, first part, I (Vienna, 1907), 250–264.

[6] John B. Wolf, *The Emergence of the Great Powers 1685–1715* (New York, 1951), 8.

ments as the continuation of war in time of peace, as the core of an emerging dynastic-military dictatorship, and, hence, as a monstrous innovation. And that, no doubt, it was. The political enervation of the Estates, the destruction of territorial autonomy, and the seizure of arbitrary authority over the making of "Prussian" policy signified the dawn of a new era. The rise of dynastic ownership and control of the means of administration with regard to foreign relations, the armed forces and the newly instituted permanent taxes was the beginning of a revolution in the direction and management of public affairs which profoundly affected the way of life of all social classes.

The founding of an "all-Prussian" central government and the centralization of financial and military administration were the most important institutional results of the advent of bureaucratized Hohenzollern absolutism. The transition was facilitated by certain organizational changes which had crystallized within the framework of the old political order. Through the reconstruction of the privy council of Brandenburg, in 1651, this originally sectional body of dynastic officials had become the embryo of an interterritorial government.[7] The more numerous professional class of field agents who carried out for Frederick William the revolution in public administration had their forerunners in the war commissars who had first appeared in Hohenzollern lands in the early seventeenth century.[8]

By taking charge of the evolving military-fiscal apparatus under exclusive monarchical control and by forging thereby administrative bonds of common statehood, the "new bureaucrats" eventually gained the upper hand over the old authorities. From the outset, the "Prussian" war commissars and their like, in conspicuous contrast to their colleagues in Austria, Bavaria, and Saxony, the other sizable German polities reconstituted in the image of absolute government, did not confine their work to military administration. They

[7] For a detailed account, see G. Oestreich, *Der brandenburg-preussische Geheime Rat vom Regierungsantritt des Grossen Kurfürsten bis zu der Neuordnung im Jahr 1651* (Würzburg, 1937).

[8] See Curt Breysig, "Die Organisation der brandenburgischen Kommissariate in der Zeit von 1660–1697," *Forschungen*, V (1892), 136–156; F. L. Carsten, *Origins of Prussia*, 222ff., 259ff.

also were tax officials, and as instruments of the central administration, they subjected social and economic life to steadily growing regimentation. In this blending of the management of military and civil affairs and in the methodical subordination of civil government to military considerations lies the distinctively militaristic character of Prussian public administration in the age of autocratic Hohenzollern rule.[9]

The consolidation of this system was the accomplishment of King Frederick William I. A dangerous, uncouth, and irascible but shrewd psychoneurotic haunted by delusions of grandeur, he was nevertheless the most remarkable administrative reformer ever produced by the Hohenzollern family. In this strange Pietist descendant of a Lutheran dynasty which, in 1613, had turned Calvinist, were combined certain elements of the Lutheran spirit of the "calling" and of the Calvinist idea of kingship and office as a public trust with the intolerant zeal, the austere demands, and the ever active inner compulsion of the fighting Puritan. Despite his highly erratic behavior and despite the premature squandering of his unusual energies—he died at the age of fifty-two—in his professional life as chief architect of Prussia's political institutions and as her alert top bureaucrat, Frederick William I proved an exceptionally singleminded drillmaster. For a whole generation, the Hohenzollern subjects were victimized by a royal bully, imbued with an obsessive bent for military organization and military scales of value. This left a deep mark upon the institutions of Prussiandom and upon the molding of the "Prussian spirit."

"The soldiers' king," as Frederick William I came to be called, regarded the army as "the basis of his temporal bliss," on which rested "his true interest as well as security, but equally his glory and prestige."[10] He made the aggrandizement of military power the center of all state activity. He did everything in his power to construct a huge human automaton, a bureaucratic state machine,

---

[9] See Otto Hintze, *Staat und Verfassung,* 233–236; Gustav Schmoller, *Deutsches Städtewesen in älterer Zeit* (Bonn and Leipzig, 1922), 415–425.

[10] *Acta Borussica. Behördenorganisation,* VI, part 2, 2. Hereafter cited as *A.B.B.*

superior in efficiency and reliability to that for which, until then, the wily builders of the monarchy of Louis XIV, Charles XI of Sweden, and Peter of Russia had furnished the most alluring examples.

Frederick William I stiffened the arbitrary character of political top leadership. Monarchical rule by "the absolute prince in council," as typified by the regime of the Elector Frederick William and by the French system of policy and law-making by royal councils, was replaced with the monocratic exercise of authority. Personal one-man rule; dynastic autocracy in the more strict sense; coördinating dictation "from the cabinet," the king's personal office, by means of edicts and written instructions to ministers and other "servants," were under Frederick William I and Frederick II characteristic traits of the Prussian government.

Frederick William I welded into a single hierarchical system the older offices, concerned with the administration of the dynastic estates and traditional regalian rights, and the new military-fiscal agencies of the absolute state. He reorganized the whole machinery of executive royal power on the central, provincial, and local level. As chief organ of central administration he founded the collegiate General Directory, headed by four ministers who were supervisors, not directors of the state's bureaucratic activity. The transformation of the Hohenzollern principalities into administrative provinces found institutional expression in the newly established Boards of War and Domains. The functions and jurisdictions of these boards, made up of councilors having the status of "commissars" (*Kriegs- und Domänenräte*), were in many ways similar to those of the French *intendants*. In the realm of local government, the crucial field agents of the central administration and the symbols of its growing power were the tax commissars (*Steuerräte*) in the sub-jugated towns, where even the ghost of self-government disappeared, and the invariably noble county commissioners (*Landräte*) in the rural districts (*Kreise*), made up by the local Junker *seigneuries*, the *Gutsherrschaften*. The power of the monarch and the bureaucracy and, thus, of the dynastic state ended with the semibureaucratic *Landrat*.

As directed by Frederick William I and Frederick II, civil admini-

stration tended to be identical with centrally planned and systemati-
cally organized fiscal exploitation in the service of the military police
state. The crown's drive for economic "prosperity by compulsion"
was concerned with raising the tax-paying power of the subjects. The
paternalistic features of public administration were incidental to this
end. Political education, too, reflected the overpowering influence of
narrow garrison standards. It was confined to teaching the duty to
work, to obey, to keep quiet—"to keep quiet is the first civic duty"
(*Ruhe ist die erste Bürgerpflicht*), as Minister von Schulenburg-
Kehnert reasserted in 1806, after the collapse of the Prussian power
machine. It would be absurd to suggest that the builders of Prussian
absolutism, as contrasted with the men in control of the old
Ständestaaten, had a higher regard for community problems and the
general welfare or were superior in humanity of feeling and action.

Frederick William I created a first-rate army which had to be
supported by a country which was third-rate in terms of manpower,
natural wealth, capital supply, and economic skills. The existence
of a large standing army had consequences for Prussia different from
those for the other absolute monarchies. Around 1800, the enlightened Minister von Schrötter, a former professional soldier, summed
up the peculiarity of the polity of the Hohenzollerns: "Prussia was
not a country with an army, but an army with a country which
served as headquarters and food magazine."

The Prussian experiment in royal monocracy resulted in the excessive militarization of society.[11] Military organization expanded out
of proportion both to the security needs of the public and Prussia's
material and demographic inferiority. Militarism grew more intensive and pervasive than elsewhere largely because of the personal
idiosyncrasy, the mad, pitiless stubbornness of the two kings who
presided over "the Sparta of the North" from 1713 to 1786.

---

[11] This aspect has been explored more fully by Otto Büsch, "Die soziale
Militarisierung im alten Preussen" (am Beispiel der Agrarverhältnisse). Un-
published Ph. D. thesis, Free University of Berlin, 1952. See also the thought-
provoking comments on the important distinction between *"Gesinnungs-
militarismus"* and *"Zweckmilitarismus"* in Max Scheler, *Die Ursachen des
Deutschenhasses* (Leipzig, 1917), 139–143, 153; *idem, Der Genius des Krieges
und der Deutsche Krieg* (Leipzig, 1915), 243–44, and *passim*.

Under Frederick William I, passionate soldier and fanatical militarist, yet in international politics the most peaceable of the Hohenzollerns of the seventeenth and eighteeenth centuries, military power gained priority over everything else in the social order and became an object of irrational idolatry. Stiffly martial concepts of authority and of military virtues were established as the models for peacetime civil government and for civil life in general. Closely tied to peasant bondage and to harsh local Junker rule, the Prussian military images exerted a harmful influence upon social ideals and political attitudes. They fostered a hideous spirit of fearful obedience to authority which, under the conditions of the nineteenth century, made for a deplorable lack of *Zivilcourage* and, in the Second Reich, for the inner surrender of most civilians to military fetishism.[12] Prussia-Germany evolved into the most militaristic country of modern times because of forces that originated in the regimes of Frederick William I and Frederick II.

Leading German intellectuals of the eighteenth century were appalled by the excesses of the Prussian garrison state. Criticism of the barbarous methods of military discipline and punishment and the insolent behavior of men in uniform toward civilians were but aspects of a more general disapproval. These critics accepted the judgment of Hugh Elliot, British ambassador during the closing years of the reign of Frederick II: "The Prussian monarchy reminds me of a vast prison in the center of which appears the great keeper, occupied in the care of his captives."[13] Let some one appear in Berlin, Lessing wrote in a private letter in 1769, "and raise his voice for the rights of the subjects and against exploitation and despotism as nowadays is being done even in France and Denmark, and you would find out very soon which is the most enslaved country of Europe

[12] See Postscript, note 2, *infra*, and F. C. Endres, "Soziologische Struktur und ihr entsprechende Ideologien des deutschen Offizierkorps vor dem Weltkriege," *Archiv für Sozialwissenschaft und Sozialpolitik*, LVIII (1927), 282–319; H. Fick, *Der Deutsche Militarismus der Vorkriegszeit* (Potsdam, 1932), 7–11, 39–46.

[13] Quoted in G. P. Gooch, *Frederick The Great* (London and New York, 1947), 104.

until the present day."[14] A sensitive lover of humanity like Winckelmann, the great classicist, evidently overstated his case, when he
characterized his "fatherland" as the incarnation of "the greatest
despotism that has ever been conceived. . . . I think with horror of
this country; at any rate I have felt the slavery more than others. I
shudder from head to foot when I think of Prussian despotism and
of that oppressor of the nations who will make his country, damned
by nature itself and covered with Libyan sand, an object of eternal
curse and horror among men."[15] Negative criticism was not universal
among men of letters. But those who extolled the merits of the Great
Frederick, among them Goethe, were fascinated by his versatility
and personal heroism; they did not like his system.

III

Dynastic absolutism in Prussia modified the traditional political
order and fortified the essentials of the preëxisting social and
economic *status quo*. In effect, the transition from parochial Junker
rule to the centralizing and bureaucratizing Hohenzollern regime
further strengthened the repressive structure of political and social
organization. Absolute government ushered in a more advanced
stage in organized coercion.

With the growth of unaccountable princely powers the representative territorial assemblies of estates were reduced to political im-
potence. The modest remnants of municipal home rule were
destroyed. Urban local government was "nationalized" by the
Hohenzollerns and turned over to the "new bureaucrats." But except
for these major qualifications, the newly devised monarchical

---

[14] *Gotthold Ephraim Lessings sämmtliche Schriften*, XXVII (Berlin, 1794),
257. See also Hermann Hettner, *Geschichte der Deutschen Literatur im 18.
Jahrhundert*, ed. G. Witkowski, second part (Leipzig, 1929), 219.

[15] Carl Justi, *Winckelmann und seine Zeitgenossen* (Leipzig, 1898), I,
176–77; III, 263ff. See also Rudolf Unger, *Hamann und die Aufklärung* (Jena,
1911), I, 177ff.; R. Haym, *Herder nach seinem Leben und seinen Werken*, I
(Berlin, 1877), 333; II (1885), 465; Roy Pascal, *The German Sturm und Drang*
(Manchester, 1953), 8, 42, 48; W. Bussmann, in *Historische Zeitschrift*, CLXV
(1953), 344.

machinery of domination supplemented rather than supplanted the old organs of executive government. The Junker-directed *Regierungen*, the courts of law, and the existing ecclesiastical authorities were encroached upon but retained. In spite of the rigorous "police" character of the Hohenzollern state, the range of administrative centralization and hence of bureaucratic *étatisme* was more restricted than in the French absolute monarchy. The "Prussian" government did not swallow up the local authorities of the countryside. In fact if not in law, the squires retained the essentials of their position as potentates of rural units of local government (*Gutsbezirke*) far into the twentieth century, long after the *Gutsherrschaften* had been dissolved in consequence of the agrarian legislation from 1807 to 1850. In altered forms, therefore, the dual structure of the *Ständestaat* lived on in the Prussian body politic.

The most characteristic mark of this dualism was the coexistence of the Hohenzollern military-bureaucratic power apparatus and of the landed nobility's dominion of private proprietary government. The vast aggregate landholdings, legal privileges, and public jurisdictions of the latter constituted a formidable "private law state" vis-a-vis the dynastic "public law state." There was thus a twofold division of real power over the bulk of the common people. The Prussian polity was sustained by a compromise between bureaucratized monarchical autocracy and the Junker aristocracy which further consolidated the local bases of its power. The fleeting interrelations between the two forces, partly conflicting partly coalescing, form the basic theme of the history of rulership under the Old Regime.

It was possible in France, after the collapse of the *Fronde*, to exclude the perplexed, disorganized, and mauled old nobility of descent (*noblesse de race*) from the seats of administrative influence and political power, at least for two generations. Similarly, in the German-Slav territories of Ferdinand II, most decisively in Bohemia and Moravia, it was possible to inflict an even more devastating defeat upon the indigenous aristocracy. Here monarchical absolutism arose in alliance with the victorious Catholic Counter-Reformation and under the political and spiritual guidance of the Jesuits. Here the rebellious Protestant nobility, who had exercised the commanding influence in the old *Ständestaaten*, was either physically annihilated or dispossessed and replaced with a new, cosmopolitan immigrant nobility, who began their ascendancy in subservience to the Crown. In Prussia such policies were not feasible. Here "noble resistance to oppression," opposition to the rise of arbitrary royal power and its legal corollary, "public law," did not flare up in organized rebellion and bloody civil war. The three great Hohenzollerns never pushed the Junkers too far. They did not follow the example of Louis XIV, who excluded the old nobility almost altogether from the commissar class. They did not act like Charles XI who through his "reduction" of 1680 effected a momentous redistribution of wealth, income, and political power by depriving the Swedish aristocracy of a large part of its landed possessions.[16] They refrained from going as far as Peter of Russia, who impressed all nobles into dynastic service.

Strong words, vitriolic threats, and occasional bursts of terror notwithstanding, the Hohenzollerns were not hostile to the nobility, as such. Extremists in some respects, moderates in others, as empirical realists they did not attempt to force the squirearchy into unconditional surrender. They rested content with a reasonably stable compromise with the strongest of the existing social forces. Here lies the real spring of their historic "greatness."[17] They aimed to improve the terms of coöperation in order to further their aspirations as "sovereigns" and to make the subjects of the landed *seigneurs* furnish taxes, services, and soldiers to the Crown; and these aims they achieved.

In these matters the stage was set by the Elector Frederick William

[16] See Pontus E. Fahlbeck, *Der Adel Schwedens und Finlands* (Jena, 1903), 14–15; B. J. Hovde, *The Scandinavian Countries*, I, 177–78; Eli F. Heckscher, *An Economic History of Sweden* (Cambridge, 1954), 120ff.

[17] The producers of historic legends, sometimes classified as "posterity," have not labeled King Frederick William "the Great," possibly because he did not win glory in military battles and conquer new provinces by force. Among the statesmen of modern times, the prestige title "the Great" has been conferred only upon two Prussian and two Russian autocrats, upon the Elector Frederick William, upon Frederick II, Peter I, and Catherine II. Why?

who antagonized as well as appeased the Junkers. The founder of modern Prussia picked off or by-passed the territorial Estates one by one, but also compensated the politically humbled nobility. He confirmed and enlarged its customary fiscal, economic, and social privileges and its *de facto* freedom to tyrannize the tillers of the soil and the rural craftsmen, and he gave priority to members of the old ruling elite in filling up the higher ranks of his civil and military bureaucracies. Even a "radical" like King Frederick William I—in his younger, exuberant days he had thought that he could establish his sovereignty like a *rocher de bronze* by clipping at will the wings of the First Estate—came to realize that far-reaching concessions were needed to make his nobles "acknowledge no master but God and the King in Prussia."[18] In consequence, the basic social institution of agrarian Prussia, peasant serfdom, increased in severity until the latter part of the eighteenth century.

Centralizing Hohenzollern absolutism intensified authoritarian propensities and also multiplied, transplanted, and coördinated authoritarian pressures that originated in the local squire autocracies of the fifteenth and sixteenth centuries. But as seen from the anti-absolutist vantage point of a thoughtful and humane Junker conservative of the early 1840's: under Frederick William I "the spirit of despotism was transmitted to the aristocracy from above and reacted upon the lower classes through this medium. Thus really no part of the people remained that was not more or less exposed to autocratic pressure. For precisely this is the quintessence of a despotic regime that the oppressed himself becomes an oppressor and, hence, all lose their liberty. Frederick William was a despot: his will stood above the law, as is shown by his deeds, often completely arbitrary, and by the unusually harsh treatment of his family."[19]

[18] *A.B.B.*, III, 451.
[19] C. T. Freiherr Gans Edler Herr zu Putlitz, *Der Nationalcharakter des preussischen Volkes und seine historische Entwicklung* (Leipzig, 1843), 35-36. See also Carl Gustav von Platen, in *Grossgrundbesitz im Umbruch der Zeit*, ed. Dr. von Rohr (Berlin, 1935), 20.

Chapter Two

The Rise of Public Law and the Old Official Hierarchy

I

With the emergence of bureaucratized monarchical autocracy, the state's relationship to law underwent a radical change. The personal authority of the sovereign prince became the source of all law. The authority of law was grounded not on its content but on the will of the unaccountable political commander-in-chief. In principle, and as under totalitarianism, this placed the ruled at the mercy of the ruler.[1] In practice, however, and in contrast to totalitarianism, the judicial, the legislative, and even the executive power of the ruler remained subject to various customary limitations.

The absolute monarchy did not stand for lawless government but for authoritarian government by "public law" and its supremacy over traditional law, inherited from a time when the chief form of recorded law was the privilege. The making of a separate body of public law and its growing preponderance over customary law signified the evolution of a dual system of law and justice. On the one hand arose the differentiation between "state" and "society" and the separation between "public" and "private" affairs, public and private rights, public and private activities. On the other hand, dynastic interests and exigencies were identified with public interests and needs, and the princely government with the state.

[1] See A. D. Lindsay, "Absolutism," in *Encyclopaedia of the Social Sciences*, I, 380; Otto Gierke, *Natural Law and the Theory of Society, 1500–1800* (Cambridge, England, 1934), I, 41; Jules Monnerot, *Sociology and Psychology of Communism* (Boston, 1953), 180.

Public law gave focus to the concentration of usurped supreme authority. Public law under absolutism had nothing to do with "the rule of law" over government and was concerned not with justice, but with political power. It was not necessarily antimoral, but it was amoral. Its function was to subjugate the public to the will of the monarch. Through it the absolute ruler encroached, as he saw fit, upon life, liberty, property, and the pursuit of happiness. Public law simply meant ruling the governed through law, however independently and irresponsibly, as distinct from sheer terroristic coercion. Its primary initial purpose was the destruction of the constitutional government of the *Ständestaat* and the curtailment of the authority of traditional law. Through this means the monarch removed himself, the "nationalized" armed forces and the "commissars" acting in his name from the jurisdiction of the regular courts of law.

For practical purposes public law was virtually identical with administrative law. It regulated the jurisdictions, organization, and activities of the executive agencies of the sovereign and their relationships to the old authorities and the governed. Public law placed the despotic ruler and his officials above and outside the traditional law, which in substance was reduced to "private law," and applied only to matters which the crown did not draw to itself. In consequence, the adjustment of law suits between private persons and the administration of customary criminal law remained in the hands of the old established courts of law.

Public law was executed and, in part, made by the new bureaucrats, the "royal servants" (*Königliche Bediente*), as they were officially classified in eighteenth-century Prussia. In content, it extended to all affairs over which the king exercised control. In form, it consisted of a medley of mostly secret legislation, royal directives and executive decrees, of their interpretation, and of specific rulings and orders worked out by the administrative departments themselves. The monarch endowed his executives with fixed authority, strong and comprehensive enough to function as judges in their own cause, wherever the subjects flouted their will and disobeyed orders.

At the same time, however, the royal autocrat, to assure unquestioning submission, imposed legal restraints upon his bureaucracy. The administrators themselves, entrusted with the administration of public law, were subjected to general norms and prescribed procedures and committed to impersonal efficiency. This type of administrative law was concerned with the effective centralization of supreme command; with the control of professional conduct by means of legal rules and disciplinary codes; with the definition of official rights and duties; and with the conversion of appointed public administrators into "royal servants" in the literal sense.

Thus arose a hierarchical system of regulated administrative discretion which standardized, to a substantial degree, the modes of exercising absolute authority. The development of such a system was an essential part of the making of the modern bureaucratic state. Under absolutism, however, the legal authorization of administrative measures and the operation of the bureaucracy, as determined by the crown, were completely divorced from public liability and accountability. Administrative law did not provide redress against arbitrary commands. Its function was to manufacture obedience, not to protect human and civic rights. It is therefore grossly misleading to inject the liberal ideals of government of, by, and under law (*Rechtsstaat*) into the Prussian police state of the Old Regime.[2]

The growth of public law in the absolute monarchy gave legal expression to the expansion of authoritarian, not responsible administration. The legal regulation of executive government activity made for a system of orderly oppression by aggressive bureaucrats, intolerant of private initiative and voluntary association. The agents and comakers of administrative law were the official foes of individual liberty and home rule, which only landed aristocrats enjoyed. They

---

[2] Concerning this whole controversial problem, see Edgar Loening, "Gerichte und Verwaltungsbehörden in Brandenburg-Preussen," *Verwaltungsarchiv*, II (1894), 217–289, 437–473; III (1895), 94–176, 510–577; Rudolf von Gneist, *Die nationale Rechtsidee von den Ständen* (Berlin, 1894), 89ff.; Otto Hintze, "Preussens Entwicklung zum Rechtsstaat," in his *Geist und Epochen*, 105–171; Kurt Wolzendorff, *Der Polizeigedanke des modernen Staats* (Breslau, 1918), 10ff., 39ff., 72ff.; H. Finer, *Theory and Practice of Modern Government*, 729, 927ff.

stifled the community spirit, kept, with few exceptions, both townsmen and peasants in a state of abject poverty, and condemned the
great bulk of the subjects to helpless apathy. Thus the absolute
monarchy was built at an exorbitant cost. In view of the general
upward trend of economic life during the last three fifths of the
eighteenth century in almost the whole of Europe, the explanation
of the limited economic growth in Prussia remains a moot problem.
A little less red tape, monopoly, dictation, and "political economy"
and a little more individual and collective freedom and respect for
human dignity might have produced even more gains than the
bureaucratic taskmaster with a big stick.

Administrative law was a means to develop economic statism.
The predominantly fiscal functions of the new bureaucracy were
not limited to army affairs or to the management of the public taxes
introduced after 1660—the permanent direct taxes and the bewildering hodgepodge of excise and sales levies, the hated *Akzise*.[3] The
royal servants further extended their dominion by putting the administration of the pre-absolutist dynastic revenues on a more business-
like basis. They overhauled the regalian rights, yielding tolls, dues,
fees, export and import duties, and fines, and they effected a
thorough and, in its way, brilliant reorganization of the vast royal
domain.

Fiscal centralization by public law broadened and intensified police
interference with the productive and distributive process. "Inspect-
ing, authorizing, prohibiting, encouraging, ruling, and adjudi-
cating," the administrative bureaus acquired direct influence over the
economy. Prices, wages, forests, mills, breweries, manufactures, local
markets and fairs, long-distance trade, and the use of roads, rivers,
and harbors all were regimented.[4]

Bureaucratic functions included the operation of royal monopolies
such as salt and the postal service and, under Frederick II, also the
coffee, tobacco, silk, and china trades. Furthermore, the new official
hierarchy, in the eighteenth century, fostered the impressive, though
not always profitable growth of government enterprise in the mining,

---

[3] See F. K. Mann, *Steuerpolitische Ideale* 1600–1935 (Jena, 1937), 50–51.
[4] See *Acta Borussica. Handels-, Zoll- und Akzisepolitik*, I, 769ff.

textile, and armaments industries, and in banking. These activities gave rise to a combination of "public" ownership, bureaucratic entre-preneurship and management, and business operations for dynastic ends, until "the State" as an abstract bearer of sovereign prerogatives and the creator of legal norms replaced the personal royal master.

II

The differentiation of traditional law from the body of law which dealt with the exercise of governmental power was not a peculiarity of Prussian history. This dualism and the dominance of public over private law were characteristic of the absolute state and of the Roman-ized system of continental law, as distinguished from the system of common law which developed in most English-speaking countries. The profound difference between dictation and subordination on the one hand and self-determined coördination and free coöperation on the other hand as generating principles of the modern state and of social organization in general is sharply reflected in the lack of a public law tradition in the Anglo-American countries.[5]

England, through the evolution of Parliament from an assembly of estates into a national legislature, became a unified constitutional monarchy at an early date. "Tudor absolutism," Stuart pretensions, and Cromwell's military dictatorship notwithstanding, it was the resurgent parliamentary state, the reformed *Ständestaat*, which won out in England. Throughout the age of continental absolutism, England, though ridden with abuses of power and corrupt political practices, maintained, in principle, a single, undivided, and in-divisible system of national law, based upon the supremacy of the common law over government and public administration. Political liberty in England was the privilege of limited economic groups, not

---

[5] See Otto Hintze, *Staat und Verfassung*, 28ff., 386ff., 420ff.; Adolf Gasser, *Gemeindefreiheit als Rettung Europas*, 2nd ed. (Basel, 1947), 12ff., 174–183; Heinrich Heffter, *Die deutsche Selbstverwaltung im 19. Jahrhundert* (Stutt-gart, 1950), 11–41; Franz Wieacker, *Privatrechtsgeschichte der Neuzeit* (Göttingen, 1952), 129ff.

the birthright of a nation. But personal freedom and basic civil rights were already the legal possession of almost all men.[6]

Since England had no special public law and since English constitutional law was an integral part of a monistic legal order, there was no room for the commissar type of government official. The "placemen," paid out of the royal civil list, were but a special category of patrimonial *officiers*. "Places" were conferred for life and were deemed, by the lawyers and by Parliament, the freehold of the incumbent. "Therefore no Government post could be taken from its occupant or suppressed, nor even could its character be changed without violating the right of private property."[7] The "placemen," sometimes euphemistically classified as "civil servants," were, in reality, more or less parasitical cobeneficiaries of the rule of aristocratic patronage.

Nowhere was the influence of the proprietary principle in public life more tenacious than in parliamentary England. This was revealed by the text of the Reform Bills of 1832 and 1867 and by the attendant parliamentary debates. The delay of serious civil service reform until the 1850's and the failure to abolish the sale of army officers' commissions until 1872 were further evidence of the tenacity of the proprietary principle. England reached the great flowering of

[6] See Josef Redlich, *Local Government in England*, II (London, 1903), 323ff.; *Encyclopaedia of the Social Sciences*, I, 452ff.; Ernest Barker, *National Character and the Factors in its Formation* (London, 1927), 152–160; Ernst Fraenkel, *The Dual State. A Contribution to the Theory of Dictatorship* (New York, 1941), 153ff.; T. H. Marshall, *Citizenship and Social Class* (Cambridge, England, 1950), 10–20. A glance at the Scottish collier serfs of the eighteenth century whose legal status was similar to that of the "possessional serfs" in Russian industry, and at the miners' bonding system in the north of England should dispel any doubt as to the fact that personal liberty in Britain under the Old Regime was not yet the "natural right" of all men. See T. S. Ashton and J. Sykes, *The Coal Industry of the Eighteenth Century* (Manchester, 1929), 70–99; J. U. Nef, *The Rise of the British Coal Industry*, II (London, 1932), 157–165.

[7] Elie Halévy, *A History of the English People*, I (New York, 1924), 14ff. See also Julius Hatschek, "Der englische Staatsdienst," *Schmollers Jahrbuch für Gesetzgebung, Verwaltung und Volkswirtschaft*, XXX (1906), 643–713; J. Donald Kingsley, *Representative Bureaucracy. An Interpretation of the British Civil Service* (Yellow Springs, 1944), 27–38; K. W. Swart, *Sale of Offices in the Seventeenth Century* (The Hague, 1949), 54–67.

direct aristocratic rulership in the eighteenth and early nineteenth centuries, perhaps because of her early success in national unification on a constitutional basis. Hence the arrested growth of administrative centralization. Hence the postponement of England's transformation into a modern bureaucratic state until the second half of the nineteenth century.

In contrast to backward England, "placemen" in Prussia were on the verge of becoming extinct by the mid-eighteenth century. The making of public law had ramified effects. The ascendancy of centralizing practices in administration, finance, and economic policy effected a drastic redistribution of governmental power at the expense of the old official hierarchy and to the benefit of the reforming new bureaucrats. The latter, under the shield of administrative law, assailed the old bodies of patrimonial officials and, in course of time, enforced their conversion into royal servants.

III

Favoritism and nepotism and, consequently, an aristocratic spoils system had dominated the personnel administration of the *Ständestaat*. In the good old days, the executive agencies of territorial government were staffed with *officiers* who were the nominees and trustees of the Estates rather than of the prince.

Among these officials was a tiny group of professional experts who combined knowledge, experience, and achievement. They came from the urban patriciate, here and there, from the nobility, and, in exceptional instances, from the petty bourgeoisie.[8] They were men who really worked at the job and who were in possession of an intellectual technique acquired by special training as jurists. This band of executives formed the elite, in the normative sense, of the official hierarchy. They were "the bureaucrats before the bureaucrats."

[8] See S. Isaacsohn, *Geschichte des preussischen Beamtentums vom Anfang des 15. Jahrhunderts*, I–II (Berlin, 1874–78), *passim*; F. Holtze, "Die ältesten märkischen Kanzler und ihre Familien," *Forschungen*, VII (1894), 479–531; G. Oestreich, *Der brandenburg-preussische Geheime Rat*, 16–31.

The vast majority of professional government administrators, however, were cavaliers and noble "spoilsmen" who had obtained their appointments on account of the venerable "right of the native-born." The *Indigenatsrecht* prescribed that all public officeholders should be recruited exclusively from the native inhabitants of the *Ständestaat* and hold landed property therein. The Estates of East Prussia defined, in 1657, this privilege as "the whole country's but, above all, the indigenous nobility's greatest benefices."[9]

In actual practice the *Indigenatsrecht* meant that, as a rule, the wealthiest and hence the most prominent noble landowners functioned as the political leaders and big patronage dispensers. Like the Wallenrodts, Kreytzens, and Tettaus in East Prussia, they passed on jobs, sinecures, and other favors to their poorer relatives and their squire friends. These satellites formed the bulk of the landed nobility, that is, of a mendicant political order on the lookout for a lucky chance. Whoever managed to take possession of one of the leading offices was, as an openminded observer with inside information remarked in 1690, "well taken care of, together with all his uncles and brothers-in-law, and the petty co-Junkers must worship the Herrn *Hauptmann* and the Herrn *Landrat* like a god."[10] This pleasing state of affairs was challenged by the Hohenzollerns, bent on recovering the princely landed domain and on asserting their absolute authority.

It had been relatively easy to turn the territorial legislatures into phantom assemblies and to take away parliamentary privileges. Thenceforth the noble landowners, acting as organized groups, had to content themselves with exerting some political pressure through their small local county assemblies (*Kreistage*) and through the *Landräte* and, on the provincial level, through the supreme courts of law.

To come to terms with these *Regierungen*, constituted as corporate bodies and operated by the permanently organized *Ständestaat officiers*, and to integrate these defenders of the old regime of local

---

[9] *Urkunden und Aktenstücke zur Geschichte des Kurfürsten Friedrich Wilhelm von Brandenburg*, XV (1894), 402.

[10] *Ibid.*, XVI (1899), 1058.

and territorial autonomy into the fabric of the absolute monarchy proved more difficult. Occasional deserters climbed on the Hohenzollern bandwagon as commissars. Still, the old official oligarchy remained powerful enough to prevent the princely aggressor from occupying entirely the political vacuum that had been created by the breakdown of parliamentary institutions.

This long entrenched governing elite was dominated by nativeborn squires. Self-assured and refractory, often parasitical, and sometimes functioning through poorly paid substitutes, they had come to form almost a closed caste. They were lords themselves rather than the servants of their princely overlord. The management of territorial state affairs was not the principal occupation of their lives but a pastime. Many offices were, in fact, hereditary family possessions, while others showed a high degree of mobility. Within the narrow circle of the ruling group it was quite common to use the office as an object of trade, a transferable commodity, and a tool of acquisitive speculation. In East Prussia, for example, both types of "exploitation" were still in use by the middle of the eighteenth century.[11]

Because of the matter-of-course confusion of public business with private enterprise, the holders of offices, though technically appointees, regarded the authority and the resources of the territorial prince as the hereditable and exchangeable usufruct of the native nobility. They were concerned more with the emoluments than with duties. Public service was a valuable source of income, a means of making or retrieving one's fortune, and a spring of social prestige, of personal comfort and of leisurely enjoyment. Their idea of justice was rooted in the conviction that ordinary mortals had been created for no loftier purpose than to serve for their benefit. Because they were superior in law, they thought that they were superior in fact. They took for granted the privileges derived from "gentle blood," that is, in the classic definition of Thorstein Veblen, "blood which has been ennobled by protracted contact with accumu-

---

[11] Eduard Uderstädt, *Die ostpreussische Kammerverwaltung 1713–1756* (Königsberg, 1911), 58–59, 84–92; R. Ecker, *Die Entwicklung der Kgl. Preussischen Regierung von 1701 bis 1756* (Königsberg, 1908), 97–104. See also *A.B.B.*, II, 334–35; IV, part 2, 393ff., 447–48.

lated wealth or unbroken prerogative."[12] Addicted to a dilatory and irregular management of the affairs of state, unhampered by detailed rules and regulations, and accustomed to working only when they felt like working, their way of life and loyalties hardly inclined them to sacrifice their liberties to the boundless appetites of a royal "despot."

The old official hierarchy was led by the high judiciary. This group functioned as a conservative and distinctly anti-Prussian force far into the eighteenth century, since "Prussification" tended to jeopardize its independence, income, and social exclusiveness. It bent its efforts to preserve regionalism, neighborhood solidarity among separate groups of nobles, and the "spoils system" in public administration. It clung to the traditional law, now threatened with enervation by the public law. In a sense, these haughty dignitaries were a modest group. All they wanted was to remain in business and to be left alone, to be allowed to do what they had done before as *Herrenmenschen*.

Institutionally, organized Junker opposition to the absolute monarchy had its stronghold in the *Regierungen*, which were primarily supreme courts of law and had served, above all, the economic and social interests of the squirearchy. Like the French *parlements* of the seventeenth and eighteenth centuries, save for the age of Louis XIV, the *Regierungen*, prior to their reorganization, combined with their judicial power other administrative as well as certain legislative and policy-making functions. And as the *parlements*, composed of *officiers*, engaged in a bitter fight for supremacy with the rival bureaucracy of *commissaires*, the *Regierungen* concentrated their energies on a defensive war, designed to contain the aggressive tactics of the royal servants.

In the pursuit of their professional work as royal agents of centralization and regimentation, the new bureaucrats constantly interfered with the ancient prerogatives of the *Regierungen* and with the economic and administrative preserves of their Junker-controlled hinterland. For several generations the fluid relationship between the two power groups was marked by chronic tension replete with

[12] *The Theory of the Leisure Class* (The Modern Library), 55.

mutual acrimony and vindictiveness. More was involved than just a clash of ill-defined and overlapping spheres of authority and colliding interests. At bottom, this struggle was a contest for administrative influence, social preëminence, pecuniary profit, and the ultimate control of civic life.

Through this cleavage two different conceptions and standards of leadership in public life were brought into bold relief. Disparate usages and procedures regulated the selection and training, the working conditions, security and tenure, the supervision and career chances of the members of these two executive elites. Furthermore, they were distinct groups by virtue of their largely antagonistic professional interests and political functions, their loyalties and bonds of allegiance. Nevertheless, in real life, and especially in the area of personnel recruitment, there was no hard and fast line between the old entrenched *officiers* and the upstart "commissars." From the outset, some of those who merged with the new administrative bureaucracy came from the disturbed army of *Ständestaat* officials.

Chapter Three

The Composition of the New Bureaucratic Elite

I

Who, then, were the "new bureaucrats" who gave administrative form to the absolute monarchy and gradually reduced the old line officials to a subsidiary position? It is impossible to identify precisely the personnel of this managerial elite. Its members were hard-pressed commissars, councilors, board presidents, and ministers, who were occasionally lifted up by a word of appreciation but were, far more frequently, called by their suspicious, explosive, and exacting employers "fools, stupid devils, idiots, dogs, school boys, crooks, thieves, scoundrels, rebels, rascals."[1]

The available printed records, despite their abundance and factual richness, contain many gaps and pitfalls. The blurring of *officier* and *commissaire* status; the tenure of multiple positions by a single person, the reappearance of the same man, not always identifiable

[1] Frederick William I, noted for his coarse language and merciless butchering of German grammar and spelling, added other vilifying appellations to this list, "nicknames" such as *"Erzfickfacker, Konfusrat, Galgenschelm, miserabler Schurke, Köter, Kanaille, Retinent, verfluchter Blagkscheisser,"* words which are difficult or impossible to translate into English. See *Forschungen*, XXX (1918), 43–44; *A.B.B.*, II, 130ff.; III, 164; VI, 2, 739. The Great Frederick, great also as a temperamental expert in name calling, was, like his father, not overly inclined to give a clean bill of moral health and professional fitness to the "lazy and idiotic war councilors who, unfortunately, are numerous in all boards" and only too often prove to be "vile human trash who steal like magpies." "Among one hundred war councilors ninety-nine always deserve to be hanged, for if a single honest man is among them it is much." See *A.B.B.*, VII, 563, 617; XV, 363; *Preussische Jahrbücher*, CXXX (1907), 286.

by name, in different departments; the conferment and sale of official titles unaccompanied by commissioned duty; the persistence of absentee jobs and sinecures even in the new executive service— such practices preclude exact quantitative measurement.

No less difficult is the gauging of qualitative factors, such as the determination of educational group or subgroup attributes. For instance, many civil bureaucrats who came from the native nobility had previously received a "university education."[2] Actually, these select noble children who registered as university students, usually at the age of fourteen or fifteen, hardly went through a modest secondary school curriculum, even if they were uncommon enough to concentrate on their studies. To obtain an academic degree was such a rare occurrence that it almost implied conduct unbecoming a nobleman. Less exacting methods of asserting social exclusiveness were preferred.

The prevocational training of the intellectual *haute volée* of the Junker nobility was no better. It provided highborn students of law with a smattering of the rudiments of this discipline. The "culture" produced by the lengthy "cavalier's tour" through France and Italy, and now and then also Holland and England, was no less superficial.[3] Only too often this splendid opportunity simply took the rough edges off rustic squire scions, endowed them with snobbish manners, and taught them the courtly arts of debauchery.

Throughout the formative period of Hohenzollern absolutism from 1660 to 1740, the Prussian nobles as a group stood far below their south German and Austrian "class equals" in cultural refinement.[4] In the straightforward judgment of Frederick William I,

---

[2] For a more detailed illustration, confined to the *Kammergericht*, the supreme court of Brandenburg, which under the Elector Frederick William functioned as a training center for top level executives, see Hans Saring, "Die Mitglieder des Kammergerichts zu Berlin unter dem Grossen Kurfürsten," *Forschungen*, LIV (1943), 69–114, 217–256; Friedrich Holtze, *Geschichte des Kammergerichts in Brandenburg-Preussen*, II (Berlin, 1891), 303ff.; G. Oestreich, *Der brandenburg-preussische Geheime Rat*, 23ff.

[3] See C. Gebauer, in *Archiv für Kulturgeschichte*, V (1907), 457ff.

[4] There were, undoubtedly, notable exceptions on both sides. Among the Dohnas of East Prussia and the Arnims of Brandenburg, for example, were several truly distinguished persons who had embraced both the courtly customs

himself but slightly touched by Germany's ancient *Kultur*, the "vassals" of his north Rhenish principalities were "dumb oxen but as malicious as the devil"; they "drink like beasts, and this is all they know."[5]

As a matter of fact, until the mid-eighteenth century the expansion of dynastic state service lowered the educational level of the Junkers. Since the traditional education was expensive, this deterioration was partly a consequence of the great economic depression which had been particularly persistent in Brandenburg and Pomerania. But in the long run more important was the rise of the "Royal Prussian Army" with its very modest entrance and promotion requirements for men of noble origin. After some initial hesitation, the new poor among the wellborn in the heartlands of the Hohenzollern monarchy seized the military job opportunities which gave a fresh lease on life to illiterate noble boys, landless noble bumpkins, unemployed nobles returned from service in foreign armies, and impoverished or bankrupt squires with little or no formal education.[6]

For a quarter of a century after 1680, this social movement was checked by heavy competition. The sudden immigration of aristocratic Huguenots after the repeal of the Edict of Nantes—by 1688, 29 per cent of the "Prussian" military officers were Frenchmen—and, then, the short-lived practice of promoting numerous commoners to commissioned rank restricted the openings for the Junker nobility. Some of its members now had to be content to serve many years as simple privates or noncommissioned officers.

The turn of the tide came with "the soldiers' king." He methodically neutralized the political restlessness, allayed the fears, and

---

and much of the higher learning of their time. Conversely, within the ranks of the south German nobility were elements who did anything but excel in either the social graces or in mental, spiritual, and vocational attainments.

[5] *A.B.B.*, III, 453. As for the virtual illiteracy of this segment of the nobility, see also Cocceji's judgment *ibid.*, VI, part 1, 462. No less devastating were the comments of Frederick II. See his "Politische Testamente," *Klassiker der Politik*, V (Munich, 1922), 32, 188.

[6] R. Frhr. v. Schrötter, "Das preussische Offizierkorps unter dem ersten Könige von Preussen," *Forschungen*, XXVII (1914), 97–167, espec. 126ff. See also *Monumenta Germaniae Paedagogica*, XIII (1896), 45–46, 56.

reconciled most of the Junker clans to the growth of autocratic central power by inviting the noble "reserve army" to regain a secure and highly honored position in society by joining the ranks of the professional military service aristocracy.[7]

Many of these experts in local tyranny were experienced in whipping the backs, hitting the faces, and breaking the bones of "disrespectful" and "disobedient" peasant serfs. Thus they were eminently fitted to be the drillmasters of common Prussian soldiers who, as Frederick II envisaged their proper status, should "fear their officers more than any danger to which they might be exposed."[8] The outdoor relief provided by the rapid growth of the "all-Prussian" army reduced the pressure for positions in the civil state service, where a certain modicum of formal schooling had become almost indispensable for admission to the higher brackets.

II

One primary fact emerges from an examination of the credentials and social antecedents of the personnel that converted the administrative mechanism of early Prussian absolutism into a going concern. It was indeed an unusual *mélange* of individuals who managed to enter the evolving elite of "public law bureaucrats." This small band comprised a few dozen men by the end of the 1660's and a few hundred by 1740, when the total population of the Prussian monarchy amounted to two and a half million. Drawn from many walks of life, these social stragglers, when thrown together into the hierarchy of commissioned Hohenzollern servants, suddenly faced each other as professional associates in a joint enterprise. Collectively, they formed a distinct functional status group. As individuals, however, they differed sharply among themselves in class origin, educational and occupational background, personal ability and achieve-

---

[7] *Acta Borussica. Getreidehandelspolitik*, III, 241; Gerhard Czybulka, *Die Lage der ländlichen Klassen Ostdeutschlands im 18. Jahrhundert* (Braunschweig, 1949), 10. For more minute detail, see P. Schwartz, "Die Klassifikation von 1718/19," *Die Neumark. Jahrbuch des Vereins für Geschichte der Neumark*, III (1926), 1–96; IV (1927), 1–191; V (1928), 1–211.

[8] *Die Werke Friedrichs des Grossen*, ed. G. B. Volz (Berlin, 1913), VI, 233.

ment, the amount and sources of income, and, consequently, also in their tastes, attitudes, loyalties, and modes of living.

Under the Elector Frederick William, the most noteworthy component of this service class, in numbers, prestige, and ease of opportunity, consisted of indigenous nobles. Prior to their appointment as councilors or commissars, these "new men" had been judges, courtiers, army officers, plain squires and agricultural entrepreneurs, or young university students. These Junker elements were joined by noble immigrants, attracted by the career prospects of the rapidly growing Hohenzollern dominions, who had previously been employed by other German potentates or by the rulers of France, Austria, and Sweden, the three countries which most influenced the early development of the institutions of Prussian absolutism.[9]

Alongside the beneficiaries of noble pedigrees were some commoners, mostly jurists. Among the Elector's top aides were several bourgeois intellectuals, the former law professors Fuchs, Rhetz, and the Jena brothers, and the son of an obscure tax collector, Franz Meinders, a student of the classics who likewise was thoroughly familiar with the literary and learned culture of contemporary France.

The social sources for replenishing the upper layers of the administrative bureaucracy broadened under Frederick William's successor. Though he was destined to become the first Prussian king, Frederick I was anything but a monocrat. The political confusion and the unstable social relations which marked the "interregnum" from 1688 to 1713 provided an excellent opportunity for the pushing and thriving dynastic servants to learn to stand on their own feet. Unhampered by effective royal control, they filled up their swiftly growing membership mainly by coöptation. But the gates of admission were not closed to new social elements.

Little men who had started out in Prussian government employment as office clerks, tax collectors, or cashiers, men like Levin Schardius and Christian Schöning, now got their chance of being elevated to the higher ranks. No less significant was the influx of

[9] See Friedrich Wolters, *Geschichte der brandenburgischen Finanzen 1640-1697*, II (Leipzig, 1915), 7ff.

self-made merchants and business entrepreneurs. The most out-standing member of this tiny subgroup was Johann Andreas Krautt who died, in 1723, as a minister of Frederick William I and, next to his sovereign, the richest man in Berlin.

Throughout the inconclusive political interlude from 1688 to 1713, the reins of Prussian state power were held, on short tenure, by rival court cliques. The permanently organized bureaucracy acquired massive strength precisely because of the instability and growing dilettantism of political leadership at the center. This indispensable body of executive technicians was then also the guardian of con-tinuity in administrative state activity and, hence, of institutional consolidation. Under these circumstances, the key men of the central government could be career bureaucrats such as the foreign-born and foreign-trained Baron Bodo von Knyphausen and the newly en-nobled administrators Meinders, Fuchs, Luben, Krautt, and Ilgen; or they could be lowborn but exceptionally gifted and strategically placed, like the former tutor of the king, Eberhard von Danckel-mann; or blue-blooded "political generals" like Barfuss, Dohna, Dönhoff, and Wartensleben; or professional civilian courtiers such as the counts Wartenberg and Wittgenstein.

Significantly enough, not even during the abortive "noble reaction" to the halfway rise of dynastic absolutism which followed Danckelmann's dismissal could the cavalier-directors of the govern-ment dispense with the services of social upstarts. They had to share influence and booty with expert members of the regular bureau-cracy, with men like Fuchs, Krautt, and Ilgen, with an ex-professor, with an international merchant-banker, and with a former petty official. This situation foreshadowed the flowering of limited com-petition which made possible the administrative reorganization of the Prussian state under Frederick William I.

When Frederick William I ascended the throne, he found in existence a civil bureaucracy which his careless father had allowed to become a serious contender for supreme power in the dynastic state. Frederick William I, chief designer of the Prussian "style" and indefatigable champion of the garrison state, pursued a personnel policy which both restricted and widened the avenues of appointment to the upper grades of the executive hierarchy. In general, the number of jurists and of "civilian" nobles declined while the ascent of businessmen, petty officials, and noble army officers accelerated. To be sure, former judges and lawyers continued to be a substantial subgroup. Even personalities with scholarly interests, mostly men with Latinized names (Cellarius, Cortrejus, Mylius, Ursinus) were occasionally given prominent positions. Although in general Frederick William held book learning in contempt, two former university professors (Fuchs and Cocceji) managed to rise to the rank of minister. But relative to the meteoric advance of the "cameralists" and of the military elements, the jurists lost importance in a system of state management which was dominated by fiscal and military considerations. Hence many of the newly nominated councilors were businessmen, who had made a place for themselves in trade, industry, mining and, above all, large-scale farming before they became "royal servants." These men of affairs who knew how to produce, what Frederick William I admiringly called a "plus," signified the intensified drive for efficiency.

Another group of favored commoners was made up of men who were lifted by the grace of their king from positions as bureaucratic subalterns. Posts of trust and profit were occasionally accessible to former municipal officials and, more frequently, to clerks thoroughly familiar with technical detail and the routines of "red tape" who were able enough to run an office or to direct a field branch.

Among the clerical employees and petty functionaries of the Prussian government of the eighteenth century were many who were subordinates in official rank only. In fact, these inferiors surpassed many of their nominal superiors in education, vocational skills, and executive ability. Men of such caliber often did the real work for which the high-ranking officials took credit. Yet, the Prussian Old Regime, in matters of professional careermaking and advancement in social status, provided infinitely better opportunities to gifted "subalterns" than the far more restrictive personnel practices of the "progressive" nineteenth century, which made it impossible, in law and in fact, to pass from the lower to the upper grades of the civil service.[10]

Particularly striking features of the recruitment and promotion policies under Frederick William I were the heavy influx of military bureaucrats and the curb on the career prospects for the old nobility who had no special connections and were not army officers. Both Frederick William I and Frederick II filled many of the nonnoble upper positions in the civil administration with *Regimentsquartiermeister*, the successors of the old "march commissars," and with *Auditeure*, military judicial officials. These army functionaries, often men with some legal training, were professional administrators. They were not, however, "civilians in uniform," for their stiffly authoritarian mentality, their conceptions of efficiency, leadership, and obedience had been molded in close association with senior members of the army officers' corps and in the image of the grim Prussian military service regulations. For this very reason these men were transferred to permanent positions in the civil state service.

The War and Domains Board of Brandenburg, as of 1767, furnishes a representative sample of the relative position which militarized commoners and former petty officials came to occupy in the upper ranks of the bureaucracy. Of the twenty-three councilors, five had previously served as *Auditeure*. One was a former sergeant major, while five others had risen from the lower grades of the regular administrative hierarchy.[11]

The employment of professional soldiers and ex-soldiers in the civil branches of the government also became a methodically pursued policy in the eighteenth century. This entailed a fourfold utilization of military manpower for nonmilitary functions. In the first place, noble army officers, because they were expected to set a model for

---

[10] See W. Naudé, "Zur Geschichte des preussischen Subalternbeamtentums," *Forschungen*, XVIII (1905), 365–386; Johannes Ziekursch, *Beiträge zur Charakteristik der preussischen Verwaltungsbeamten in Schlesien bis zum Untergang des friderizianischen Staates* (Breslau, 1907), 64ff., 93; Rolf Grabower, *Preussens Steuern vor und nach dem Befreiungskriege* (Berlin, 1932), 112. For the corresponding personnel trend in the military bureaucracy, see Freiherr Ferdinand von Ledebur, *Die Geschichte des deutschen Unteroffiziers* (Berlin, 1939), 85, 94ff., 104, 113, and *passim*.

[11] *A.B.B.*, XIV, 433ff. See also *ibid.*, X, 349; XIII, 683; XV, 488–499.

blind obedience and quick action, were transferred to ranking posts in the regular administrative service. Secondly, trusted staff officers and generals were often appointed members or chairmen of special royal committees and boards and given temporary assignments or commissions with special powers, whether only of report or of decision and executive action.[12] These tasks frequently included the obligation to "investigate" civilian functionaries. Thirdly, the military exercised a strong influence in urban administration. Regular army officers sat on municipal committees, usually as chairmen. In garrison towns the military commander regulated the local retail trade and fixed, in coöperation with the *Steuerrat*, the prices of basic foodstuffs.[13] Finally, numerous subordinate posts in the civil bureaucracy were set aside in place of a pension for the upkeep of uneducated noble soldiers and of nonnoble noncommissioned officers who had lost their physical fitness for active military service and who were without private income.

III

With the formation of large administrative and military bureaucracies, a delicate and unstable balance was struck in government employment between commoners and the heirs of superior social rank. It was generally characteristic of the rising absolute monarchies that a considerable percentage of the "new bureaucrats" was supplied by "illborn" persons and, except for France, also by foreign, in preference to native, nobles. Men of such defective background were more dependent upon, and therefore more obedient to, the royal authority.

The diverse composition of the executive elite of the Hohenzollerns reflected, in accord with this continental trend, the bewildering currents of social mobility. However, the gathering of a

[12] There was a striking parallel to this practice in Russian administrative history. See B. H. Sumner, *Survey of Russian History* (London, 1947), 109–10.

[13] See *A.B.B.*, III, 603; V,2, 5–6, 200. See also *Preussische Jahrbücher*, CXXX (1907), 287; Johannes Ziekursch, *Das Ergebnis der friderizianischen Städteverwaltung* (Jena, 1908), 61ff.; G. Schmoller, *Städtewesen*, 414ff.; *Acta Borussica. Handels-, Zoll- und Akzisepolitik*, III, part 1, 18.

"Prussian" staff of professional administrators under monarchical control did not involve a sudden or radical break with the past when almost only men with long pedigrees had access to the spoils of "public service." A more flexible policy had gained ground in parochial Brandenburg during the first half of the seventeenth century. Almost all the members of the elector's privy council, founded in 1604 to circumvent the influence of Junkerdom, were either foreign noblemen or commoners. Yet it was here that the ancient *status quo* was restored on the eve of the transition to monarchical absolutism by reserving the majority of all significant government positions for native nobles. The reorganization of the privy council, in 1651, was preceded by a social purge. In 1640, the ratio of non-nobles to nobles in the council had been five to three. A decade later it was only one to five. Of the thirty-four privy councilors appointed from 1653 until 1687, only seven were commoners.[14] Some of the latter, moreover, felt themselves suppressed and stigmatized by their ancestor-conscious colleagues. The relative position of the lowborn in the upper ranks of the General War Commissariat was stronger, if not only the War Commissars proper, but also the *commissarii loci*, the predecessors of the *Steuerräte*, are included in the reckoning.[15] But on the whole, the founder of Prussian absolutism, because of social prejudice, personal preference, and political expediency, set aside the most distinguished civil state employments for nobles of old lineage, mostly Junkers.

Even accurate statistics can be quite deceptive. The numerical preponderance of the "blood nobility" in the councils of Elector Frederick William obscures the fact that after 1660, during the absolutist phase of his career, bureaucrats of middle class origin were his chief political advisers and diplomatic assistants. In the 1640's, a Brandenburgian Junker soldier, von Burgsdorff, had guided his young prince. In the 1650's, Count Waldeck and, then, a Pomeranian nobleman, Otto von Schwerin, served virtually as a one-man "brain

---

[14] G. Oestreich, *Der brandenburg-preussische Geheime Rat,* 29–30; F. L. Carsten, *Origins of Prussia,* 178, 180, 182, 257–58.

[15] For the details see F. Wolters, *Brandenburgischen Finanzen,* II, 106ff., 112ff., 145ff., 159ff.

trust." But after 1660 the tide turned against the increasingly anachronistic survivors of the old *Ständestaat* regime. During the 1660's, a former university professor, Friedrich Jena, was the "suggesting" deputy prime minister. When his star declined, he gave way to another commoner, Franz Meinders, who held his own for about fifteen years, until he was overshadowed by still another scheming ex-professor, Paul Fuchs.

The numerical balance between the high and lowborn in the civil bureaucracy was reversed in the course of the first half of the eighteenth century. The political entrepreneurship of Frederick William I turned out to be a golden age for select men of common origin. He created chances for advancement unmatched in Prussian government employment until the 1920's when the Prussian state was a stronghold of the Social Democrats. To increase his personal power and to speed up the subjugation of the old official hierarchy; to demonstrate to the titled aristocracy that there were limits to its indispensability; to prevent a sagging of ambitions in the service of the crown, he gave qualified priority to pliable nonnobles in the civil establishments.

Thus, in filling the functionally important positions in the administrative bureaucracy, he largely relied on men who could not boast of ancestors who, even before the Hohenzollerns had settled down in eastern Germany, had been masters of the land. Frederick William I was bent on preventing monarchical absolutism from being a mockery. Like Frederick III of Denmark, Charles XI of Sweden, Louis XIV of France, and Peter of Russia, he was drawn to men whom he could make and unmake and, therefore, use effectively as tools in the pursuit of a policy of domesticating the native nobility. Hence the "common intruders" were called upon to keep a watchful eye on the predatory *seigneurs*, the Junker *officiers* and the squire judges in the higher courts who, in the past, had banded together in converting a large part of the dynastic patrimony into a wonderful means of making a cavalier-like living. All this, combined with the drive for the raising of professional quality, accounts for the sharply marked ascendancy of social parvenus in the civil state service from 1713 to 1740.

All the private secretaries and personal assistants of Frederick William I, holding the rank of secretary or councilor in his "cabinet" (*Kabinettssekretär* or *Kabinettsrat*), were commoners.[16] Even Frederick II, who otherwise yielded to the resurgence of the nobility in government, did not touch this job monopoly set apart for men of low birth. Although he broke away from the practice of his predecessor to make ministers (Creutz, Thulemeier, Marschall, Boden) out of cabinet officers, he did not allow a nobleman to become a cabinet councilor, that is, to be a clerk, one able to pull wires behind the curtain in the king's personal office, the cabinet.

Of the one hundred and eighteen functionaries outside Berlin listed in 1737 as councilors and directors of the various Boards of War and Domains, only thirty-six were noble.[17] No other Prussian government until the destruction of the monarchy had at the summit of the executive hierarchy a larger percentage of social *nouveaux arrivés* than Frederick William's General Directory, foreign office, and department of justice and church affairs, the three collegiate agencies which had come to constitute the chief divisions of the reorganized central administration.[18]

In 1723, in the newly founded General Directory, the nine noble privy councilors, whose function and official rank corresponded to that of the *maîtres des requêtes* in France, still held the margin over their eight nonnoble colleagues. Conversely, by 1740, of eighteen privy councilors only three were wellborn.[19] And as for the ministers themselves, the men with common parents rose as a group to a relative position which put them slightly above parity with those of their professional peers who came from old noble families. The numerical superiority of the lowborn in the upper ranks of the administrative bureaucracy of King Frederick William did not make them the politically most effective group in the monocratically directed state, let alone in the Prussian community. Reversely, their

[16] Hermann Hüffer, "Die Beamten des älteren preussischen Kabinetts von 1713–1808," *Forschungen*, V (1892), 157–190.

[17] *Forschungen*, XLIX (1937), 233–34.

[18] For a complete list of the Prussian ministers from 1848 to 1918, see *Handbuch über den preussischen Staat*, CXXXVI (Berlin, 1930), 99–104.

[19] *A.B.B.*, VI, part 1, 283.

numerical insignificance in the days of the Elector Frederick William had been disproportionate to the strong political role which men of their kind had played after 1660. Thus, the nobility of descent had lost ground, in terms of influence and numbers, in the exercise of the powers of leadership.

But in several crucial corners of the professionalized state service the First Estate reasserted under Frederick William I its time-honored claim to preëminence and privileged treatment in public life. Of the presidencies of the new Boards of War and Domains all but one were held by noblemen of old lineage. Within the framework of the absolute monarchy's provincial administration, therefore, the richest rewards and the highest responsibilities were from the beginning a noble preserve. In order to facilitate, on the provincial level, the enforcement of royal policy, it proved indeed opportune to appoint as top officials old-established Junkers, especially if they had been reoriented in the Royal Prussian Army prior to their transfer to the civil bureaucracy.

These board presidents were not merely key administrators who happened to own landed estates. They were also "commissioned professional politicians," who had a political function which was as important as it was difficult. It was their job to end antagonism and conflict in the rural districts by securing the loyal support of the squire-*Landräte*, who linked the central administration to the mighty village masters who had to be won over to the royal cause. Within their private law dominion these local autocrats continued to unite in a single focus of power landownership, proprietary public authority, and high social position. Thus, the presidents were strategically placed liaison officers in aristocratic public relations. They were intimately associated with the cardinal task of cementing the interpenetration of the new political system of centralized despotism and of the old order of Junker home rule. Consequently, the board presidents were, throughout the eighteenth century, often the equals and sometimes even the superiors of the ministers in Berlin in prestige, influence, and official recognition.

More clearcut than the uneven distribution of administrative "commissions" among the high and lowborn was the trend of personnel replenishment in the military service class. Under the resolute leadership of Frederick William I, the heterogeneous body of mercenary army officers was converted into a closely knit corps of aristocrats. Formerly the opportunities accorded to "talent" or, in other words, to "illborn" *officiers de fortune* had been broad enough to bring to the dinner table of the Elector Frederick William three peasant sons, the generals Derfflinger, Hennigs, and Lüdcke. The avenues were now closed by the same Frederick William I who opened the gates of the civil state to careerists of humble social origin. He restricted or eliminated altogether the "undesirables" in the armed forces, that is, in the tactful language of Frederick II, the "nonnoble riff-raff."[20] In consequence, the nobility gradually attained almost a complete monopoly over all commissions from the rank of captain upwards.[21] This was political capital profitably invested: it lured the hitherto decisive social force in the community, the independent Junker class, into the dynastic–bureaucratic state where, as Frederick II put it, *"la guerre est un métier de gens d'honneur."*[22]

IV

The composition of the civil and military service elites of the Hohenzollern state was indicative of some of the major social changes which crystallized everywhere with the growth of the monarch's personal powers and of bureaucratic organization on a large scale. Since absolute government and the expansion of the dynastic labor market opened up fresh sources of differentiation, the stratification of society grew more complex. By giving rise to novel

[20] *Ibid.*, XIV, 452.
[21] See Max Lehmann, *Scharnhorst,* II (Leipzig, 1887), 56–57, 644; Reinhold Koser, *König Friedrich der Grosse,* I (Stuttgart, 1893), 531ff.; II, 2 (1903), 505–6; Curt Jany, *Geschichte der Königlich Preussischen Armee bis zum Jahre 1807,* I (Berlin, 1928), 722–725; Max Jähns, *Geschichte der Kriegswissenschaften,* II (Munich, 1890), 1635–36. By 1804, there were only two nonnobles among the 422 staff and general officers of the infantry. Of the corresponding 276 cavalry officers, only four hussars were without noble rank. Calculated on the basis of *Kurzgefasste Stamm- und Rangliste der Kgl. Preussischen Armee 1804* (Berlin, 1805).
[22] *Oeuvres de Frédéric le Grand,* IX (Berlin, 1848), 106.

segments of the governing class, absolutism disturbed and confused the old social system, built on birth and privilege, on hierarchy and hereditary estate distinctions (*ständische Gesellschaft*).

The new civil and military bureaucracies constituted professional classes of great functional and political importance. Hence they were recognized by their creator, the sovereign ruler, as superior status groups. Having like organizational status and a common way of life as "royal servants," they formed two distinct occupational estates (*Berufsstände*), an estate of administrative government officials (*Beamtenstand*) and an estate of military officers (*Offiziersstand*). These hierarchies of appointed and removable dynastic employees did not fit into the neatly defined divisions of the traditional society of northeastern Germany, the essential features of which had been the rigorous partition into hereditary estates (*Geburtsstände*), into closed, caste-like legal classes. In such a society "man was not man"; he was either superior, common, or inferior.

The nobility, being superior to all other groups in power, privilege, and prestige, had formed the First Estate (*Adelsstand*), the upper class. The commoners or burghers, i.e., the permanent town residents subject to municipal law and administration, being only "second class people" in influence and rights, had constituted the Second Estate (*Bürgerstand*), the middle class, inferior to the nobility but superior to the peasantry. At the bottom of the scale had stood the "inferiors," the Third Estate (*Bauernstand*), identical with the rural masses, mostly peasant serfs.[23]

The formation of new upper class strata, made up of the holders of the higher positions in the civil and military bureaucracies, complicated social rankings. But their emergence also reacted on the relations between social stratification and political hierarchy. By their very existence and by virtue of the heterogeneous social antecedents of their personnel, the service estates challenged the complacent illusion that inherited superior status and ownership of a

---

[23] These social status divisions continued to prevail until 1807 when they were largely liquidated by the famous October Edict. As for the numerical strength of the hereditary estates and the occupational estates on the eve of the Stein-Hardenberg reforms, see Leopold Krug, *Abriss der neuesten Statistik des preussischen Staats* (Halle, 1804), 18.

landed estate as such assured the right to rule as well as fitness for leadership and managerial ability.

Even titled aristocrats were now impelled, before they were entrusted with definite duties, to give the impression of competence. This requirement often aroused hurt feelings in the circles of the large landed proprietors, infuriated by any violation of noble privileges, especially where "places" and the "right of the native-born" were at stake.[24]

The competitive struggle for professional advancement and individual social success among the bureaucratic partisans of absolute government gave birth to a type of functionary more opportunistic and more "rational" than the *Ständestaat officier* had been. Within the royal service careful calculation of personal chances and the adoption of rules of behavior designed to outwit and trip up rivals by shrewdness, superior performance, intrigue, or eel-like maneuvering, came to be typical ingredients of "personal ability," "special skills," and "efficiency."[25] For the persevering climber it was not enough to learn self-discipline. He had to make a methodical attempt to appraise his professional colleagues and superiors in terms of their fluctuating "value" and the influence of their relatives, friends, and cliques. In short, he had to be a special kind of social and political arithmetician. He could not get ahead without the favor of prominent influence peddlers in the good graces of the absolute prince, the chief dispenser of power, emoluments, social prestige, and other favors.

---

[24] For a typical illustration, see *Urkunden und Aktenstücke zur Geschichte des Kurfürsten Friedrich Wilhelm*, XVI (1899), 1004ff., 1014.

[25] For descriptive detail, see M. Philippson, *Der Grosse Kurfürst Friedrich Wilhelm von Brandenburg*, III (Berlin, 1903), 14–15, 40–55; C. Hinrichs, *Friedrich Wilhelm I*, 111ff.; Theodor Fontane, *Wanderungen durch die Mark Brandenburg*, II (Berlin, 1868), 90ff. A penetrating generalized comment on this process of readjusting the modes of social behavior to the trend of political centralization under dynastic leadership, in Norbert Elias, *Ueber den Prozess der Zivilisation*, II (Basel, 1939), 370ff. See also Max Handman, "The Bureaucratic Culture Pattern and Political Revolution," *The American Journal of Sociology*, XXXIX (1933), 301–313; Alexander Rüstow, *Ortsbestimmung der Gegenwart. Eine universalgeschichtliche Kulturkritik*, I (Erlenbach-Zürich, 1950), 241–246.

The "new bureaucrat," as a social type, was well represented by the aides of Frederick William, the Elector, and of his immediate successor. These restless, intensely selfish men played their cards with cold-blooded efficiency. They were ardent collectors of tips, bribes, and valuable gifts. They had to be unscrupulous, ever suspicious, sharp-witted careerists to come out on top for a while in the turmoil and controversy following the harrowing decades after the Thirty Years' War. The "servants" of King Frederick William I were certainly not superior in intelligence or energy, let alone in forcefulness of personality to the early pioneers, but they had grown conscious of the burdensome proprieties of "Prussian Puritanism."

Although the nobles of descent continued to enjoy great initial advantage, their rise in the official hierarchy was often impeded or blocked by the successful competition of "immodest" commoners of some distinguishing personal quality. This trespassing on traditional class functions and monopolies and the ensuing rivalry between nobles and nonnobles were a notable phenomenon only in a little, though extremely important niche of the social order: in the realm of dynastic employment. Here, from the outset, a major problem presented itself, the problem of the compatibility of two coexistent, disparate social ladders of advancement.

In view of this situation, some *modus vivendi* had to be found between the antagonistic claims to social position which arose from the old, simple way of equating noble birth with superior social worth and personal excellence and the new, more individualized and more fluid practice of rating man on the basis of his vocational qualities, political utility, and official grade in the state service.

The ancient social rank order was regulated by inherited privilege, landownership, and genealogical considerations. The new service rank order was determined by office, function, and the will of the autocratic prince. In government employment, official position as a fountain of social esteem and self-respect competed with rank derived from exalted birth. Men of "poor extraction" frequently became the supervisory or commanding officers of old-established aristocrats.

This impertinent innovation, the growth of "unfair competition," gave rise to new and knotty relationships between nobles and commoners. Unabating irritation and friction were bound to emanate from the fact that the holding of significant posts under the authority of the crown became an important determinant of social status. In accordance with the novel yardstick for gauging merit and excellence, the upper service grades and the more imposing official titles *per se* became conspicuous symbols of high social standing. Thus organizational status, relative to hereditary prestige, gained vastly in significance as a social ranking device with the rise of the modern bureaucratic state.

Chapter Four

The Alliance between the Merit and the Spoils System

I

Since the Hohenzollern monarchy was built on compromise with the Junkers, the emergence of the class of "royal servants" was not a radical departure from the traditional usages in the manning of government administration. Patronage appointment, mitigated by limited competition, was the basis of recruitment in the career service of the Prussian state. Through trial and error and after much confusion, there developed an untidy and disjointed amalgamation of the new merit system with the old "spoils system." The former was founded on centralized royal patronage, trained "experts," and discretionary appointments. The latter was sustained by aristocratic patronage, social heredity, amateurism, and, often, proprietary tenure.

With the connivance of Frederick William I, this synthesis between the new and the old order was consolidated into a long enduring "system." Frederick William spelled out the practical maxims of public personnel administration and formulated the qualifications for holding royal commissions. Resolved on fortifying his authority by any means, he was concerned with assuring subservience and getting things done. He gave much thought and energy to the task of raising the standards and perfecting the techniques of staffing professional government service. In his passionate search for greater efficiency and probity he dimly anticipated the goal which, a century later, in the age of the British Civil Service reform, John Stuart Mill put into golden words, "the business of finding the fittest persons to fill public employment—not merely selecting the best who offer, but looking out for the absolutely best, and taking note of all fit persons who are met with, that they may be found when wanted."[1]

Time and again, Frederick William I instructed his ministers and board presidents to nominate for admission and to recommend for higher rank only persons who were not merely "loyal and honest" and endowed with "native intelligence" and "mental alertness" but who also had the requisite vocational fitness for the responsibilities to be entrusted to them. "They must be as capable people as can be found anywhere," or, in the words of Frederick II, men "who possess the necessary capacity, talent, and experience and, at the same time, are honest, diligent, and incorruptible." Hence no weight was to be given to the fact that the candidate for office might be "the brother, cousin, brother-in-law, or any other in-law or client" of the sponsor.[2] Yet, in the same breath and in recognition of the utility of deep-rooted usages, the royal controller general of patronage promised his officials, if respectful of the prescribed professional code, not only to protect them against adversaries but also "to take care of them and their relatives and to miss no opportunity to extend indeed special favors to them."[3]

Little wonder that, whatever the new ideals for the identification and harnessing of ability, "the career open to talent" often meant, above all, careers open to kinsmen, in-laws, and similarly "qualified" protégés. Neither special education, nor special examinations, nor special preparatory in-service training, nor any other adequately defined test of fitness were, in fact, general prerequisites to getting well established in the bureaucracy. Not even the introduction of civil service examinations, in 1770, wrought a substantial change for the immediately following generation.

A jumble of expedients, of coexisting, coalescing, and often hopelessly antagonistic criteria served as yardsticks for measuring the worth of men for professional government administration at a high level. "Merit," as actually recognized by the king, meant various

[1] Mill, *Representative Government* (Everyman's Library), 336.
[2] *A.B.B.*, III, 577–78, V, part 2, 432, 537, 564, 614; VII, 649.
[3] *Ibid.*, IV, part 2, 401.

things: the possession of ranking ancestors and influential social connections; the aptitude to follow, as well as to lead and domineer; the ability to bluff, to push, to plot, to ingratiate, and to sell one's personality; the capacity and willingness to pay cash; and last but not least, individual distinction on account of superior training, mental acumen, outstanding professional performance, and personal stamina.

There were many ways, then, of gaining access to places of influence, dignity, and profit in the "new bureaucracy." In comparison with the clear, simple, and straightforward devices, typical of the *Ständestaat* arrangements, the modes of public career making had indeed grown more intricate. This was due to the concentration of office patronage in the monarch, the ensuing regulated competition, and the growing emphasis on fact-finding procedures in screening candidates for commissions.

A noteworthy way of joining the bureaucracy and of assuring security of tenure and advancement to places of authority in it was the direct purchase of positions or, at least, the payment of money to the crown. In his arbitrary promotion of the "merit system" Frederick William I, swaying between the drive for efficiency and submission and the quest for hard cash, succeeded where his two "absolute" predecessors had failed. He emancipated himself from the financial tutelage of the small band of high functionaries who, during the first half century of Hohenzollern despotism, had made their official position more secure by extending loans, at interest, to their princely employer.[4]

Frederick William preferred "sovereign" devices in extracting money from the enterprising and ambitious. He made it a standard practice that whoever gained a government post or advanced in official rank had to make a financial contribution to the Recruiting Chest (*Rekrutenkasse*).[5] In effect, this entailed both the extension

[4] Hugo Rachel and Paul Wallich, *Berliner Grosskaufleute und Kapitalisten*, II (Berlin, 1938), 103–108; *Forschungen*, XXXVIII (1926), 3; M. Hein, *Johann v. Hoverbeck* (Königsberg, 1925), 229; F. Wolters, *Brandenburgischen Finanzen*, II, 328–29.

[5] See A. Lotz, *Geschichte des Deutschen Beamtentums*, 2nd ed. (Berlin, 1914), 162ff.; *A.B.B.*, V, part 2, 749–50; *Forschungen*, XXX (1918), 41–42.

and the nationalization of the long-standing "kickback" practice by applying it to almost all new appointees as well as to the newly promoted, while at the same time converting it from a species of private enterprise into an exclusive royal monopoly. More substantial was the tribute collected from the few who gained an administrative councilorship by means of outright purchase.[6] And quite formidable was the redemption price charged, in the early eighteenth century, to dismissed felonious bureaucrats for reinstatement or, sometimes, even promotion.[7] But by and large, the commercial exploitation of royal patronage affected the new administrative hierarchy above the local level only superficially.

The fiscal cupidity of the crown was strongest in the old courts of law and in local government. While Frederick William I thundered against the judiciary's corruption and incompetence, in action he strengthened the commodity character of justice by putting many judgeships and court positions up for sale.[8] And in municipal administration the introduction of the royal merit system meant that many local offices were auctioned off to the highest bidder under the leadership of the *Steuerrat*.[9] Finally, the opportunity of exchanging money for official luster was not denied to squires, bent on managing the public affairs of their county from the private manor house. Frederick William I was not particularly squeamish in opening his palms to the landed plutocrats who desired appointments as *Landrat*.[10]

In spite of these weaknesses of the emerging merit system, the venality of officeholding did not become firmly rooted in the civil state of Prussia. As early as 1743, Frederick II restricted the sale of government jobs to his outlying Rhenish-Westphalian provinces, where financial burgher strength, although it had declined under Hohenzollern rule, was more than a memory of the past. Only here

---

[6] *A.B.B.*, IV, part 1, 606–7; IV, part 2, 27, 72.
[7] *Ibid.*, I, 46, and *passim*. See also *Acta Borussica. Die Briefe König Friedrich Wilhelms I. an den Fürsten Leopold zu Anhalt-Dessau* (Berlin, 1905), 185–192, 329.
[8] *A.B.B.*, IV, part 1, 491ff.; V, part 2, 293, 796; VI, part 1, 204–5, 208, 278, 439; VIII, 47.
[9] *Ibid.*, VI, part 1, 248.
[10] *Ibid.*, IV, part 2, 472; V, part 2, 836ff., and *passim*.

was it now officially permissible to continue the old practice of accepting bids from the applicants, of boosting such offers "as much as most likely used to be done," and of actually appointing "the highest bidders." Furthermore, soon thereafter this method was done away with altogether in order to prevent "inferior, incompetent, and inexperienced people from sneaking into public employment."[11]

Far more retardative and incomplete was the process of disengaging professional public functions from the rights of private property in the Junker dominated army. In the military establishments the private exploitation of delegated royal authority lived on for another half century in the particularly vicious and brutalizing form of "company management" (*Kompagniewirtschaft*). Newly appointed company commanders, whether they discharged their duties in person or, when promoted to higher service rank, by means of deputies, purchased from their predecessors the entrepreneurial rights of farming their unit under the crown not without risk but, as a rule, at a considerable profit.[12] Thus, until the military reforms after 1806, bureaucratic administration continued to be on a limited scale an object of private ownership and a source of personal gain within the "nationalized" domain of the Prussian state under the central direction of the king, who had staked his political fortune upon the army.

Yet, all things considered, it was not so much the venality but rather the heredity of its membership which became the typical trait of the status of the Prussian bureaucracy. Of course, royal servants had no permanently guaranteed legal rights. But heredity by custom was sanctioned by qualified royal approval. The pattern of heredity which permeated the administrative service of the absolute monarchy rested on a more precarious foundation than in the old days when the incumbent usually passed on his "patrimony" to a member of his family. The beneficiaries of the modified pattern

[11] *Ibid.*, VI, part 2, 585; VII, 648–49, 746–47; IX, 68–69.
[12] M. Lehmann, *Scharnhorst*, II, 136–140; C. Jany, *Geschichte der Armee*, III, 47; M. Jähns, *Geschichte der Kriegswissenschaften*, III, 2259ff., Otto Büsch, "Die soziale Militarisierung," 128–136.

were constantly threatened by royal whim and kept on the perpetual alert against infiltration by successful *homines novi.* The merit system gained sufficient impetus to prevent "commissioned" government service from becoming more than, at best, a hereditable family profession. In principle inheritance claims to particular offices in particular departments and localities were no longer recognized. For the most fortunate families, whether of noble or nonnoble background, it did not prove too difficult to hold on to one or several positions over generations or even centuries. Thus sons stepped into the posts previously held by their fathers. Sometimes sons, sons-in-law, nephews, cousins, and grandsons had to rest content with a lower service grade and with residence in a less desirable community. Sometimes they came to equal or higher rank. In any event, accelerated social mobility in the form of incessant downgrading or upgrading under the impact of limited competition was an essential attribute of this species of occupational heredity which shaped the character of the new bureaucratic elite and gave a strong patrimonial touch to it.

Less typical, yet very real was the development of a hereditary family monopoly over a particular branch of the service. Such a situation could serve the general interest. For several consecutive generations the upper levels of the exceptionally competent, enterprising, and high-spirited Prussian mining administration, for instance, were completely dominated by a tiny, intermarried group of firmly entrenched noble and nonnoble families.[13] Wherever in the Prussian economy salt and coal mining, iron making, and the metallurgical industry had become more important than grain, cattle, and vegetables, the von Heinitzs, von Redens, von Hardenbergs, von Steins, Dechens, Gerhards, and their kinsmen were prominent. In the late eighteenth century the German coal and iron industries had their main center in the hitherto neglected corner of Silesia which Baron von Heinitz, a noble man not only in social rank, wanted to transform into "a pearl of the Prussian crown" and "its inhabitants

---

[13] See Walter Serlo, *Bergmannsfamilien in Rheinland und Westfalen* (Münster, 1936), 1–22, 56–73.

from poor, oppressed slaves into educated and happy human beings."[14]

Even a family of social parvenus sometimes succeeded in developing a hereditary claim to a particular office of distinction. Thus the Danckelmanns, who after their entry into the Prussian service in the late seventeenth century had fortified their newly acquired title of nobility by establishing themselves also as wealthy landowners, furnished four ministers of justice from 1695 until 1825.[15]

Whatever the road to success, arrival carried in its train another resounding victory for nepotism and for patronage. The "commissars" managed to share this useful inheritance with the old official hierarchy. Whether they had started out near the top or had come up the hard way, the farther they advanced in service rank, the better was their chance to pass their status on to their descendants, in-laws, or personal favorites.

This practice fulfilled important functions in the dynastic state. It promoted continuity and stability in bureaucratic administration and thus facilitated the drive for political integration. It made less burdensome the difficult job of educating novices in the service to their duties. It was a powerful aid in cultivating a sense of common tradition, in strengthening the social homogeneity of personnel, and reducing some of the barriers to the growth of *esprit de corps*.

Frederick II was aware of all these implications. For this very reason he revised the directives for staff recruitment in all grades by urging the top executives to recommend for employment primarily the sons of established functionaries because of their "inbred qualities" and "natural fitness." This reinterpretation of the "merit system" was not to mean, however, that henceforth "government positions should become completely hereditary and always pass from the father to the son."[16]

Power over access to permanent offices and their spoils was a royal monopoly more in name than in fact. To be sure, the final

[14] Quoted in Conrad Matschoss, *Die Entwicklung der Dampfmaschine*, I (Berlin, 1908), 153.

[15] Adolf Stölzel, *Brandenburg-Preussens Rechtsverwaltung und Rechtsverfassung*, I (Berlin, 1888), XXXIV–V.

[16] *A.B.B.*, VII, 168.

decision in these matters continued to rest with the king, who occasionally acted on his own initiative and against the wishes of his chief executives. This was, however, not the prevalent method. Even under Frederick William I, before the vast growth of the monarchy in size and the further expansion of governmental activity fortified the power of the nominating top bureaucrats, most appointments and promotions were made in compliance with the requests of the ministers, board presidents, and more irresponsible, but similarly well-placed men of consequence.

It is impossible to determine precisely, on the basis of the official records, the role which "loans," "gifts," "gratuities," and other undercover payments played in the recruitment and advancement of Prussian government personnel. Frequent royal ordinances, directed against ranking functionaries borrowing money from subordinates, testify to the tenacity of the nonprofessional private loan business in state employment.[17] Clearly, these practices, if undetected, did not impede the lender's chances of "earning" his elevation to higher rank. That "recognition fees," in cash or in kind, were often paid to nominating officials, there can be no doubt. Although these usages declined and may have disappeared altogether in the latter part of the eighteenth century, the mentality lingered on for some time. For example, *Steuerrat* Ludendorff, in 1764, sent 120 ducats as a token of his gratitude to President von Schlabrendorff to whose recommendation he owed his promotion. Ludendorff's sponsor, noted for his exacting professional standards, returned the present with the terse comment: "I am not in the habit of selling public employments."[18]

II

A cursory glance at some typical representatives of the high-ranking bureaucracy in the central state administration (*Ministerialbürokratie*) will illustrate the incongruous factors and values which influenced the attainment of executive elite status.

[17] *Ibid.*, IV, part 2, 460–61; X, 392–93; XI, part 1, 81; XII, 351ff., and *passim.*

[18] *Ibid.*, XIII, 93, 249.

The ministerial bureaucracy was continuously, if slightly, rejuvenated by intruders unrelated by blood or friendship to established insiders. The original core of the new leadership group was, by force of circumstances, composed of "self-made" men. They however made nepotism the prevailing practice of personnel recruitment. Just as the most important positions in the central executive of the monarchy of Louis XIV were monopolized by a very few family dynasties, headed by the Colberts and the Le Telliers, so in the Prussia of Frederick I and Frederick William I the ranking posts in the central administration were the preserve of a few select families.[19]

In the Hohenzollern state, the scion of an old Junker family like von Blumenthal could in 1661, at the age of twenty-three, become a member of the elector's privy council because he had the right father-in-law in Otto von Schwerin. Two generations later, this way of singling out "noble merit" for accelerated promotions had not lost its magic. Friedrich Wilhelm von Grumbkow was indeed born with a silver spoon in his mouth. An army general at the age of thirty, as a young man he also obtained the precious presidency of the General War Commissariat, to which, in view of his heritage, he had a two-fold claim of priority. This position had belonged both to his father, Joachim Ernst von Grumbkow, and to his stepfather, the neonoble Franz von Meinders. In 1723, upon the establishment of the General Directory, Grumbkow, the younger, being on intimate terms with Frederick William I, became its most influential minister. Hence he found at once in this department a privy councilorship waiting for his colorless son-in-law, von Podewils.

Grumbkow was a competent and assiduous administrator. This could not be said of the charlatan von Viereck. His "qualifications" were manifold. He was a wealthy Mecklenburgian landowner who had brought capital to Prussia. He was the darling of the ladies of the Royal Court, and was known as a *roué*, a card player, and a pompous social snob. But like Blumenthal and Podewils, he had an

---

[19] See *A.B.B.*, VI, part 1, 71–78, 157–178, and the very informative index to vol. VI, as well as to the preceding volumes of this invaluable collection of documents.

even more decisive credit to his account, namely, the father of his spouse. And it was "in recognition of his father-in-law," an army general who had lost his only son on the battlefield, that Frederick William I entrusted Viereck with the presidency of the War Commissariat of Brandenburg. On this particular occasion the royal master, who could be quite lenient toward the weaknesses of the highborn, did not refrain from admonishing the new appointee to give up excessive gambling and to be "exact, vigilant, and prompt in his work and not so tardy and lazy as he had been hitherto."[20]

This good advice went unheeded. Nevertheless, eight years later, Viereck rose to the very top of the hierarchy as a minister. This felicitous event occurred in the age of "the creator of the proverbial efficiency of the Prussian civil service," whose "greatest deed," according to Gustav Schmoller, was "the moral purification of the administration."[21] As a minister of the General Directory, Viereck, a memorable symbol of conspicuous waste, lived happily for a whole generation, after he had snatched up a number of remunerative sinecures and made his position even more untouchable through his second marriage with the daughter of Field Marshal General Count Finckenstein. Special favors extended to "meritorious" cavaliers could be quite a boon also to relatives in distress. For example, when Viereck's brother lost his councilorship because of "insubordination," the blow was cushioned by discharging him with full salary, "until another opportunity of finding a berth for him may develop."[22]

Illborn bureaucrats, only too eager to prove their mettle as patrons of talent by "building up" their relatives, usually had to wait much longer than their genteel competitors. But in the end the spoils were sometimes even more considerable. The famous case of the Danckelmanns in the 1690's was extravagant, not only because it involved seven brothers within a few years, but also because their highborn rivals managed to bring disgrace and ruin to some of them. A more typical example is furnished by the Ilgen clan.

[20] *Ibid.*, III, 664.
[21] Schmoller, in *Preussische Jahrbücher*, XXV (1870), 589.
[22] *A.B.B.*, V, part 1, 25; see also V, part 2, 913.

Rüdiger von Ilgen, a commoner by birth, had been a Hohenzollern servant for half a century when, in 1728, his happiest opportunity arose. This shrewd old fox had been the "omnipotent" managing director of the foreign office for several decades. That, at least, was the contention of his enemies, of whom, as he himself remarked, "unfortunately I have only too many."[23] In 1728, now almost eighty years of age, Ilgen was given by his sovereign a virtually free hand in reorganizing the small department of external affairs. He used the occasion to intrench his relatives in their careers. Ilgen's son-in-law, Baron von Cnyphausen, now became one of the two ministers in charge.[24] Ilgen's nephew Thulemeier, a career diplomat like Cnyphausen, served as chief councilor, and another nephew as councilor junior grade. When, after Ilgen's death, Cnyphausen was replaced by Grumbkow's protégé, Heinrich von Podewils, an amateur like his co-minister General von Borcke, Thulemeier was raised to equal rank. But by virtue of his superior experience and mastery of detail the latter was, in fact, the real head of the reconstituted collegial top of the foreign office, the *Kabinettsministerium*.

Old Ilgen, in 1728, had been prudent enough to turn down Frederick William's generous offer to fill all the three councilorships of the department with kinsmen. For he had come to the considered conclusion that among a total of five ranking officials, "three of one family" were "great enough a blessing." He did not deem it wise further to strengthen the impression that "I wanted to take over this *département des affaires étrangères* lock, stock, and barrel and to pack it only with people chosen from among my relatives."[25] Thus, for the sake of cover, two outsiders were allowed to benefit from reform. However, to assure supreme influence over the department for his family, Ilgen recommended for the position of second minister General von Borcke, a decent but ignorant and decrepit man who, aware of his limitations and just on the verge of enjoying a leisurely

[23] *Ibid.*, IV, part 2, 386.
[24] Minister von Cnyphausen was the father-in-law of von Hertzberg, Prussian minister of foreign affairs in the age of the French Revolution.
[25] *A.B.B.*, IV, part 2, 386. See also R. Koser, "Die Gründung des Auswärtigen Amtes durch König Friedrich Wilhelm I. im Jahre 1728," *Forschungen*, II (1890), 160–197.

old age, at first refused to accept. After much ado—Frederick William I paid Borcke the rare honor of calling him an "honest man," a compliment to which the latter responded with the naïve or, perhaps, slightly acid comment: "This distinction, as honorable as it is, is not enough"—the general had to be drafted.[26]

As a result of caution and restraint in the years of ultimate triumph, the prominent position of the Ilgen dynasty in the *Ministerialbürokratie* did not end with the passing away of "the old man," as it did in the case of the Krautts, to whom the Ilgens were related by marriage. Johann Andreas Krautt, merchant, banker, industrialist, and minister of state, was a master in the blending of human avarice and public enterprise or, as Frederick William I characterized him to his son and political heir, "able and efficient but astute as the devil in money matters. So you must keep your eye open that he doesn't cheat you."[27]

Chronologically, and certainly not by accident, the Prussian beginnings of sizable units of commercial, financial, and even manufacturing enterprise coincided with the great speculative boom which, in western Europe, reached its peak in the South Sea Bubble and the inflationary system of John Law. In Prussia, Krautt ingeniously experimented with theretofore unknown forms of economic organization which, like the *Lagerhaus*, a huge textile manufactory, operated through "mixed," public-private business units. At the same time Krautt placed practically all his numerous relatives in the upper brackets of the bureaucracy. But he had risen too fast from obscure beginnings to preëminence. He had grown too wealthy, too independent, and too impetuous to secure long-enduring success for his family. A highhanded moneymaker like Frederick William I, a despot not only by profession but also by inclination, did not miss the opportunity, opened up to him by Krautt's death, of doing something for "the moral purification of the administration." He diverted a handsome portion of the accumulations of this formidable accumulator into his own pockets and he inflicted heavy blows upon the

26 *A.B.B.*, IV, part 2, 396.
27 *Ibid.*, III, 457.

"royal servants" who happened to be members of the Krautt family.[28]

It would not be profitable to go on with this drab and rather redundant tale of family appointments. The art of nepotism was, of course, not a unique feature of the Prussian system. In all the reorganized polities of western and eastern Europe the unleashing of limited competition by the sovereign had altered, but certainly not blotted out the ancient aristocratic tradition of making the powers of government belong to certain families. The transition to a system of absolute government had broadened the social base for the recruitment of the bureaucratic elite. That led to an influx of new men, new concepts, and new values; the introduction of more exacting standards and of improved techniques for the measurement of professional qualifications and personal achievements; and the adoption of new devices of personnel supervision. But all these innovations or modifications proved compatible, in the world of facts, with favoritism and the persistence of the nepotist practices of hereditary officeholding. Hence there arose the many "new bureaucrats," whether nobles or commoners by origin, who, even if they were able, were chosen not so much because they were able but because of their special connections with those who stood at the top or near the top of the hierarchy of "commissars."

Thus, in the age of the emergence of the modern merit system in government employment, no fixed line separated "spoils" from "merit," privilege from proficiency, patronage from appointment for competence only, and "artificial" from "natural" aristocracy.

[28] For further detail see G. Wentz, "Die Familie Krautt in Berlin und Magdeburg," *Forschungen*, XXXVII (1926), 1–29; *Acta Borussica. Wollindustrie* (Berlin, 1933), 15–37; Rachel and Wallich, *Berliner Grosskaufleute*, II, 134–174.

Chapter Five

Discipline and Loyalty:
Incentives, Rewards, and Penalties

I

It was a stupendous undertaking to whip into shape the mixed crowd of career bureaucrats who represented greatly divergent qualities, habits, aspirations, interests, loyalties, values, and traditions. However contemptible some of the means used to make the "royal servants" function as servile instruments of dynastic policy, the fact that the effort was partly successful was an impressive historic achievement. The new bureaucrats learned to act as an organized group and as reasonably efficient team workers. The collective pursuit of a common professional task and political function was made compatible with the disruptive influences stemming from individual differences- and jealousies and from intragroup antagonisms.

The Prussian kings based their personnel management on a flexible combination of calculated external pressures and inducements and internal incentives. They put a premium on dictation and terrorization, mitigated by occasional bribes and paternal deeds, and on the manipulatory efficacy of human selfishness. Both pessimism and optimism—distrust in self-imposed restraints on the one hand and a qualified belief in progress and human perfectibility on the other—sustained the pragmatic personnel administration of Frederick William I and of Frederick II.

In their direct personal contacts mostly limited to flatterers and opportunists, their idea of the best way to manage men rested on a few hasty and primitive generalizations. It sprang from the assumption that, save for a few—a very few—no one was to be trusted, that, "human nature being what it is," government officials were likely to be evil rather than good, corrupt rather than honest, lazy rather than diligent, irresponsible rather than dutiful. In order to make the personal will of the ruler supreme, his agents, therefore, were to be regimented with an iron hand, driven to their work, compelled to acquire a new frame of mind and attitude of service, watched all the time and spurred to greater exertions by the hope of material reward and social honors and the fear of stern punishment.

Carefully planned, neatly defined, and minutely detailed official codes of professional behavior, of disciplinary rules, and of moral proprieties were worked out for the major service branches in the age of Frederick William I.[1] These sets of standardized regulations and the efforts to enforce them had more than local and episodical significance. These were not merely the visionary schemes of a temperamental, eccentric, and frantic crusader, intoxicated with militaristic logic and outraged by lax standards of conduct, who was bent on turning his hired assistants into spineless marionettes. By his threats and blandishments, it is true, Frederick William thought that he might bring the dynastic enforcement squads into line: "They shall dance to my music or the devil take me. Like the Czar I will hang and roast and treat them as rebels."[2]

But this experiment in fabricating a novel kind of nodding conformist had broad human and social significance. It provided a substantial clue to the understanding of the knotty problem of when, where, how, and why there was born, outside the acquisitive business community, the ceaselessly efficient, rationally tempered modern "vocational man" (*Berufsmensch*), who did not work in order to live but who lived in order to work. Collectivist Prussia made a remarkable contribution to the creation of this new species

[1] The text of the service codes for the General Directory and the Boards of War and Domains in *A.B.B.*, III, 532–651, 681–714. The amended codes, *ibid.*, VII, 572–839. As for the professional duties of the *Landräte*, *ibid.*, V, part 1, 464–65; VI, part 1, 260–269; VI, part 2, 64–65, 278–286; IX, 437–445; XIV, 105ff.

[2] *Ibid.*, II, 130–31.

of thoroughly disciplined man, activated by quasi-moral compulsions and chained to a large-scale apparatus and thus to the collective pursuit of objectified, utilitarian tasks. In line with the conception of the bureaucratic state as a machine, man himself was destined to become an automaton.

In Prussia the bureaucrats were supposed to function as figures on the royal chessboard. In this martial state the campaign against individual self-will, slovenliness, waste, corruption, and falsehood in dynastic employment received its distinctive texture from the deification of military values. These furnished the central theme for the legal regulations and the moral canons which the Hohenzollerns imposed upon their civilian servants in the attempt to mold their behavior.

In the poor and backward Prussian state the impatient and over-ambitious royal leaders, apt to overtax the strength of their subjects, did not rest content with the mere improvement of discipline and efficiency. They aimed at superdiscipline, superconformity, and superefficiency. Compliance with garrison standards (*"Kommiss!"*) was the ideal discipline in civil employment. In consequence, they regarded self-resilient initiative, let alone criticism of their orders, as an act of insubordination bordering on mutiny. Loyalty, therefore, they confounded with unquestioning submission to the service code and unconditional subservience to the machine of compulsion, directed by the autocratic commander-in-chief.

II

The norms of vocational conduct, as laid down from above, were largely concerned with the regulation of the technical terms of employment and of functional duties. The *règlements*, in spelling out uniform rules for particular categories of officials and bureaus, provided a meticulous specification of the division of labor within the service and a minutely defined allocation of individual and collective tasks and responsibilities. The service codes also regulated the hours of labor, many small particulars of the working methods, and the ways of using administrative time.

Frederick William I, with his passion for concrete detail, did not overlook anything. When, for instance, he imposed a mandatory eight-and-a-half-hour day for the summer period and a seven-and-a-half-hour day for the winter season upon his servants, he did not forget to map out the whole day even for the ministers of the General Directory. As for the latter, he gave his stringent requirements a human touch by guaranteeing a complimentary luncheon, consisting of "four substantial courses with the necessary wine and beer."[3]

The standards of efficiency and sober practicality laid down by Frederick II were more ascetic and demanding but also more impersonal and egalitarian. Having gained through his spies and his tours of inspection a comprehensive picture as to how things worked out in daily life, he made Prussian government service even more humorless by dispensing with state-financed sumptuous living during the luncheon period. Thus he terminated the friendly alliance between the royal household as a generous supplier of culinary pleasures to the elite of the *Ministerialbürokratie* and the state as an austere and pedantic extractor of expeditious labor from all dynastic employees. For with regard to upper officialdom as a whole he had arrived at the considered judgment that "if everybody does his duty and works diligently, all current business can be disposed of in three hours during the morning. However, the whole day will not be long enough to get through with the work in hand, if the members of the board tell each other stories, read the newspapers, go for a walk or keep themselves busy with other matters which have nothing to do with the functions of the board."[4]

Infinitely more consequential were the moral obligations which all Prussian bureaucrats were ordered to meet. The building up of an apparatus of vastly extended, legally irresponsible royal power was accompanied by changing conceptions and standards of public morality subordinate to dynastic interests and political utility. In the old days of the supremacy of traditional law and of the private proprietary state it was perfectly respectable, cavalier-like and, in

[3] *Ibid.*, III, 583, 669.
[4] *Ibid.*, VII, 572.

fact, the thing to do for an administrator of the princely domain to alienate its yield. Conduct of this kind, in terms of the new, dynastically decreed public law, was a crime. To clear up the legal and moral confusion that had arisen; to provide a specific guide to human behavior in the new complex organization; to redefine rights and duties, permissible and nonpermissible ways of thinking and of acting—this was the function of the Hohenzollerns' dexterous attempt at effecting a "moral purification of the administration."

The official code of vocational proprieties and professional ethics lumped together, in rather abstract fashion, "loyalty, diligence, restraint, discretion, conscientiousness, adroitness" as particularly desirable qualities. It sought to promote a peculiar attitude of career service, pervading the whole of one's activities and resulting in hard and faithful work and superior performance. Although, time and again, the state bureaucrats were scornfully treated like valets, naughty school boys, and prospective criminals, they were constantly reminded of their special status as a distinctive and superior occupational group. Membership in the powerful organization to which they belonged carried with it singular responsibilities. Their appointment to the select body entailed the duty to be scrupulous and vigilant in the execution of their assignments and to band harmoniously together in the coöperative pursuit of a common end. Theirs was the obligation to practice in their calling unswerving submission, thrift, sobriety, repression of the passions, and stern self-discipline.

The royal drillmasters knew that man does not live by bread alone. They were not unaware of the utility of nonmaterial incentives for both individual and group discipline, loyalty, and efficiency. In fact, to get things done they did not rely exclusively on external coercive controls and sanctions, on the lure of strictly material stimuli, on the exploitation of human vanity, and on the use of ethical norms as technical expedients. In order to reduce expenses, to tap additional sources of energy, and to forge politically indispensable bonds of allegiance, they also attempted to arouse sentimental attachment to the royal service, a spirit of affectionate, selfless dedication, of coöperation freely and eagerly rendered.

In his desperate search for workable means of making his civilian employees and his army officers serve "with great advantage" to himself and his ends, Frederick William I almost drifted into the camp of the "idealists," although he was incapable of conceiving of the state in other than personal terms. The idea that the "vocational man" might come to practice self-denial in the service of an idea and to devote himself to impersonal tasks for their own sake was beyond his grasp. Yet, in his own peculiar way he tried to breed individual idealism. He urged the royal servant not only to give his technical skill, but to merge his personal desires and opinions, his very individuality and whole personality with his professional work. He called upon the bureaucrat to take pride in his vocational activity and to find through it an ideal content of life by functioning as "an intelligent, assiduous, and alert person who after God values nothing higher than his king's pleasure and serves him out of love and for the sake of honor rather than money and who in his conduct solely seeks and constantly bears in mind his king's service and interest, who, moreover, abhors all intrigues and emotional deterrents."[5]

Despite the enormous gulf between fiction and fact and the conflict between intended and unintended results, it was not merely a matter of wishful thinking to expect the administrative executives at all times to give their undivided allegiance to the concerns of the ruler and to stake upon their profession "everything but their salvation."[6] Plans for the "moral purification of the administration" and for the unconditional inner surrender of the administrators advanced faster on paper than in the minds and deeds of the officials. Still, Prussian state service, slowly and inexorably, evolved not merely into a specialized full-time vocation for life but into a rigorously circumscribed professional career. The new bureaucrats were indeed more than common job holders, as their supreme commanders were more than ordinary large-scale employers.

Here were the early historic roots of some of the peculiarities which distinguished the Prussian service estates of the nineteenth century from the government bureaucracies of the West. The

[5] *Ibid.*, II, 128.
[6] *Ibid.*, III, 645.

authoritarian political outlook, the professional superiority complex and the social group vanity, as developed by the Royal Prussian Bureaucracy and the Royal Prussian Army, were supported by conceptions and illusions which went back to the reign of Frederick William I. For it became a matter-of-course part of the bureaucracy's creed and ideology to advance the argument that the permanent civil official or military officer was a distinctive and particularly valuable type of man, since he sacrificed his whole life to a collective lofty cause instead of selling his labor to a particular employer. Like the monarch himself, he was the bearer of state authority. He deserved therefore special security, special rights, and a special position of dignity and honor. Hence the inclination to segregate the bureaucracy from the general public, to regard the former as the embodiment of the state and to equate its privileges and power with the public interest.

III

The elaborate machinery for the enforcement of the disciplinary code was formidable enough to assure a substantial measure of superficial conformity. Nevertheless, the striving for discipline and subordination interfered with the goal of consolidating monocratic leadership, of perfecting efficiency and promoting personal integrity. Excessive royal demands were simply self-defeating. They had a harmful influence upon group morale and an evil effect upon human character training.

Bombarded with edicts, ordinances, rules, regulations and, if something went wrong, at once humiliated in snarling language, the oppressed royal servants needed a thick skin to put up with the outbursts of their masters. Flattery and servility belonged in the defense mechanism of upper officialdom. But in protecting their right to self-preservation these well paid and high ranking yet withal pitiable creatures learned to camouflage their real lives, to resort to subterfuges and doubledealing, and to practice calculated deceit. Thus moral obtuseness and degradation became an essential feature of employer-employee relations in the most austere of all the European states of the Old Regime, its respectable façade notwithstanding. The cunning and bad temper of the mighty leaders found an insurmountable obstacle in the crafty and obstinate responses of the subordinates. Those who had enough backbone to refuse to be turned into puppets found manifold ways to revenge themselves for being treated, occasionally, like the scum of the earth.

Even in technical and organizational matters the Hohenzollerns overshot their mark. Their harsh methods failed to eliminate many cumbersome and wasteful forms of management. In fact, the superfluity of regulations, checks, and controls kept alive or produced unnecessary jobs and overlapping functions as well as administrative confusion and jurisdictional disputes which dissipated energy.[7] Nevertheless, incessant drill, underpinned by the dissemination of hope and fear, of promises and threats, produced certain enduring results. Many of the "permanent probationers," for reasons of their own, found it to their advantage to exert themselves fully. The vigorous assault of the autocracy upon the bureaucracy, combined with the forces boring from within, gave rise to infinitely more routinized and more efficient working habits than had evolved in the age of the *Ständestaat*. Regular, standardized individual and team work tended to become a matter of habit. And in the long run, the sense of duty which developed with the changing style of work made for the glorification of duty as such, often devoid however of critical thinking about ultimate purposes.

In the young and artificial Prussian state, more so than in the modernized old monarchies of western Europe, it was the salient political function of the bureaucracy to hold the scattered dominions together by cultivating the arts of government regimentation and by teaching the subjects unquestioning obedience to the central power. But since the bureaucrats themselves had first to be taught subservience and the working rules of large-scale authoritarian collectivism, even the outward forms of the administrative institutions reflected their function as strict disciplinary agencies.

The administrative colleges, though adopted in imitation of the

[7] As for the problem of overstaffing, see *Forschungen*, XV (1902), 416; XX (1907), 275ff.

old collegial courts of law and of foreign models, were contrived to produce both pliability and efficiency. The collegial principle in central and provincial administration played an important role in Prussia, and also in the leading monarchies of central, northern, and eastern Europe, in Austria, Sweden, and Russia. This unwieldy instrument of absolutist statecraft was not designed to provide "the public" with legal protection against government by dictation. It was the monarch who was to be protected against idlers, saboteurs, liars, crooks, and rebels on the royal payroll.

The stress on the collaborative efforts and the responsibility of administrative boards was a constructive means of ensuring steadiness, greater uniformity, coöperation, and accountability in the discharge of common professional duties. Group action under central supervision reduced the dangers of graft, favoritism, and personal arbitrariness. The service code tied the individual official to his department colleagues. All matters falling within the jurisdiction of a particular board and calling for corporate action upon the completion of the preparatory work by an individual or small subcommittee were, if regulations were followed, freely discussed in a meeting of the whole department and resolved by simple majority vote. This democratic intraservice procedure, though sometimes farcical in actual operation, did much to make administrative management more scientific by basing decisions on facts and the critical examination of information rather than on loose personal opinions, preconceived notions, and individual fancy.[8]

The board pattern of transacting executive business facilitated the education of bureaucrats for discipline in a mutual undertaking and for routinized servicing of the administrative machine. Group pressure hampered the few strong and imaginative individuals, but when brought to bear upon timorous and slothful workers, it tended to stir these to greater efforts, and to thereby raise the level of trained mediocrity.

Collegial organization also proved a valuable instrument for

[8] For the corresponding developments in France, see James E. King, *Science and Rationalism in the Government of Louis XIV 1661–1683* (Baltimore, 1949), Chs. V and VI.

strengthening the bonds of group solidarity. At the same time, however, it had a disruptive and demoralizing effect upon intragroup life in consequence of the disciplinary functions which the colleges were requested to perform. In accordance with its policy of divide and rule, the crown used the boards as a double barrier against insubordination by methodically organizing mutual vigilance and distrust through the medium of both corporate and individual checks.

In the first place, each department was made the responsible sponsor of efficient and honest standards of work. It was the self-governing vehicle for enforcing discipline upon all its members, and for maintaining and refining professional honor under the service code. Highly diversified modes of behavior emerged from this collective guardianship of duty, decorum, and probity which have endured to the present day and, in varied forms, have spread to all modern bureaucracies. Sustained by interservice contacts, by the transfer of individual functionaries from one agency to another, and by the manner with which the administrators dealt with the subjects, the bureaucratic ways of living profoundly influenced the making of a tradition of service. They deeply affected the characteristics typical of the Prussian bureaucracy as a whole.

In the second place, the collegial principle in public administration fostered *esprit de parti* rather than "that complex pattern of emotion and thought which is *esprit de corps*."[9] Both Frederick William I and Frederick II overshot their target when they incited their bureaucratic assistants to engage in little wars of all against all. The royal tactics turned the administrative hierarchy into a hothouse of disharmony, suspicion, animosity, and underhand plotting. The kings inadvertently encouraged the very paralyzing intraservice strife against which they often thundered. In fact, in their attempt to turn human weaknesses into dynastic assets, they converted the bureaucracy into an informer and spy-ridden association.

It was one thing to invest the ministers and privy councilors of the General Directory, the presidents, directors, and councilors of the

[9] G. L. Coyle, *Social Process in Organized Groups* (New York, 1930), 165.

various Boards of War and Domains and the members of special committees with the responsibility of acting individually as guardians of professional discipline by restraining defective fellow workers and offenders of the service codes. It was quite another matter to call upon them to watch closely and unceasingly their rank equals, subordinates, and superiors and to turn informer upon their brethren by reporting, secretly though not anonymously, weaknesses, irregularities, and misdemeanors, let alone felonies.[10] And it was still another matter to make this sort of "alertness" and "faithfulness" not only part of their normal professional duty, but to offer as an inducement to "qualified informers" the prospect of higher salaries, accelerated promotions, or other special favors.

Other devices were likewise designed to produce formal obedience and internal constraints. The inventive Hohenzollerns made organized spying a major instrument of disciplinary pressure in the new bureaucratic state. To ensure central control over the councilors in the realm of provincial administration, the members of the General Directory were duty-bound to develop a maze of mutual suspicion by working in intimate coöperation with a whole host of secret field agents and petty local informers, such as "substantial tenant farmers, burghers and subaltern royal domain officials, peasants and village officers. . . . By means of such clandestine intelligence they often will get better information as to what is going on in the provinces than from the reports of the Commissariats and Boards."[11]

In addition, throughout the upper service particular career men, mostly of high official rank and of nonnoble origin, were given secret assignments to act as royal watchdogs and informers upon promise of protecting them against all possible adversaries. For these henchmen this task of shadowing their associates was but a by-employment. Part of their assignments they met by doing, so to

---

[10] *A.B.B.*, III, 625, 666, and *passim*; see also *Forschungen*, XXI (1908), 146ff., 602ff.; August Skalweit, *Die ostpreussische Domänenverwaltung unter Friedrich Wilhelm I.* (Leipzig, 1906), 110.

[11] *A.B.B.*, III, 611.

speak, overtime without expectation of any immediate extra compensation.

Viebahn, for example, when made a minister of state, in 1729, at the same time was appointed special secret agent in the General Directory. As undercover agent of His Serene Highness it was his job to submit confidential memoranda on all fellow ministers who tended to deviate from the instructions, were slack in their work, or engaged in "intrigues" and "malicious gossip." Significantly enough, Viebahn did not express any distaste for the onerous burden imposed on him. On the contrary, he recalled the "happy experience" of his predecessor, the minister-spy Katsch, who, by living up to royal expectations, had managed "to overcome all jealousy and persecutions, to enjoy a pleasant life and to die in a state of unbroken bliss and honors."[12]

Neither Frederick William I nor Frederick II were content with the services of such informers. Discipline through intimidation and fear of reprisals received an additional impetus from the *Fiskale*. These rather ominous men, aside from being ordinary state attorneys, functioned as professional in-service spies in every branch of the central and provincial administration.[13] They formed a special little bureaucratic hierarchy of their own, acting at once as a secret administrative police and as a body of public prosecutors under the direction of the *Generalfiskal*.

This impressive array of controls carried in its train the threat of humiliation, degradation, and more severe punishment. Penalties, as distinct from simple reprimands and mere indignities, varied widely. They ranged from the denial, temporary or permanent, of further professional advancement or the transfer to undesirable positions to money fines, salary cuts, suspension, outright dismissal, jail sentences with or without discharge, mostly without even the semblance of a hearing or trial, and, finally, to death on the gallows.

[12] *Ibid.*, IV, part 2, 481–82. See also X, 225; XV, 469ff.

[13] *Ibid.*, VI, part 1, 236–37. Strikingly similar were the status and function of the *Fiskale* in Petrine Russia. See M. N. Pokrovsky, *History of Russia* (New York, 1931), 298ff.; Valentin Gitermann, *Geschichte Russlands*, II (Zürich, 1945), 140.

These penalties were not a dead letter. Frederick William I and Frederick II dealt summarily with some of the more obnoxious offenders of the disciplinary rules. The brutal Frederick William I dared even to hang a noble councilor guilty of petty embezzlement and for a few weeks displayed the corpse in front of the building of the Board of War and Domains in Königsberg as a little memento to his, temporarily, frightened colleagues.[14] Yet, one should not take too seriously Frederick William's promise "to hang and roast" like the czar, "to singe and burn," to inflict "exemplary punishment and in good Russian fashion."[15] Utterances of this kind were but the impotent threats of a frightened individual who from time to time sublimated his rage by getting tipsy on words and expurgatory fantasies.

A consistently serious and strict enforcement of the stark unwritten penal code, which was held like a club over the heads of the Prussian bureaucrats, would have meant the disbanding of the administrative service altogether and the killing of many of its members. The autocratic monarchs of Prussia could oust, banish, jail, or even put to death individual bureaucrats, but they were utterly helpless without the bureaucracy. In real life, therefore, leniency and sluggishness dominated. Rewards proved far more instrumental than penalties in producing the fact as well as the fiction of competent work and of compliance with royal orders. Hope as an incentive to effort, allied, in certain cases, with creative instincts, prevailed over fear. Paradoxically enough, the much talked about "superior efficiency" of the Prussian bureaucracy in the age of dynastic absolutism was at least as much due to the evasion of the disciplinary codes as to their actual enforcement.

IV

The need for attracting and holding capable administrators could not possibly be met solely by coercive methods. In fact, in gathering and disciplining their executive staff, monarchs relied primarily on

---

[14] *A.B.B.*, V, part 1, 261–62.
[15] *Ibid.*, II, 130–31; III, 649.

the irresistible influence of external inducements and rewards as incentives for productive work and obedience.

The resourceful personnel policy of the Hohenzollerns was based on the matter-of-course premise that self-seeking individual interests and the will to "get ahead" in the world were at the center of human motivation. In line with this policy the royal employers left no stone unturned in luring their servants into conformity and in spurring them on to extra efforts. The "commissars" were not only bullied, they were also bribed into coöperation and subservience. There was rich compensation for the personal sacrifice of learning to keep self-will under control toward the end of the common enterprise for the prescribed collective aim of making the bureaucratic police state the master of the entire life of the community.

No single prime motive prompted the vastly different social types of functionaries *"travailler pour le Roi de Prusse."* The major incentives, of necessity varying in efficacy, consisted in the enticing chance of rising in the world by obtaining conspicuous positions of prestige carrying with them august service titles, high incomes, and premiums of vanity; in the active sharing in managerial power and authoritarian leadership; in the feeling of "belonging" to a select class of "very important persons" whose worth, in the hierarchy of social status groups, as recognized by the crown, found tangible expression in the bestowal of high corporate standing.

Permanent tenure upon satisfactory behavior was, as a matter of standard practice, a regular attribute of all service officers. It was, in effect, a group privilege which, in 1794, was further solidified by being converted into a qualified legal right. For the bourgeois bureaucrats, moreover, admission to this functional aristocracy entailed elevation to seminoble status by virtue of the automatic conferment of certain noble class privileges, such as exemption from the payment of most taxes and from the jurisdiction of the lower courts of law.

Some prosperous members of the elite of old-established Junker squires also drifted into the administrative bureaucracy. These men who possessed high social status gave up, in some degree, their independence by seeking ranking, yet dependent and vulnerable positions. Personages of this type substantially buttressed their political influence as well as their social standing and personal reputation by holding posts as key executives of the absolute monarchy.

Money was not everything in Prussian state service. For many bureaucrats, beyond doubt, it was not the decisive factor. Nevertheless, government careers provided an excellent avenue to affluence. Throughout the *ancien régime*, everywhere in Europe employment under the crown, in administration, the courts of law, and the armed services, was permeated with commercialism. Ill-payment in the higher grades is a "democratic," not an "aristocratic" historic phenomenon. Aristocratic disdain for the emoluments of office, being a particularly subtle and costly form of social snobbery and political exclusiveness, did not become relevant until the traditional position of the privileged in government was seriously challenged by liberal and democratic movements.

Contrary to widely held misconceptions which have beclouded many issues, work for the King of Prussia could be most gratifying to material ambition. Relative to the limited economic opportunities available in German society, administrative service in the upper and, sometimes, even in the middle brackets was a way to make money rather easily and to enjoy the things money could buy. Under the conditions of the seventeenth and eighteenth centuries it was one of the best and shortest ways either of getting rich or of adding to one's riches. With the more prosperous members of the squirearchy, the army officers' hierarchy from captain upwards, the small band of invariably nonnoble capitalist tenant farmers of the state domain, and some isolated merchants and professional financiers, including a few Jews, the higher civil bureaucracy formed the "upper ten thousand" of the economic society of Prussia.

As to income, an enormous gulf separated the superior from the lowest echelons of the administrative personnel.[16] In spite of sharp inequalities of income between the upper service grades, between the various departments, and among officials holding identical rank in the same department, the salaries and official allowances paid to upper bureaucrats were unusually high, if measured in terms of the

[16] For a typical statistical illustration, see *A.B.B.*, VIII, 190–223.

purchasing power of money of the time and in relation to the comparatively low salary schedules of the nineteenth century.[17] Aside from the army officers, the civil bureaucracy was the chief direct beneficiary of the service-extracting and service-rendering activities of the fiscal state. Furthermore, as in all the European monarchies and aristocratic polities of the Old Regime, office, as such, remained to some extent a species of private enterprise. Apart from receiving fixed salaries, the "royal servants" were the legitimate collectors of elastic and often very lucrative emoluments of office which entitled them to the private appropriation of a certain share in the fees and fines collected, in the proceeds from the beer tax or salt monopoly, in urban gild funds, in the revenues of municipal treasuries and ecclesiastical foundations, and in the charges levied on Jews for their "protection."[18] In addition, for royal favorites and particularly privileged top officials and their protégés there were special allowances, subsidies, bonuses, and handsome gifts in kind.

This system of remuneration had a pernicious effect upon the public service spirit of the bureaucracy, once it had attained a consolidated position. The prevalent modes of compensation impaired the zeal for administrative and social reforms. Most innovations in the direction of greater rationality and economy proved detrimental to the monetary self-interests of officialdom, exercising, in numerous instances, both enforcement and judicial functions. Besides, bureaucratic dignitaries frequently yielded to the temptation of violating the service codes by exploiting their authority for personal ends or vested group interests. All over Europe there was still ample room for peculation in government administration.

The well-paid Prussian bureaucracy, though it could afford to be honest, was not free from shady usages. Both Frederick William I and Frederick II, time and again, blasted their executives. Sometimes the royal accusations were unsupported by the facts. On the other hand, petty graft as well as criminal conduct in the civil

[17] For details see *ibid.*, V, part 1, 16ff.; V, part 2, 745–46, 866–892; VI, part 1, 284ff.; VII, 234–35; VIII, 190–223; *Forschungen*, XV, 415–16.
[18] J. Ziekursch, *Beiträge*, 32–62, 74–75, 92; A. Skalweit, *Die ostpreussische Domänenverwaltung*, 63, 96; *Forschungen*, XXI (1908), 327–331, 550–51; *A.B.B.*, IV, part 2, 406; XI, 213; XIV, 450.

administration only too often remained undetected and, even if detected, were not always followed by disciplinary action.

The charging of "travelling expenses" for fictitious "official" trips, for instance, or the acceptance of bribes from leaseholders of state estates and from merchants and manufacturers seem to have been rather popular. Less frequent but more serious criminal acts involved extortion, blackmail, embezzlement, and larceny, sometimes on a considerable scale.[19] A particularly noteworthy record was established by highborn *Landräte* who cheated the peasants out of tax refunds, relief money, and payments due to them for services rendered to the state.[20] Influential army generals, courtiers, and high ranking members of the civil bureaucracy employed unscrupulous methods in grabbing vast landed estates upon the special opportunity provided by the second and third partitions of Poland.[21]

Officials, playing a lone hand or joining a dissolute association of booty-hungry prospectors, and even whole regular departments, acting as a body, were rather reluctant to adjust their sense of proprieties and their professional habits to the dividing line between "private" and "public" administration, as defined by the royal interpreter of *"raison d'état."* When, for example, Frederick II ordered the abolition of all "fees," except for the petty "service charges" (*Expeditionsgebühren*), the members of the Boards of War and Domains in Silesia, unperturbed by the royal request, continued to collect and to pocket the old "fees" under the name of "service charges."[22]

Practices of this kind were not Prussian peculiarities. On the contrary, compared with the usages in other, diverse polities, in *Ständestaaten* such as Hanover and Mecklenburg, in autocratic Russia and in parliamentary England, the old-fashioned paradise of aristocratic

[19] *A.B.B.*, IX, 1–30; XIII, 122–23; XIV, 174ff., 258, 311, 473–74, 477, and *passim*; *A. B. Handels-, Zoll- und Akzisepolitik*, III, part 1, 368–376; *Forschungen*, II, 499ff.; XXIII, 271.
[20] *A.B.B.*, VIII, 254, 339ff., 689ff.; X, 35ff., 489–90; XII, 382ff., 453–54, 497–98; XIII, 477, and *passim*.
[21] Martin Philippson, *Geschichte des Preussischen Staatswesens vom Tode Friedrichs des Grossen*, II (Berlin, 1882), 284–292.
[22] *Preussische Jahrbücher*, CXXX (1907), 300; *A.B.B.*, XV, 130ff.

spoilsmen in the West, in the Hohenzollern monarchy a far sharper line was drawn between private assets and dynastic funds, private persons and public officials. The Prussian system of administration erected massive, though surmountable barriers against bureaucrats, bent on engaging in business for profit. These sanctions were reinforced by the new concepts of authority, allegiance, and public responsibility which crystallized, partly in protest to the widespread existence of disreputable practices in government management, during the age of the Enlightenment. Nonetheless, even by the dawn of the nineteenth century, the Prussian bureaucracy was still far remote from that ideal of high-spirited devotion which called for "men wholly set apart and dedicated for public purposes, without any other than public duties and public principles; men without the possibility of converting the estate of the community into a private fortune; men denied to self-interests, whose avarice is for some community; men to whom personal poverty is honor, and implicit obedience stands in the place of freedom."[23]

One must not, however, overlook the social differentiation implied in the famous Prussian motto of *suum cuique* ("to each his own") during the epoch of dynastic absolutism. Just as the royal policy of staff selection and of promotions linked the official merit basis to family patronage and aristocratic spoils politics, so, too, the practices of dispensing rewards, honors, and other plums had their own pattern. There was room for limited competition only. Even under Frederick William I the democratization of bureaucratic career chances was partly offset by the custom of granting various extras to titled aristocrats. This policy became more accentuated under Frederick II, although he sometimes pretended to rate his subordinates not in accordance with their "social rank but their service and merit."[24]

The differential treatment of nobles and nonnobles found expression also in the inequities of the income structure. In this ticklish area a special value, as a rule, continued to be attached to noble

[23] Edmund Burke, *Reflections on the French Revolution* (Everyman's Library), 154.
[24] *A.B.B.*, VII, 34.

status, even if it was of recent origin. For example, Councilor von Nüssler was granted special income privileges "in recognition of the merits of his late father-in-law," the newly ennobled educational bureaucrat von Ludewig, Chancellor of the University of Halle.[25] Conversely, a plain Mr. Cautius, while serving with distinction as First Director of a Board of War and Domains, for a long time received a decidedly lower salary than his subordinate von Boden, who had the good fortune to be the son of a newly ennobled minister. Boden, jr., was not only the inferior of Cautius with regard to both service rank and seniority, he also was an indolent, incompetent, and impertinent dandy, or, as his president, von Schlabrendorff, pictured him: "He is exactly as Your Majesty has characterized him to me and as the late president, too, has described him, namely, utterly unfit and unable to do any good, but excelling in malice, arrogance, and underhand plotting. His absence, therefore, is always of greater usefulness to the department than his presence."[26]

Conditions in Silesia in the late eighteenth century bore eloquent witness to the consolidated pattern of social class favoritism. Not only did the noble councilors enjoy a higher salary than their non-noble colleagues, the former also got their appointment, on the average, at the age of twenty-seven, the commoners when they were forty-two.[27] Little wonder that the idea of social reform and of abolishing privileges of birth found favor among frustrated bureaucrats of poor extraction who had no reason to think lightly of the merit system. In general, however, their faith in the principles of equality of opportunity and of freedom from social discrimination hardly went beyond the desire of gaining equality with their superiors.

Such was the all-pervasive influence of social status distinctions as regulators of the distribution of rewards and penalties that even dipsomaniacs and royal mistresses came to feel its impact. Non-noble councilors, if addicted to the excessive consumption of intoxi-

---

[25] *Ibid.*, VI, part 1, 333.
[26] *Ibid.*, IX, 718–19; X, 154ff.
[27] J. Ziekursch, *Beiträge*, 9, 84. Under Frederick II it was by no means unusual that nobles were promoted to councilorships at the age of twenty-one or twenty-two. See *A.B.B.*, X, 53, 128, 157, 171, and *passim*.

cating beverages, sometimes were chastised by being dismissed. By the mid-eighteenth century, this could happen even to a judicial councilor (*Regierungsrat*) "because he hangs around the saloons and is mostly drunk."[28] A professional ignoramus but an expert at the card table like the Herr von Voss, on the other hand, who had a high score in the lineage test and "practised drinking" in the salon rather than in the saloon, "went upstairs." He was made president of a *Regierung*.[29]

Wilhelmine Enke, because she was of low birth, was severely censured when her philandering royal lover (Frederick William II) passed away.[30] Her rivals, whom the old nobility had been obliging enough to supply to the king, were more fortunate. Julie von Voss and Countess Sophie Dönhoff did not have to defend themselves against the charge of immorality, nor were they forced to surrender the more precious tokens of royal generosity. Moreover, their relatives and illegitimate children rose to great wealth and honors and walked the earth lordly and secure.

Yet, when all is said, the old order of social ranks, partly conflicting and partly converging with the new ladder of professional ranks and titles, exercised a counteracting rather than a merely dividing influence upon the administrative bureaucracy. The continued primacy of the greater prestige of the wellborn was helpful as well as hurtful to the formation of *esprit de corps* among the upper ranges of officialdom. The noble ways of measuring social worth, rectified by the royal use of titled privilege as a reward for obedient, well-deserving, or just long service, displayed considerable unifying and assimilating power. Reinforced by the rivalry with the socially more exclusive *Regierungen*, they gave more definite direction to the great endeavor for social climbing in the administrative hierarchy, an endeavor that was oriented towards the entrenched aristocracy, the hereditary nobility.

[28] *Ibid.*, IX, 285; XI, 282–285.
[29] *Ibid.*, X, 323–327.
[30] Otto Tschirch, *Geschichte der öffentlichen Meinung in Preussen* (1795–1806), I (Weimar, 1933), 255, 262.

Significantly enough, the high regard paid to inherited rank penetrated the minds of the chief contestants of the traditional First Estate. Jealousy, friction, and the dramatization of differences between the nobly born and the "nonnoble riff-raff" in the bureaucracy notwithstanding, the commoners were primarily concerned with their careers and their further advance in the social scale by getting established, if possible, as nobles of ascent. At least for their own immediate practical ends, many of the pushing parvenus simply succumbed to the mores of the nobles of descent by copying as best they could the mannerisms and style of life of those with the higher social standing. This pattern of behavior facilitated the diffusion of a sense of aristocratic status within the bureaucratic elite as a group.

Chapter Six

Inter- and Intraservice Relations and the Reorganization of the Old Hierarchy

I

The development of the Royal Prussian Bureaucracy set it off, as a body, from the competing elites of political power holders: the independent landed nobility, the semi-independent old official hierarchy, and the new professional estate of dependent army officers. These four functional and social elites, put together, made up the Prussian political aristocracy, the governing class. Each of them, demarcated by a different, though partly overlapping and coalescing combination of external and internal attributes, had a curiously peculiar group character and mentality, a special way of life and social reputation.

The executive officials of the absolute monarchy acquired their most distinguishing group traits through a complex process which set in motion an ever renewed regrouping of the governing elements of Prussian society. These career administrators had originated as a fighting occupational group. They came into being and rose to prominence as co-makers, executors, and custodians of "public law." *De jure*, they were hired servants, but they also were, *de facto*, bureaucratic empire builders and powerful partners of the new system of dynastic authoritarianism. They personified the sensational ascendancy of the centralized mechanism of government based on monarchical *raison d'état*, on the scientific calculation and manipulation of political utility.

Being aggressive and self-assertive *nouveaux arrivés*, subjected to both indoctrination and hierarchical discipline, the royal servants developed a sense of status. They grew conscious of their increasingly eminent and indispensable calling. However, the evolution of their corporate solidarity and of their internal dissensions was deeply influenced by relations with the other three leadership groups of the Prussian body politic.

As a tyro group, the new bureaucrats were impelled to jockey for position and to struggle for social recognition. In the pursuit of their professional tasks and personal ambitions they came into contact with their rivals for status and power. In competition and conflict with the old state service dignitaries, the makers of modern Prussia developed a feeling of community of interests and aspirations. By the very nature of their origin and political function, the crusaders of administrative law, being champions of centralized government by executive order, were at first the natural antagonists of the *officiers* of the *Regierungen*. The latter, reluctant to part with their ancient prerogatives, greeted the rising fraternity of commissars with hostility.

II

The old official aristocracy was partitioned into a string of small sectional groups which were headed by particularly prominent noble squires. These leaders came from the oldest and wealthiest and, consequently, the "best" Junker families. These men could afford to indulge in "insubordination" and "noble resistance to oppression." Clinging to traditional notions of social value and to customary methods of political control, they had fixed ideas as to the proper functions of government and decided opinions as to what should not be done. Tied to their once autonomous regions, they could not easily detach themselves from the memory of the golden days of the *Ständestaat*. Accordingly, most of them for a long time regarded the makers and operators of the evolving "Prussian" machinery of dynastic public administration as dangerous political adventurers and repulsive parvenus.

It took a whole century to reform this headstrong power group. "Reorientation," the transformation of group outlook and habits of living was a slow and incomplete process. The persistent prodding of the Hohenzollerns and of their status and power hungry executive aides was needed to turn these proprietary *officiers* into accountable and removable "commissioned officers," to make them develop an occasional interest in long hours and hard and efficient work, and to give their avocational activities a more vocational complexion. In the end, external pressure, combined with readjustment by rejuvenation from within, resolved the dilemma which the rise of Prussia had produced. By the mid-eighteenth century, the high judiciary made its peace with the new political order through assimilation with the institutions of the absolute monarchy. Instead of struggling from without for preëminence, it now girded itself within to resume the battle of noble reaction.

Until then, the civil government of the Hohenzollern state was disrupted by the interservice conflict between the representatives of the contracting old system of managing public affairs and the executives of the expanding administrative order of absolutism. Both contending factions, in the heat of their campaign for supremacy, exaggerated their differences. In fact, this bitter feud was but a dispute over the terms of coöperation. The eventual outcome was a process of bargaining and compromise.

The immediate object of intergroup warfare was the fixing of jurisdictions and spheres of competency.[1] More simple but far more serious was the underlying issue: each group wanted commanding influence. Each wished to control and manage the administrative and judicial means of organized domination and to appropriate the lion's share of the profits of public service. Each desired the more distinguished social position and the respect and, perhaps, the gratitude and admiration of men of consequence.

The old leaders, on the defensive, tended to curb, wherever

---

[1] These aspects are well explored. See E. Loening, "Gerichte und Verwaltungsbehörden"; O. Hintze, *Geist und Epochen*, 105–131, 352–434; *idem*, *A.B.B.*, VI, part 1, 227–233; G. Schmoller, in *Jahrbuch für Gesetzgebung, Verwaltung und Rechtsprechung*, X (1886), 32–35.

possible, the unquenchable appetites of the upstart bureaucrats. The gradual emasculation of the territorial legislatures as effective organs of the political will of the Junkers and of what was left of the urban patriciate under the Elector Frederick William had virtually removed this organized check upon the activities of the rising service class. For the "royal servants" this opened the road to centralized authoritarian power. Holding the initiative, they were not content to extend the functional boundaries of their administrative dominion. They wanted to make their newly gained position secure by becoming, under the aegis of the political commander-in-chief, the dominant oligarchy, the managing directors of the whole civil polity, at least outside the unconquerable Junker domain of rural local government. And this goal could not be reached without reducing the placemen of the *Regierungen* to a subsidiary position.

In waging an intensive campaign against the upholders of the *Ständestaat* interests and ideals, the new bureaucrats were knit together into a cohesive and purposeful power group. Chronic friction with the rival hierarchy in matters of day-to-day routine and frequent disagreements in matters of policy led to the subordination of individual differences among the members of the administrative class. Competition promoted professional as well as political *esprit de corps* among the commissars.

At the same time, however, the crystallization of group solidarity was held in check by stubborn *esprit de parti*. The "royal servants" had much to fight and worry about among themselves. The Prussian government executives were not a particularly virtuous or high-spirited group, but rather a perplexing association of jealous, intensely selfish, and often mean and treacherous individuals whose day-to-day life was embittered by spies, informers, self-appointed snipers, and experts in intrigue.

Internal disunity and conflict sprang from many sources. There was no lack of contriving "team workers" who needed a little entertainment to break the dullness of the regular routine. Thus intra-departmental brawls over the service codes and the allocation of the work load were enlivened by differences of opinion, the clash of personalities and temperaments, the flaring up of vanity, avarice, and envy. Feuds had ugly overtones since the contestants did not recoil from calumny, anonymous denunciations, and outbursts of hate.[2] Hazards to staff morale and decent human relations also arose from nepotism and favoritism. These usages, too, fostered cliques and countercliques.

Most of these manifestations of internal discord, upon close examination, turn out to be derivations from more deeply seated influences. They were linked to an obsessive preoccupation with social status. Craving for social position was the most persistent as well as the most potent generator of disharmony in the Prussian bureaucracy. Individual distinction, manifested in nobility of character or creative ability, as yet counted for nothing unless backed up by rank or title. Consonant with the aristocratic class structure of their time, career administrators, in Prussia as elsewhere, attached the utmost importance to inequalities of rank, precedence, propriety, and reputation. Accordingly, they were extremely touchy when it came to any infringement of their "rights," privileges of service rank and precious symbols of pride and vanity.

The bickering over the ornaments of social position was not just a matter of personal fancy or an idle quest for mere prestige. The unabating struggle over the assessment of social class distinctions had an objective foundation. It rested on actual status inequality in professional life and in society at large and on strong awareness of these differences, which were sustained by the prevalent practice of according differential treatment to nobles and nonnobles. Although after the early eighteenth century all board members in the reconstructed or newly created collegial administrative bodies were officially rated and seated according to their service grade and seniority and, therefore, irrespective of birth and original social position, the conflict between the old social rank scale and the new professional service ladder was patched up rather than resolved. This situation produced a host of delicate problems, and it encouraged a

---

[2] *A.B.B.*, IV, part 1, 588, 655–56; V, part 1, 545ff., 623ff.; VII, 666; XII, 464, and *passim*; *Forschungen*, XXI (1908), 602ff.; A. Skalweit, *Die ostpreussische Domänenverwaltung*, 110.

pattern of interpersonal relationships which was replete with self-assertive scheming, watchful animosity, meticulous rank disputes, and ponderous, interminable quibbling over social etiquette.

A few illustrations, chosen at random, will throw light on the feelings and claims of the representatives of some bureaucratic social types. Promotion to the post of *Steuerrat* frequently went to the head of the elated new incumbents who had come up the hard way and now learned to treat disdainfully those who hitherto had been their equals. They gave themselves the airs of swaggering parvenus. When on circuit, these social peacocks traveled in style with an entourage of "admirers," made up of petty town mayors and greasy aldermen on the lookout for special favors from their patron. Some *Steuerräte,* when advanced to a higher position, lost their sense of proportions altogether. Their stilted vanity and, particularly, their overbearing attitude towards subordinate noble and nonnoble service officers made them objects of ridicule.[3]

Conversely, wealthy pedigreed snobs of the von Viereck type, in their contacts with "common" associates of equal or higher service grade, did not easily lose their haughty ancient faith in their own ingrained superiority. Undaunted by the rules pertaining to the official rank scale, they found ways and means to express the thought that the higher class, made up of old-established noble landowners, was *per se* the socially more valuable one.

In consequence of the divergence of attitudes and in frequent defiance of royal orders "to refrain once and for all from all wrangle and rancorous quarrels," controversies over "proper" seating arrangements or over the question as to whether a nonnoble functionary had the right to substitute for a noble official in certain meetings on certain occasions, time and again grew from molehills into mountains. Sharp skirmishes grew out of the thorny problem as to whether signatures should be affixed to a document in the order of seniority, the service grade, or social rank.[4] For several genera-

---

[3] *Forschungen*, XXIII (1909), 596ff. See also W. Naudé, "Die merkantilistische Wirtschaftspolitik Friedrich Wilhelms I. und der Küstriner Kammerdirektor Hille," *Historische Zeitschrift*, XC (1903), 38–39.

[4] *A.B.B.*, II, 387; III, 625, 726ff.

tions, disputes of this kind were the object of personal and social rivalry.

Reclassifications in the professional hierarchy sometimes caused much resentment. Thus, in 1723, the noble *Landräte* felt tormented when Frederick William I, in his revised "table of ranks," dared to accord a higher grade to the largely nonnoble War and Domains councilors than to themselves. And this pill was the more bitter to swallow since both the wellborn and the newly ennobled ministers of the General Directory had certified the social preëminence of the Herren *Landräte* by reminding the capricious overlord that gentlemen of this type "represent the whole county and, as a rule, are socially the most distinguished members of the *noblesse* in it."[5]

Argument and strife extended far into the reign of Frederick II who made it known that he "hated" these "trifles."[6] Until the 1720's the administrative bureaucracy was a house divided against itself. Chronic discord over areas of competence and questions of corporate prestige, aside from their effect upon efficiency, discipline, and loyalty, proved quite important for the self-esteem and the purse of the members of the group.

The chief contenders were the War Commissariats and the Domains boards. The former, among many other activities, were in charge of collecting the municipal state taxes, the *Akzise*. To increase the aggregate amount and to demonstrate thereby their fiscal effectiveness, they tended to foster the urban industrial and commercial interests. The Domains boards, on the other hand, were intimately tied to the agrarian economy. This made for incessant altercation between the two bureaucratic groups.[7] The founding of the General Directory and of the Boards of War and Domains brought about the merger of the two service branches, so that "if they want to amuse themselves, there is no need any more to wage war against each other through law suits."[8]

[5] *Ibid.*, IV, part 1, 234, 483ff.
[6] *Ibid.*, VII, 34; VIII, 188.
[7] *Ibid.*, III, 532–33. For an excellent summary, see O. Hintze, *Die Hohenzollern und ihr Werk*, 8th ed. (Berlin, 1916), 287–291; Carl Hinrichs, in *Acta Borussica. Wollindustrie*, 55.
[8] *A.B.B.*, III, 625.

Unification by compulsion, by dictatorial decree of the royal top bureaucrat, dried up one of the most formidable springs of intra-group hostilities which had sapped the strength of both factions and retarded their combined triumph over the high judiciary. This closing of ranks immeasurably deepened the sense of solidarity and, hence, the political striking power of the administrative class as a whole. The long-standing conflict with the *Regierungen* now reached its climax. The way was paved for the settling of accounts between the two vying state service oligarchies.

III

During their long war the antagonists excelled in the use of provocative tactics. Spiteful litigation, trickery, and sabotage were favorite fighting techniques. Time and again, the struggle was enlivened by personality and prestige squabbles, descending, occasionally, to fisticuffs. Such questions as who should occupy the best office rooms set off fierce debates and character assassination. Thus, in the realm of interservice relations, too, endless wrangling over social precedence and the intricacies of professional decorum and the social amenities gave plenty of exercise to sharp pens, malicious tongues, and mocking eyebrows.[9]

The balance of power in this contest turned against the defenders of the pre-absolutist regime slowly at first, but more rapidly after the early 1720's. The arrival of the new bureaucrats found expression in the partial political displacement of the old bureaucrats. The latter gradually lost all their traditional policy-making and nonjudicial administrative functions, retaining only a somewhat curtailed hold over the ecclesiastical and educational establishments. They were even stripped of a considerable portion of the judicial authority which had been the core of their professional activities.

Conversely, the new official hierarchy assumed vast judicial powers as members of administrative boards in the provinces and of the central executive in Berlin. The royal servants initiated and carried out judicial action, whenever and wherever a public, that is,

[9] Particularly revealing illustrations in *ibid.*, IV, part 1, 557ff.; IV, part 2, 374ff.; V, part 1, 134; XIII, 709–10.

a dynastic or bureau interest was involved. Every expansion of their authority, every victory won over the retreating *officiers* brought to the commissars handsome compensations: improvement of their career prospects; expansion of their salary, fee and bonus-yielding positions; and growth of corporate power and of individual and collective self-esteem.

The debasement of the high judiciary had noteworthy financial aspects. Frederick William I, in his drive for royal autocracy, helped to smoke out the obstinate dignitaries of the supreme courts. In certain instances he refused to give his approval to the filling of vacancies. More frequently, when new appointments were actually made, he sponsored "intruders" or more loathsome "undesirables" who through purchase established themselves as "trading justices" or served as royal minions. Sometimes, he confiscated whole salary lines and transferred them as a permanent bonus to ranking members of his administrative staff.[10] Furthermore, the contracting volume of business of the *Regierungen* entailed a substantial loss in fees and gifts to the detriment of the administrators of the pre-absolutist law. The indignation and anger which embittered the conflict between the two service hierarchies were, in no small measure, rooted in their competitive acquisitive interests.

Disintegration from within furthered the process. While the royal servants gradually gained in group unity, the old officials lost much of their former cohesion and solidarity. The old governing elite failed to maintain a united front even against attack. Torn between conflicting desires, its members had to make difficult personal and political choices. Ever since the pursuit of arbitrary policies by the Elector Frederick William, adaptable deserters had come to the fore. Less hampered by class custom and class prejudice, they had enlisted in the stronger battalions. Those who gave aid and comfort to the founder of Hohenzollern absolutism by leaving the decentralized judicial service and joining the centralizing administrative service of commissars retained the influence in public life to which they had been accustomed.

[10] *Ibid.*, VI, part 1, 208, 441–42; A. Skalweit, *Die ostpreussische Domänen-verwaltung*, 63.

Another distinctive group of Junker nobles which identified itself with the absolute state consisted of disgruntled elements who, previously, had been politically boycotted, although they came, like the Dohnas, Dönhoffs, and Schliebens, from wealthy and renowned families. Because they were Calvinists, they had been shut off from office in the *Ständestaat* government by the parochial-minded Lutheran majority of the community of fellow squires. Frustrated noblemen of this type were cordially welcomed and richly rewarded by the crown, eager for support by the highborn. They in turn availed themselves of the opportunity to break out of the political ghetto by gaining a leading position in dynastic service, commensurate with their social rank and economic position.

The bait of accelerated promotions and special favors held out to Junker renegades also attracted a few venturesome, energetic, and ambitious dissidents who lived above their means. Such a man, for example, was Count Truchsess von Waldburg, who at the age of thirty-five reached the peak of his government career by becoming the administrative top official with the title *Oberpräsident* in the province of East Prussia. A squire and a former army lieutenant, he was a forceful and persevering organizer. At the same time, however, he was extraordinarily resourceful in selling his services at a high price.[11] Upon entry into the civil state service he had indicated, politely yet pointedly, the terms of collaboration. His Royal Majesty, instead of harboring the strange idea "that I should sacrifice part of my private income in His service, rather would provide for me most generously in such a way that, with regard to my private interest, I can be at ease and, therefore, without handicap can be all the better equipped to watch out in all matters for Your Royal Majesty's welfare."[12]

Increasingly numerous defections from the ranks of the judiciary and territorial *Ständestaat* officials jeopardized group morale and the chances of successful collective defense against the attacks of the commissars. Intragroup unity was further impaired by a revolt of the "learned bench" against the "noble bench." The nonnoble

---

[11] A. Skalweit, *Die ostpreussische Domänenverwaltung*, 48–64.
[12] *A.B.B.*, II, 151.

judges showed signs of considerable unrest after the new administrative bureaucracy seriously challenged the traditional preëminence of predetermined social rank derived from birth. They were jealous of the fact that a *roturier* official could give orders to a nobleman inferior in service rank. Thereafter, the common judiciary aspired to status equality with their noble fellow workers, especially since some of the latter were merely sinecure-holding proprietary parasites.

This disruptive social duel bred mutual distrust, chicanery, and hatred. It gave rise to trivial and seemingly absurd, yet very revealing controversies, to interminable hairsplitting over social rights and customs and the delicate, circuitous ways of measuring social distance. In the *Regierung* of Cleves, for instance, a veritable uproar was caused in 1715 by the simple fact that a freshly ennobled councilor "forgot himself" by venturing to take a seat in church on the bench reserved to the nobly born.[13]

Assailed from different quarters, with functions curtailed, sources of income trimmed, and real power largely lost, the retreating placemen of the *Regierungen* clung more desperately than ever to their claim to superior social rank. Indeed, they had little left in which to take pride except their ancestors and their assured social status. For the time being, even Frederick William I proved powerless in his attempt to impose his utilitarian scale of social values. Although his revised "table of ranks" accorded precedence to the administrative councilors (*Kriegs- und Domänenräte*) over the judicial councilors (*Regierungsräte*) and he often expressed contempt for the latter, these vilified men, as a group, retained the flavor of superior social prestige until the remaking of Prussian institutions under the leadership of Stein and Hardenberg.[14]

Thus for two more generations the members of the *Regierungen* continued to be recognized as the more "distinguished" bureaucrats by the landed nobility of Prussia. And this aristocracy of serf-masters was still, as in the Habsburg empire and in post-Petrine Russia, the

---

[13] *Ibid.*, II, 228ff. See also XIII, 4–7.

[14] As for Frederick William's "table of ranks" and his caustic comments on job applicants whom he regarded "good enough to be made councilor in a *Regierung*," see *ibid.*, I, 410–419; III, 328–29; IV, part 1, 392ff.

chief determinant in gauging position in "society." With regard to its historic function, the "social" victory of the high judiciary was more than a consolation prize for political defeat. As will be seen, it also was the gratifying symbol of the triumph, limited but genuine, over the mind of the official parvenu elite which had won the battle for preponderance in the management of the civil state.

The contacts between the two oligarchies were not marked by friction and conflict only. They had various tastes in common. They acted more and more like congenial special interest groups. In their own self-seeking ways they were stirred to greater efforts under the whip of the crown. Both factions were apt to identify the public interest with the interest of their bureaus, the interest of the bureaus with the private interests of the bureau members, and the private interests of the members with their personal interests in career making, prestige hunting, and pecuniary opportunities.

Much human traffic had moved across the social barriers and the political and functional fighting lines since 1660. The ramified cross-currents of nepotism and favoritism, fortified by intermarriage, were indicative of the fact that there was room for unity in the midst of diversity. Mutual infiltration helped to pave the way for reconciliation. The intermingling of personnel speeded up the process which wrought a gradual amalgamation of conflicting values and attitudes. Occasional professional intergroup associations for coöperation against the excessive demands of the royal autocrat or against arbitrary interference by the army had been further cemented by social connections of blood, of friendship, of acquaintanceship, and by the soothing effect of convivial habits, which promoted understanding, tolerance, and readiness to bargain.

Thus Truchsess von Waldburg found conspicuous consumption, financed by the crown, fascinating. His major professional achievement was reform of the land tax in East Prussia. As it happened, his effectiveness as an administrator was intimately linked to his crowded social activities. His suave methods, made more palatable by his excellent cuisine, made a substantial contribution to the political reëducation of the adamant East Prussian squirearchy and its leaders. In view of the obstacles in the way of his effort to "Prussianize" the old ruling class of East Prussia, Waldburg had a strong point when he implored his sovereign to have pity on his "table's urgent need by supplying him most graciously with eight elks, eight stags, six wild boars, twelve deers per year" or when, shortly thereafter, he requested the royal master to give a new *élan* to his servant's professional zeal by paying his formidable debts. Even absolute kings had to be told "that it depends on God alone to change the spirit of a nation. Based on experience, I know that in my early years I accomplished more through munificence in feasting and drinking and rendered better service to Your Royal Majesty than I am capable of doing now."[15]

Whatever the effects of jovial fellowship, the gastronomic arts, and common recreation grounds in the working out of a *modus vivendi* between the high judiciary, the administrative bureaucracy, the squirearchy, and the military service aristocracy, certain chords of social affinity and mutual respect had always linked the noble career administrators to the Junker members of the *Regierungen*. From its inception, the rising elite of commissioned officers had managed to dilute the emerging "merit system." The growing practice of personnel replenishment by inbreeding gave a new turn to the hoary *Indigenatsrecht*. By broadening its social base, it now was sustained by custom rather than hereditary right.

Successful bourgeois bureaucrats who had made a place for themselves in the administrative hierarchy derived particular benefit from this readjustment of the new to the old pattern of civil government service. Inasmuch as these seminobles no longer regarded themselves as *homines novi* or feared to be identified with "the lower orders," their enthusiasm for competition sharply declined. In the latter part of the reign of Frederick William I, who was by now a disillusioned and more easygoing man, they and their noble colleagues worked out their destiny more freely. In the search for a defense mechanism that would make their personal success and the fortune of their families secure, they learned to see the mentality of their competitors, the oldstyle patrimonial *officiers*, in a new light. They yielded to the assimilating power of the idea that the

[15] *Ibid.*, III, 47, 199; see also 216ff.

state as the inheritable estate of a small, privileged group of families deserved, in altered forms, a new lease on life.

Even more far-reaching was the "mental corruption" of most of the newly ennobled among the administrative bureaucrats. For them a government career carried with it a "double social promotion," the shift, first, from common to *bourgeois gentilhomme* and, then, from seminoble to noble status and, as a rule, to membership in the wealthy brackets of the squirearchy. Striving for social approval by the highborn, aspiring to admission, on the footing of equality of treatment, to the "best circles," they had good reason to wink at the canons of Junker class bias which had been transmitted from the more distant past.

Thus, the development of the new bureaucracy's sense of social status was largely molded in the image of the aristocratic standards inherited from the *Ständestaat*. Concomitantly, the political mentality of the haughty owners of the supreme courts became more bureaucratic and more Prussian. In this connection it was significant that many of their relatives by blood and by marriage had become Prussian army officers while some others had entered the administrative service. In the course of time, the high judiciary ceased to look upon absolutism as the embodiment of injustice, tyranny, and autocracy. Slowly it adopted a more friendly attitude towards "Prussia," her institutions, policies, and conspicuous achievements. Strong traces of the old political rancor and of the distaste for bureaucratic centralization lingered on. But they did not prevent the revision of attitudes.

Thus the tensions between the two services subsided, and the antagonism between these groups was greatly attenuated. Toward the middle of the eighteenth century, cleavage gave way to a spirit of reasonable, almost amicable coöperation, of live and let live, of give and take. The subtle transmutation had important historic repercussions which greatly aided the resurgence of the nobility as the ruling social force in the polity. The appeased and reconciled official elite of the *Ständestaat* began to amalgamate with the commissioned executives of the absolute monarchy and that recast the structure of the dynastic-bureaucratic-aristocratic body politic. Under the imaginative leadership of Samuel von Cocceji (1679–1755) the stage for the new pattern was set in the 1740's and 50's.[16] Thereafter, the reconstituted body of old guard officials was a component, yet distinct and self-reliant part of the royal Prussian bureaucracy, the hierarchy of absolute government.

IV

Cocceji's career, both as a public figure and a tenacious social climber, epitomized important aspects of the process of the regrouping of the Prussian governing class. At the same time, Cocceji points to some of the major problems ushered in by the "noble reaction" against centralized and bureaucratized autocracy. Cocceji played an important role in giving a "modern" touch to the persistent struggle of the nobility for its ancient liberties.

Most Prussian ministers of the seventeenth and eighteenth centuries were men without inner culture and intellectual or aesthetic refinement. At best, they were technical experts. Cocceji, however, was a highly distinguished scholar, "an incorruptible man and eminent jurist," as Frederick II characterized him.[17] Yet, underneath the brilliant surface of Cocceji's checkered life as an author and man of learning, as an administrator, politician, and social career maker there was hidden a tragic undercurrent of shattered hopes, of weak compromises, and of elements of self-betrayal. Cocceji discovered how precarious, irritating, and demoralizing, even after a lengthy "probationary" period, were the terms of professional and social advancement for a person who was not a regular fellow.

The son of a prosperous and renowned jurist, Cocceji received a thorough higher education before he, though a commoner, made the cavalier's tour through Europe. In 1702, as a young professor of law

[16] On Cocceji see A. Stölzel, *Brandenburg-Preussens Rechtsverwaltung*, II, 50–235; O. Hintze, in *A.B.B.*, VI, part 1, 82–134; *idem., Geist und Epochen*, 118–131; E. Loening, in *Verwaltungsarchiv*, II (1894), 258–270; *Allgemeine Deutsche Biographie*, IV, 373–376; Ernst Landsberg, *Geschichte der deutschen Rechtswissenschaft*, part 3, I (Munich, 1898), 112–115; R. Koser, *König Friedrich der Grosse*, I, 322–23.

[17] *Politische Testamente*, 118.

in the University of Frankfort on the Oder, he attained noble status by virtue of the ennoblement of his father. Shortly thereafter Cocceji entered the high judiciary which at that time was made up mostly of legal amateurs. In 1727, he became a minister of justice and thus the professional colleague of the Junker von Plotho, whose noble pedigree dated back to the thirteenth century and who did his utmost to keep Cocceji in his place. Nevertheless, ten years later, the practical need of rewarding superior merit to facilitate the reorganization of the judicial service in the image of the new administrative bureaucracy overcame social prejudice and personal favoritism. In 1737, just after having been investigated by a special royal committee, Cocceji was appointed *ministre chef de justice*.[18] He owed his promotion to the recommendation of the committee which recognized the fertility of his mind, the extraordinary range of his legal knowledge, his exceptional ability as an organizer, and his tireless energy. In the years to come, however, Cocceji's official career met setbacks.

Like virtually all the other recently ennobled top officials, Cocceji had found his way into the elite of wealth within the landed aristocracy. Through his marriage with the daughter of General von Beschefer he became the owner of several large estates. In his own estimation it was a most pleasing reward for his toils that the indigenous nobility, the *Ritterschaft* of Pomerania accepted him as one of them. He managed to establish two of his sons as Prussian army officers, while two of his daughters married officers of noble lineage. In view of these gratifying manifestations of professional recognition, growing affluence, and social arrival, Cocceji's pride and vanity were deeply hurt by the fact that he continued to be treated contemptuously by caste-conscious members of the old world of gentility who continued to measure human values and the right to direct public affairs by the number of nobly born ancestors. An oldline aristocrat like the Silesian magnate and Catholic grandee von Schaffgotsch felt outraged by the mere possibility that "a man of such noble birth as myself should be confounded with somebody of

[18] *A.B.B.*, V, part 2, 275.

such poor extraction as the Lord Chancellor." To him, Cocceji was but an obnoxious parvenu, full of "perfidy and *mauvaise foi.*"[19]

That the sentiments and reservations of prominent members of the old official elite still carried a great deal of weight was brought home to Cocceji by Georg Dietloff von Arnim, one of his coministers of justice. Arnim represented the legal and political ideas, the tastes and attitudes of the traditional Junker judiciary at its very best. He was a well-educated cavalier and refined man of the world, as these terms were understood in the courtly society of western Europe at that time. Arnim was an economically independent *grand seigneur* by inheritance and habituation, a former courtier, army captain, and supreme court justice who had traveled widely. He took particular pride in the fact that he had lived for many years in masterly fashion at Boitzenburg, the country seat of his forefathers, who since the medieval German drive to the East had played a leading role in the public affairs of East Elbia.

Throughout his long-suffering professional association with Cocceji, Arnim treated his colleague with an exasperating mixture of ironic reticence and snobbish courtesy, polite amusement, sarcastic sharpness, and calculated insolence of tone, while from the dark he shot at him with poisoned arrows. Methodically Arnim built up a strong faction among the judicial dignitaries of Berlin whom he frequently entertained at dinner with mocking and derogatory remarks about Cocceji and his followers. Cocceji returned these edifying compliments by calling his rival "a Jesuit and an Italian." Arnim, a pugnacious skeptic when it came to school learning and reformers with ideas, saw in Cocceji a clumsy pusher and rootless "go-getter," a *bourgeois gentilhomme*, whose zealous, ever busy, and exacting workmanship threatened to obliterate the casual, almost flippant old ways of transacting public business. Thus the lines were clearly drawn.

In 1737, when appointed to his new post, Cocceji had been given the difficult special assignment of injecting Prussian discipline into the administration of justice by making the judiciary mend its ways

---

[19] Max Lehmann, ed., *Preussen und die katholische Kirche seit 1640*, III (Berlin, 1882), 434–35.

and by reorganizing the hopelessly inefficient and corrupt courts of law above the level of local proprietary Junker "justice."[20] At that time, save for the Rhenish territories, the predominance of the noble squire judges, though weakened, was not yet broken in the superior courts.[21] In the judicial service local right, privilege of birth, and family prestige still were the chief requirements of appointment. However, although the balance of numbers and power remained with the old, self-perpetuating noble families, their ancestral prerogative was challenged by Frederick William I's autocratic practice of selling judicial offices to the highest bidder and by threatening "disobedient" *Regierungsräte* with dismissal.

From the outset, Cocceji met the unremitting sabotage of his three cominsters in the justice department: von Arnim, von Broich, and von Brandt. His attempt to lower or abolish judicial fees and court charges made him many enemies among bench members and court officials who resented any reform to cut down their material perquisites.[22] But even the official leaders of the administrative bureaucracy, the elderly gentlemen in the General Directory, by now had lost all interest in serious innovations. In consequence, they secretly opposed Cocceji. Having evolved into "permanent politicians," these top bureaucrats had learned to turn tendencies toward reform into a spiritless defense of the *status quo*. Above all, however, the cunning intrigues of Arnim accounted for the fact that Cocceji did not get anywhere and was, in 1739, stripped of all power. Arnim directed the successful campaign against Cocceji's "overhasty" and "confused" proposals and measures. He made Cocceji appear as a man who was bent on establishing himself as the king's "co-regent" and on usurping an amount of authority as "hardly ever a prime minister has arrogated to himself."[23] For a number of years, Cocceji, smarting under the affronts and intrigues by Arnim, was put on inactive duty and thus forced to bury his plans of judicial reform.

Cocceji's comeback started on a rather modest scale, in 1742, with

[20] *A.B.B.*, V, part 2, 279–293, 317, 504ff.
[21] *Ibid.*, VI, part 1, 131, 283, 333ff., 369, 382ff., 461ff.; VI, part 2, 871–898.
[22] *Ibid.*, V, part 2, 783ff., 792ff.
[23] *Ibid.*, V, part 2, 783–797.

his short-lived appointment as "special minister of justice" for newly conquered Lower Silesia. Like most public career men in this crafty age, he was not particularly scrupulous in the choice of means. Thus he managed to ingratiate himself with Prussia's new ruler, Frederick II, by "proving," in an unsolicited, anonymously published political pamphlet, that the armed aggression of Silesia, far from being an act of violence, was in accord with "natural rights." For, "if someone wants to vindicate his property no declaration of war is necessary."[24]

Cocceji, in 1746, was triumphantly reinstated as the head of the department of justice with the title of Lord Chancellor. For the next nine years he concentrated in his hands a string of policy making and legislative and executive functions which, in effect, almost amounted to the establishment of a personal dictatorship over the professional judiciary and the administration of private and criminal law. After having lost many rounds against Arnim, his implacable enemy, Cocceji now won the last one by bringing about the "resignation" of the hated rival who to the very end thundered against Cocceji's "unbearable despotism."[25] As Lord Chancellor Cocceji was given by his young sovereign more discretionary authority than was entrusted to any Prussian minister in the eighteenth century. Only the Frenchman de Launay, the powerful chief of the reorganized Prussian excise and customs administration, the so-called *Régie* from 1766 to 1786, enjoyed a similar degree of independence from monocratic rulership.

V

Cocceji was near his seventies when he was called upon to overhaul, piece by piece, the old-fashioned and disjointed judicial structure of the Hohenzollern states and to integrate the old official hierarchy more firmly into the absolute monarchy. This task was commensurate with his unusual talents, excellent workmanship, and fierce determination to arrive, at long last, at real power.

---

[24] Quoted in Stölzel, *Brandenburg-Preussens Rechtsverwaltung*, II, 149–50.
[25] *A.B.B.*, VI, part 2, 674.

Although Cocceji did not attain all his objectives, he accomplished a great deal.

He set out to "nationalize" and, hence, to "Prussianize" the administration of justice by subjecting the professional guardians of law to centralized controls. Thereby he subjugated, though superficially, the higher courts of law to royal sovereignty. He also injected elements of unity into the mazes of legal regionalism by drafting and promulgating a new statute law which simplified and standardized the cumbersome legal procedures. He lowered the costs and accelerated the tempo of litigation by a sustained attack upon inertia, bribery, and judicial racketeering, deeply entrenched practices which even in the most civilized countries of western Europe marred the administration of justice. Frederick II hailed these reforms, although, in his considered opinion, "rapacity" was bound to appear "in a new mask, and the laws will be bypassed through arbitrary interpretation."[26] Cocceji even took steps toward the establishment of legal unity through codification. Thus he began with the preparation of a code, based upon natural law, of private, substantive law which he attempted to harmonize with Roman law as well as with the administrative law, the current needs of the absolute police state, and with the hearty appetites of the Junker squires.

In the pursuit of his policies Cocceji did not forget himself. Although he thought that his royal master might have endowed him a little more generously with authority, he actually succeeded in building up a formidable bureaucratic empire over which he ruled as chief policy maker, virtually independent managing director, and all-powerful patronage dispenser. Ironically enough, it was a former commoner and university teacher, the son and grandson of professors of law, who was destined to halt the decay of the aristocratic *Regierungen*, the battered strongholds of the *Ständestaat*. Cocceji, a middle class scholar by training, developed into a wealthy neo-Junker and, in 1749, became a baron, and made these corporations function more effectively as liaison bodies between the squire-

[26] *Pol. Testamente*, 118.

archy and the absolute monarch. He gave a new *élan* to the hard-pressed old judiciary.

The conversion of judicial *officiers* into accountable and removable royal servants was the keystone of the revitalized administration of justice. The old official aristocracy had lost much of its former power and in craftsmanship, too, had become inferior to the administrative bureaucracy. In 1737, the perturbed Prussian ministers of justice gave a caustic appraisal of the professional caliber of the members of the overstaffed courts of law. "Many presidents of judicial boards who never studied or, even if they had studied something superficially" were declared utterly unfit "to supervise the councilors and attorneys and to keep them under control." Similarly defective was the work of the great bulk of the councilors. The members of the judiciary were "mostly young, unadaptable, and inexperienced people" and but "a burden to the country," since "they attempt by all sorts of ways and methods to make profit or gain means of support at the expense of the public."[27] A decade later, Cocceji noted that "those of the nobility did not study any more for the past thirty years, but devoted themselves to military service. The *roturiers* purchased their positions through the Recruiting Chest and, consequently, neglected serious scholarly studies."[28]

In view of this state of affairs it was an extravagantly ambitious undertaking to attempt to build up in a hurry a judicial state service, composed of properly qualified and objectively tested experts of law. Cocceji had to rest content with modification of the old spoils system by the rudiments of a merit system. He abolished the venality of judgeships and concentrated the royal power of hiring and firing in his own hands.

He struck a decisive blow against the fee system of compensation which either had not yielded enough income to attract able men or had turned officeholders into plutocrats at the expense of the people. To socialize the professional administration of law, to disengage the state from private profiteering, and to transform justice into an expeditious and honest public service, Cocceji introduced

[27] *A.B.B.*, V, part 2, 279–283.
[28] *Ibid.*, VIII, 47.

a fixed remuneration for the formerly unsalaried and, on the average, doubled the salary of those councilors for whom a budget line had been available previously.[29] By securing for his *Regierungsräte* higher pay than was accorded, as a rule, to the administrative councilors, he reinsured the traditionally superior social prestige of the judicial administration (*Rechtsverwaltung*) as against the more powerful regular administration (*Kameralverwaltung*).

Cocceji also improved the relative position of the judicial councilors vis-a-vis the administrative bureaucrats by raising the professional standards of the former and thus bringing them nearer the efficiency and discipline of the latter. Cocceji carried out a purge of the judiciary by checking on credentials and by personally testing the professional performance of numerous judges. For all prospective bench members he introduced, as a matter of principle, prescribed university training in law. He also stiffened the entrance examinations.

By imposing more uniform norms and regulations upon the courts of law; by injecting an impersonal quality into the professional work of their members and by subjecting them to centralized supervision, Cocceji strengthened the bureaucratic character and the royal service complexion of the administration of private and criminal law. Thus, no doubt, he considerably accelerated the process of converting the old official hierarchy into a disciplined body of commissioned functionaries, subordinate to the directives of the ministry of justice.

Baron von Cocceji, who in the course of his career had developed a strong attachment to the landed nobility of which he had become a member, refrained from seriously attacking the aristocratic social structure of the legal system. It continued to be founded on the principles of inequality before the law and of justice as a function of graded privilege and of upper class power. The sacrosanct judicial authority of the squires, as such, was left untouched. These autocratic jurisdictions, therefore, remained an appendage of the private rights of noble landed property.

---

[29] For a detailed summary of the personnel and of the salary schedules in the higher courts, as of 1745, see *ibid.*, VI, part 2, 871–898. See also VII, 299ff.

Cocceji pursued most of his policies of reform in consultation and close coöperation with the spokesmen of the territorial estates (*Landstände*). Political acumen and diplomatic skill brought about a negotiated settlement in province after province. Thus he was instrumental in reactivating, on a modest scale, the political influence of the old territorial organs of Junkerdom's co-government which previously had disintegrated. Cocceji even managed to persuade the noble defenders of the vestiges of the *Ständestaat* to foot a substantial part of the salary bill of the reconstituted hierarchy. By becoming its principal paymaster, the squirearchy, without functioning as a bureaucracy, improved its political position within the bureaucratized monarchy. Thus the professional administrators of justice, though henceforth royal servants and mostly nonnobles, maintained the traditional, intimate alliance with the landed interest. In his dealings with the people worthy of special consideration, the Lord Chancellor could be a very affable man. Hence he did not hesitate further to cement the manifold ties that connected the supreme courts of law with the landed nobility of their region by calling upon the representatives of the First Estate to submit to him nominations for ranking appointments.[30]

Whatever his complex motives and wavering objectives, judged by his deeds, Cocceji shared the responsibility for rendering innocuous the activities of the administrative bureaucracy in the autocratic home rule of the Junkers. It was Cocceji who, in 1751, led the opposition of the noble landowners against the mild agrarian reform schemes of the crown and who, through skilful cabal and sophistry, prevented the contemplated reduction of the servile labor obligations of the peasantry. In this contest of strength Cocceji identified himself without reservations with the cause of time-honored class privilege and lent his support to the squires. He based his arguments on the complacent assertion that the proposed changes would violate venerable rights; that they would not benefit the peasants; that they would result in the economic ruin of the landed

[30] *Ibid.*, VIII, 47.

nobility and prevent it thereafter from sending its sons into the Prussian army.[31]

Even in his capacity as the master of the personnel administration of the judicial bureaucracy Cocceji appeased the defenders of old-time usages. The superiority of the old social rank order over the professional rank order in the judicial service was kept intact. Cocceji maintained the distinction between a noble and a nonnoble bench wherever it was still in existence in the higher courts.[32] And his successors, until 1809, continued to uphold the ancient order of precedence. They rejected as presumptuous and "completely erroneous" the liberal interpretation which self-assertive, lowborn judges were inclined to give to Cocceji's reforms by assuming that all bench members, without regard for their background, had the same duties and the same rights. Supported by Frederick II, the heads of the justice department adhered to the conservative maxim that from time immemorial the considered policy of the government had been "to preserve each social estate in its well-established privileges without injury and to protect it accordingly."[33]

The newly introduced official standards, designed to make appointments and promotions contingent on "merit," barely affected the top of the judicial hierarchy. High birth, valuable connections, and wealth were, as in the past, the essential prerequisites for the presidency of a *Regierung*.[34] For decades to come, therefore, some of these select gentlemen "bureaucrats" turned out to be indolent professional charlatans.[35] The conception of merit, as defined for practical purposes by Cocceji and his immediate successors, keenly reflected the priority of the noble prestige values, but also the impact of human nature in politics. Mindful of his agonizing association with von Arnim, who had a strong personality, Cocceji chose as

[31] See O. Hintze, "Zur Agrarpolitik Friedrichs des Grossen," *Forschungen*, X (1898), 281ff.

[32] *A.B.B.*, VI, part 2, 517.

[33] *Ibid.*, XIII, 4-7.

[34] *Ibid.*, XIII, 69ff., 384ff.; XIV, 167-68, 562, 595-96.

[35] But quite an exception after the middle of the eighteenth century was an odious delinquent like President von Braxein. See *A.B.B.*, XIV, 452-460, 552-555.

ranking top aides respectable but colorless mediocrities who added social luster to his department. Thus he contrived to surround himself with men like Count Reuss, whom he made attractive to Frederick II by presenting as an "honest and incorruptible man," who had "some knowledge of law" and through a Dutch inheritance promised to become "the richest cavalier in Prussian lands."[36]

Cocceji's organizational, legal, and personnel reforms had a unifying political principle. As semi-autocratic leader of the judicial bureaucracy it was Cocceji's all-absorbing ambition to resolve, once and for all, the century-old struggle for supremacy between the two civil government hierarchies, between the higher courts of law and the administrative boards. He wanted to reverse the existing balance of power between the two elites; to reconquer with royal support for the rejuvenated *Regierungen* their bygone preëminence in the control of public affairs; to strip the administrative bureaucracy of all judicial authority by transferring the administration of public law to the reorganized judicial bureaucracy. Cocceji aimed at a clean-cut separation between judicial and executive powers which, if carried out, would have entailed an administrative revolution and the practical introduction of constitutionally limited government, representative of the political will of the high judiciary and the landed aristocracy.

What Cocceji had hoped to be the crowning consummation of all his laborious efforts ended in failure. His political defeat he rightly attributed to the "ambition and vested interest" of the administrative boards, to their desire "to have a hand in every pie," and to their fear of "being regarded as a zero," if they were deprived of all judicial authority.[37] At the height of the bitter fight for the attainment of his ultimate ends Cocceji eloquently pleaded before His Royal Majesty: "I testify before God that I seek with this *règlement* nothing but the conservation of Your subjects so that they are once and for all protected against the injustices of the Boards and the tyranny" of the administrative councilors.[38]

[36] *Ibid.*, VIII, 49; IX, 286.
[37] *Ibid.*, VIII, 143.
[38] *Ibid.*, VIII, 134.

Although defeated, Cocceji was not put to rout. In the end, his political fight produced a substantial and socially significant result which further accentuated the inequality of rights in Prussian society. No group, save for the nobility, gained effective legal protection against arbitrary government action, for Cocceji, the stubborn old warrior, succeeded in recapturing for the *Regierungen* the right of handling, without interference by the agents of administrative law, all cases in which a nobleman was involved, even if the crown was the plaintiff.

Cocceji thus contributed to the working out of a relatively stable *modus vivendi.* The new compromise was welcome to Frederick II, palatable to the Junker squires and, without removing the scars of the interservice divisions, acceptable to the administrative bureaucracy, which came to realize that its judicial rival for power, though difficult to live with, was impossible to live without. The recasting of the legal institutions of Prussia and the ultimate absorption of the old official hierarchy into the ranks of the royal service gave to the high judiciary a clearly circumscribed and more definite share in the management of dynastic authority. But in the long run even more important was the fact that the judicial reforms, directly as well as indirectly, bolstered the privileged position of the nobility at large in the absolute state.

A comparable, yet quite different regrouping of the civil state service classes, accompanied by a decisive shift in the interlocked relationship to both the old and the new nobility, had run its course in France. Here, the commissioned intendants of the eighteenth century were recruited from firmly entrenched parliamentary families, usually after they had become members of the select body of the *maîtres des requêtes* in the Council of State. They rose, therefore, from the ranks of the self-willed bureaucratic *noblesse de robe* of the "sovereign courts," which supplied both the core and the leadership of the upper layers of the extraordinarily numerous hierarchy of patrimonial *officiers*. Frequently, and largely for the purpose of reducing friction between the administrative and judicial elites, the intendants remained members of the legal corporations and strongly attached to their regional and local connections.

The political implications of this interfusion of government personnel, however, were quite different in the two countries. In France, the high judiciary, starting its political resurgence under the Regency (1715–1723), functioned as a powerful check upon the absolute power of the crown and the central administrative bureaucracy.[39] In Prussia, on the other hand, the monarchical autocrat was restricted in the exercise of his sovereign authority by the self-centered squires. On the village and county district level, these masters over bondsmen retained independent jurisdictions which their French colleagues had largely lost. Frederick William I even turned over, in effect, the same tyrannical local judicial and police power to the nonnoble leasehold farmers who had come to manage the radically reorganized crown estates. Thus these agriculturists, though essentially private entrepreneurs engaged in business for profit, were elevated to the status of temporary *officiers* in possession of delegated public authority over the state serfs.[40]

In France, the absolute monarchy of the eighteenth century developed, in fact, more and more into a limited monarchy, limited by the self-perpetuating regional oligarchies of the judicial aristocracy. And indirectly, since by this time many members of the *parlements* belonged to the landed rich, the directors of the machinery of administrative centralization were restrained by the landed *noblesse*. The latter, moreover, as a bundle of organized political pressure groups, was a force to be reckoned with in the *pays d'état*. Here, the provincial estates, an institutional bequest of the French *Ständestaat*, had never been throttled completely, and

[39] See Philippe Sagnac, *La formation de la société française moderne*, II (Paris, 1946), 54–57, 166–169; Louis Gottschalk, "The French Parlements and Judicial Review," *Journal of the History of Ideas*, V (1944), 105–112; A. B. Cobban, "The Parlements of France in the Eighteenth Century," *History*, XXXV (1950), 64–80; Franklin L. Ford, *Robe and Sword. The Regrouping of the French Aristocracy after Louis XIV* (Cambridge, 1953), 246ff., and *passim*; Martin Göhring, *Geschichte der Grossen Revolution*, I (Tübingen, 1950), 91–101, 136–138.

[40] Often they were given the title *Oberamtmann*, *Amtsrat*, or *Kammerrat*. In the official cameralist vocabulary of eighteenth-century Prussia, this newly established economic elite was lumped together under the designation *Beamte*, a word which not before the very end of the century became a synonym for governmental bureaucrats.

during the second half of the eighteenth century they regained some of their former vigor. In France, accordingly, not only dynastic absolutism, but also the bureaucratic absolutism of the central administration became a matter of wishful thinking rather than of fact.

In Prussia, conversely, the absolute monarchy of the eighteenth century evolved into a peculiar species of personal royal autocracy which was gradually whittled down under the impact of a dual check: a check that came from the squirearchy itself and from the increasingly bold and independent corps of bureaucrats led by the administrative rather than the judicial service elite.

Chapter Seven

The Formation and Transformation of the Bureaucratic Nobility

I

The Prussian administrative elite had finally won the fateful battle for the manipulation of public law and thus for authoritarian government by the new bureaucracy under royal control and direction. But before it could aspire to independent action in routine administration, let alone to policy-making power, it still had to consolidate its position as an aristocratic status group within the upper class. The conquest of political leadership proved difficult since it entailed a struggle—dilatory, intricate, and intense—with the dynastic autocracy.

The transformation of the bureaucracy into a self-governing public service class and an almost autonomous political machine was not really accomplished before the age of the plebiscitary dictatorship of Napoleon I which made old-style monarchical absolutism hopelessly anachronistic. In Prussia, prior to Hardenberg's invocation, in 1807, of "democratic principles in a monarchical government," the cementing of the noble apex of the administrative service pyramid was an essential precondition to making the corporate power and political will of the authoritarian bureaucracy prevail over the absolute legal authority of the royal master.

In spite of the lessened importance of noble birth and landed property as determinants of political power and high social standing, aristocratic valuations in society, politics, and public administration retained their primacy during the eighteenth century. Noble status not only remained a special asset in professional state service, it also was a badge of any position of eminence in the governmental hierarchy. However, superiority of noble social rank, as recognized by the sovereign, was no longer identical with the priority of nobility of birth over high official position. But the influence of the traditional relationship between social status and public authority remained so powerful that those who attained leading posts under the crown and, therefore, were social notables simply had to be holders of noble rank, whether or not they were of gentle birth.

All this, with variations in standards and methods, was common European practice. In line with this trend, the new state service estates of the Hohenzollern monarchy were headed by a special segment of the nobility, the bureaucratic nobility. Throughout its formative stage, this elite was made up of two distinctive elements, of nobles of descent and of nobles of ascent. Since compromise between the Hohenzollerns and the Junkers was the cornerstone of the Prussian experiment in bureaucratic state making, the heavy weight of the latter was reflected in the evolution of the leadership personnel of the absolute monarchy.

Because the nobility by birth had been the ruling class in the society of the old *Ständestaat,* many of its members, acting as individuals, maintained or regained a special position in the absolute state simply by becoming commissioned officers and new bureaucrats on the basis of customary privilege and social favoritism. They derived special benefit from their inherited station, in tacit recognition of their claim to inborn, superior qualities of leadership. From the start it was common, and after the middle of the eighteenth century, usual practice to place these cavaliers at advantage by granting extra favors to them.

These occupationally mobile noblemen, by swamping the evolving Prussian army officers' corps, were the backbone of the traditionless military service aristocracy. In addition, a string of particularly responsive individuals and families, not infrequently recruited from the old body of officialdom, obtained prominent and gratifyingly lucrative positions as members of the much smaller new administrative elite. Throughout the history of the Prussian state, from the cradle to the grave, the armed forces, not the civil bureaucracy, were the primary mode of the Junkers' active participation in professionalized government.

Conversely, because the socially mixed upstart class of royal career administrators had a superior position in the polity as powerful, though dependent executives of rulership by dictation, all its nonnoble members from the grade of commissar or councilor upwards reduced their social distance from the old aristocracy. Hence the conferment of at least personal seminoble privileges upon all of them while in royal service and of a hereditary title of nobility upon those who attained high rank in the government. The traditional division of society into castelike estates, static in principle, was sufficiently flexible in operation to provide opportunity for ascending from the lower social orders to places of public dignity. Correspondingly, the royal system of incentives and rewards also had room for the granting of noble privileges and noble titles. In the highest service brackets the chasm between official status and social rank was thus neatly resolved. A synthesis between the new and the old concept of excellence was effected by the simple device of bestowing hereditary nobility upon all top executives who were "illborn." This soothing arrangement pleased the vanity of the *nouveaux arrivés* and, for the time being, reinforced their allegiance to the dynastic autocrat. It also raised, though not always immediately, their prestige and thereby their authority in the service and in the community at large. Whatever the more distant consequences, in the short run the policy of ennoblement facilitated the fulfillment of the cardinal task assigned to the bureaucracy: to act as transmitters of the royal will.

This fusion of two sets of values by welding together the old social rank order and the new service hierarchy went back to the original founder of Prussian absolutism, for it was the Elector Frederick William who paid tribute to the customs and prejudices of his time by inaugurating the dynastic practice of recognizing the "ennobling" character of meritorious government service through the grant of noble rank. In 1660, by becoming "sovereign" ruler of the duchy of East Prussia, which stood outside the loose nexus of the Holy Roman Empire, he acquired the legal right to "make nobles" on his own initiative.

With respect to both numbers and standards, the practice of admitting deserving individuals to the social dignity of the nobility was kept within narrow bounds in the Prussian monarchy. The policy of ennoblement, as pursued by the three leading Hohenzollerns, was a socially more restrictive and, politically, far more singleminded and purposeful affair than the thoroughly commercialized usages, which in the contemporaneous Bourbon and Habsburg monarchies resulted in multiplication of noblemen.[1] There advancement in social rank had come to rest to a large extent on a plutocratic foundation, on the ability and willingness to pay cash.[2] Although in Prussia, too, the nobility was anything but a closed caste, money, though important, was not the determining factor in gaining access to it. Significantly, in this military-bureaucratic state, dynastic service was the decisive channel of social mobility. Only a fighting career and a conspicuous position in the civil government were, with few exceptions, grounds for ennoblement. Furthermore, the acquisition of noble status was never a matter of right, even for the uppermost state managers.

Nevertheless, by the early eighteenth century it had become the established practice to confer, by royal letters patent, hereditary noble rank upon all lowborn bureaucrats at the moment of, if not prior to, their appointment as ministers of state. Especially under Frederick William I, the same favor rather frequently was extended to

[1] See Johann Georg M. von Mühlfeld, *Oesterreichisches Adels-Lexikon des 18. und 19. Jahrhunderts* (Vienna, 1822), *passim*; *idem, Ergänzungsband* (Vienna, 1824), *passim*; Ernst Kohn-Bramstedt, *Aristocracy and the Middle Classes in Germany. Social Types in German Literature 1830–1900* (London, 1937), 18–20; Jean Brissaud, *A History of French Public Law* (Boston, 1905), 297ff.; Charles Normand, *La bourgeoisie française au XVIIe siècle* (Paris, 1908), 11, 45–55, 98ff.; F. L. Ford, *Robe and Sword*, 12ff.

[2] In the words of a thoughtful contemporary: Nowadays, "the power of money is supreme. With money one can accomplish everything; with it one can purchase and become whatever one wants. . . . One should not ask whether money is a *jus quaesitum* to acquire noble status. Money *per se* already assures nobility. . . . Whoever has money demonstrates thereby, as a matter of course, that he does not lack any of the traits of noble superiority." Johann Michael von Loen, *Der Adel* (Ulm, 1752), 111, 328–29, 331.

other commoners who as administrators, diplomats, or judges had attained the nominal title of privy councilor (*Geheimrat*) in the official hierarchy.[3]

This tiny but crucial band of successful climbers, who were the intimate teammates and, by order of the king, the social equals of members of the nobility of descent, closely resembled the French "noblesse des hautes fonctions publiques." The latter, also known as "noblesse de fonctions gouvernementales," had come into its own in the days of Louis XIV. To a far larger extent than in Prussia, this newly established French bureaucratic nobility was made up of parvenus, of men like Colbert, Le Tellier, Louvois, Seignelay, Torcy, Desmarets, who either entered the nobility in the course of their government careers or came from recently ennobled state service families. A very small, unique group by virtue of its control of the machinery of the central government, its social identity, despite its singular status as the dominant political power group, was somewhat uncertain. These newly arrived leaders of the "commissar class" amalgamated with established prominent families of the increasingly interfused *noblesse de robe* and the *noblesse de race*.[4]

In Prussia throughout the eighteenth century no office or commission carried with it noble status by prescription. This was quite unlike French and Russian usages, where noble rank had become the hallmark of all the more distinguished government offices and was, therefore, automatically acquired by incumbents, if commoners by social origin.[5] Both the ancient, relatively large venal French

[3] Ernst v. Meier, *Französische Einflüsse auf die Staats- und Rechtsentwicklung Preussens im XIX. Jahrhundert*, II (Leipzig, 1908), 56–64.

[4] Ph. Sagnac, *La société française*, II, 54ff., 166ff., 216ff.

[5] See M. Marion, *Dictionnaire des institutions de la France aux XVIIe et XVIIIe siècles* (Paris, 1923), 432; F. L. Ford, *Robe and Sword*, 61–62; Henry Lévy-Bruhl, "La noblesse de la France et le commerce à la fin de l'Ancien Régime," *Revue d' Histoire Moderne*, VIII (1923), 210; V. O. Kluchevsky, *A History of Russia*, IV (London and New York, 1926), 82, 243–44; Otto Hötzsch, "Adel und Lehnswesen in Russland und Polen," *Historische Zeitschrift*, CVIII (1912), 565ff.; Peter Miljukoff, "Zur Geschichte des russischen Adels," *Archiv für Sozialwissenschaft und Sozialpolitik*, XLI (1916), 88–109; Max Beloff, "Russia," in A. Goodwin, ed., *The European Nobility in the Eighteenth Century* (London, 1953), 172–189.

noblesse de robe and the extraordinarily numerous, newly created landholding state service nobility of Petrine Russia (*dvorianstvo*) had no genuine counterparts in the Hohenzollern monarchy.

The policy of ennoblement in Prussia, whether inadvertently or by design, helped to fix the social identity and the loyalties of the civil bureaucracy as a distinctive status group within the remodeled upper class. As such, it was detached and alienated from the common and inferior people. It was imbued with the hierarchical and corporative ideals of the superior class of the preabsolutist past which had been intimately blended with the authoritarian outlook and the arrogant habits of militaristic *Herrenmenschen*. In the execution of their orders, the commissars were apt to act like commanding officers in their own right and accustomed to bending the lower orders to their will.

At the head of the administrative aristocracy stood the bureaucratic nobility. Though irregular of composition and constantly reshuffled, it nonetheless formed a lofty body *sui generis*. Its lines of demarcation were reasonably clear. It was composed of the top officials holding the most notable posts, an aristocracy within an aristocracy of probationary bureaucrats. Hence its unstable membership. In the civil state it constituted the dominant group of the governing class by exercising, under the authority of the crown, the most important managerial functions of centralized regimentation. Sometimes, however, the responsibilities of high office were actually discharged, so it was rumored, not so much by the mighty themselves, but by their secretaries or female relatives who opened the dispatches and letters and made the decisions. Financially, the group was most highly favored with the spoils of office. Socially, it was exclusively composed of men born or elevated to noble rank. Thus it was set off from the rest of the administrative aristocracy.

The latter, to be sure, included a substantial number of nobly born members. Yet since the early eighteenth century the upper bureaucracy was predominantly nonnoble in origin and its majority but seminoble in status. Clearly then, in terms of official influence, service grade, and service income, as well as titled prestige, the bureaucratic nobility was at once the most powerful and the most privileged element within the elite of professional government executives.

Bureaucratic top officialdom counted among its members several vigorous personalities of exceptional caliber, alongside many pedestrian technicians and some nonentities of the von Viereck type. Those who added real distinction to the group were mostly former *roturiers*, men like Meinders, Krautt, Ilgen, and Cocceji.[6] These "natural aristocrats" formed an elite in the normative sense, a nobility of talent and outstanding achievement within the bureaucratic nobility which, prior to the reign of Frederick II, was an "open" aristocracy.

II

The emergence of the bureaucratic nobility as a special group was linked to a wider, more ramified trend—the reconstitution of the old upper class, the hereditary nobility. The rise of the professional service estates and the struggle over the distribution of the enlarged governmental authority and intensified social controls, as engendered by the making of Prussia, divided the nobility into different status groups and factions and disrupted the whole pattern of traditional noble life. The deepening inequalities within the First Estate were visible signs of this process of readjustment. The acceleration of intraclass mobility produced its victors and its victims, nobles rising and falling in the social scale. The internal scramble for position was aggravated by competition, however imperfect, within the government service.

As a class, the established Junker nobility was revitalized by the rise of the military-bureaucratic state. As to personnel and group character, it acquired a more colorful complexion through the

---

[6] These men stand out like towering figures, especially if compared with the most infamous of their Junker colleagues: President von Borck, a notorious crook and perjurer, was dismissed by Frederick William I but reinstated and promoted by Frederick II. And Herr von Görne, Jr., was eminently successful in practicing thievery as a big business after having become, like von Borck, a minister in the General Directory. See *A.B.B.*, V, part 1, 623ff.; V, part 2, 540, 550ff.; VI, part 1, 443–44; *A.B. Handels-, Zoll- und Akzisepolitik*, III, part 2, 450ff.; *A.B. Seidenindustrie*, III, 285–288.

inflow of blueblooded and newly ennobled immigrants from a multi-
tude of German principalities and from France, Scandinavia,
Scotland, Ireland, Italy, and the Habsburg dominions. It also grew
less parochial through assimilation with the noble "vassals," gained
by the Hohenzollerns in their more recently annexed territories. The
Prussian nobility also was rejuvenated by social climbers who, as
Prussian subjects pressing from below, managed to lift themselves
up to nobles of ascent.

But what was good for the nobility as a whole was not always a
blessing for individual noblemen, even if they were the descendants
of renowned medieval families. Some of the Junkers of old lineage,
to be sure, bolstered their traditionally superior position through
professional government service. Those few who secured a place in
the bureaucratic nobility substantially enlarged their power, material
prosperity, and social standing. Far more frequently, however, wellborn bureaucrats were "frozen" in their rank of "ordinary" councilor. Though shut off from the highest service dignities, these noble
officials were recognized members of the upper bureaucracy and,
hence, of a professional elite belonging to the increasingly differen-
tiated upper class. Their aristocratic status was beyond doubt since
they combined high birth with a ranking, remunerative position
in the government.

But a wide gulf separated the nobles in actual possession of
superior status from the increasingly numerous group of common
and inferior holders of noble rank. Although the latter came from
the old upper class, as civil government employees they never rose
above the subaltern, poorly paid position of a petty excise tax official
or customs inspector or municipal police functionary or postmaster
or captain of a local fire brigade.[7] Among these were many invalid
or retired army officers who frequently could hardly read or write.[8]
Such nobles were excluded from the chance of competing with the
better educated for positions on the upper rungs of the administrative

[7] Joh. Ziekursch, *Das Ergebnis*, 201–211; Fritz Martiny, *Die Adelsfrage in
Preussen vor 1806* (Stuttgart, 1936), 70–71, 83ff.

[8] Even as late as the 1770's, among the graduates of the military cadet
schools many were, literally speaking, illiterates. See *Oeuvres de Frédéric le
Grand*, VI, 98–99; *Altpreussische Forschungen*, XVII (1940), 213.

ladder. But they had special ease of access to the lower service grades in consequence of the all-pervasive policy of differential treatment of nobles and nonnobles. Thus this species of "born aristocrats" who secured appointments as petty officials nevertheless derived only modest practical benefits from their legal class membership in the First Estate.

In exceptional cases, members of this group belonged to old noble families, previously prominent in the landed but also in the bureaucratic aristocracy. The Grumbkows, for instance, entered the downward road in the latter part of the eighteenth century. Thereafter, some of them still managed to obtain commissions in the armed services. But most of them had to make their living as subaltern employees in public or private service or as craftsmen, particularly in the printing trade.[9]

Both during and after the Old Regime, a lowly position in the government services did not necessarily imply, however, an irretrievable demotion of a noble family in public life and in the hierarchy of income groups. This was demonstrated by the great Clausewitz, the son of a former army lieutenant, who had to earn his daily bread as a minor tax collector. So too, Albrecht von Roon's sensational public career as minister of war and his rise to landed wealth in the age of Bismarck were hardly foreshadowed by his social antecedents: the rather dubious character of his noble pedigree, the mendicant status of his *déclassé* father, and his own poverty-stricken start in the army.[10]

Doubtless, the predominantly nonnoble personnel of the administrative upper class had made an exceptional place for itself vis-a-vis those "low grade" nobles of descent who, by virtue of incompetence, ignorance, indolence, or bad luck, were kicked down the ladder. The new arrivals stood out in even bolder relief when contrasted with the noble "reserve army," composed of paupers, *déclassés*, and delinquents, no longer able to obtain any position.

[9] See *Gothaisches Genealogisches Taschenbuch der Uradeligen Häuser. Der in Deutschland eingeborene Adel*, VIII (Gotha, 1907), 277ff.

[10] *Denkwürdigkeiten aus dem Leben des Generalfeldmarschalls Kriegsministers Grafen von Roon*, I (Breslau, 1892), 1–74.

The resurgence of a titled body of unemployed reached considerable proportions in the course of the eighteenth century. Among "the noble riff-raff" were social parasites who depended on the moody charity of their well-to-do relatives. Others, even more completely uprooted, were professional hoboes. Drifting from manor house to manor house, the "noble tramp" earned his livelihood as a carrier of "society" gossip and as a card player and "jolly joker." He was usually received as a welcome visitor since he pleasantly interrupted the quietude of country life and the rather monotonous conversations about dogs, horses, women, crops, the weather, and the neighbors. He had his counterpart among the dispossessed French *hoberaux* and the Spanish *hidalgos*. And he was a well-known figure in Russian society during the decades just after the peasant emancipation.

In Prussia, the process of economic deterioration and social debasement which had hit many persons of high birth during and after the Thirty Years' War was only temporarily checked by the inflationary growth of job opportunities in dynastic service. Even the Prussian army, which served with remarkable effectiveness as a vocational rehabilitation center for destitute nobles and the elegant poor, did not have at its disposal unlimited funds for expanding its facilities. And the physical growth of the Hohenzollern monarchy did not always aid in the preservation of the superior social respectability of *"l'élite de la nation,"* "the foremost and the most brilliant estate of the state," as Frederick II characterized the Prussian nobility. The three partitions of Poland brought Prussia not merely huge territories, but also a numerous and largely illiterate, indigent Polish nobility.[11]

With the passage of time, the social decline of many noblemen did much to raise the stock of official position and to lower the utility and prestige of noble status as such. Well-established nobles, inside and outside government service, watched with misgivings the deflation of their "superior" rank, as precipitated by the many

[11] C. H. Hagen, *Ueber das Agrargesetz und die Anwendbarkeit desselben* (Königsberg, 1814), 53ff.; Max Bär, ed., *Westpreussen unter Friedrich dem Grossen* (Leipzig, 1909), 361ff.

"Herren von Habenichts" (have-nots), pretending to be their "class equals." Determined to regain possession of ostentatious symbols of lofty exclusiveness, the upholders of the unwritten laws of "proper" social distance did their utmost to obtain for themselves the title of baron or count. Significantly, as early as 1800, in Brandenburg, for instance, one sixth of all the noble landowners already held such rank.[12]

The widening of the range of noble intraclass inequalities carried in its train altered relationships to competing social elements. The vacuum created by the exodus of "displaced noble persons" was filled by climbing members of *"la vile bourgeoisie."*

From an early date this had a salutary effect upon the social standing of the bureaucrats. In education, function, income, in the standards of consumption, and modes of recreation, nobles employed as petty functionaries were nothing but low class people, if contrasted with the common councilors and privy councilors who had risen in the social scale. To go a step further, those genteel members of the administrative aristocracy who failed to be admitted to the more select band of the bureaucratic nobility shared with their nonnoble service equals similar professional experiences, interests, habits, and propensities, as well as distinctive privileges, service titles, and honors. As to their actual social station, the former had far more in common with the latter than with the nobly born in the lower service brackets, nominally their social rank equals, but in real life more or less *déclassés*. Finally, the nobles of ancient descent in so far as they had reached the summit of the official hierarchy were, as to status and their style of life, more closely bound to their newly ennobled professional colleagues than to their wellborn service rank inferiors in the higher grades. In fact, nothing of significance, except for the accident of birth, separated in these two respects the social position of the top bureaucrats of old noble lineage from the bureaucratic nobles of ascent. And the stigma attached to the parvenus on account of deficiencies in genealogical inheritance, though irritating and humiliating, proved, in most cases, surmountable, even within the span of their own lifetime.

[12] F. Martiny, *Die Adelsfrage*, 78.

The predecessors of Frederick II made political capital out of the twofold composition of the bureaucratic nobility by playing out against each other the jealousies and rivalries of its two component elements. This clumsy divide-and-rule technique was of dubious utility and yielded but a diminishing return. The nobles of ascent at once stabilized their social advance by becoming founders of wealthy noble families. So overpowering was the magic spell of the combination of vanity and utility, that to be absorbed by the noble of birth became the burning desire of the newcomers. Their claim to social equality did not entail an attempt on their part to bring the highborn down to their own "inferior" standards and habits, but rather to lift themselves up to the ways of the old nobility. Preoccupied with the consolidation of their newly gained status and with the fortunes of their families in the aristocratic community, they aimed at assimilation by emulation. They surrendered to the tastes, mores, and outlook of their "superiors." And since the bureaucratic nobility, in part, was recruited from scions of the old nobility who at the same time were members of the squirearchy, the *homines novi* bent their energies toward eliminating the barriers of social distance by intermarrying with the old noble families and by availing themselves of the newly acquired legal privileges which entitled them to purchase noble estates (*Rittergüter*).

Thus the bureaucratic nobles of ascent were linked to the bureaucratic nobles of descent, as well as to the independent, nonbureaucratic Junker squires. In consequence, the administrative top authorities were intimately interlocked with the ownership and entrepreneurial exploitation of large-scale landed property. This whole pattern of amalgamation was established by Jena, Meinders, and Fuchs during the reign of the Elector Frederick William. It was followed up by the Danckelmanns, Ilgens, Krautts, Happes, and others under his successor, and was further solidified by the former commoners among the ministers and other newly ennobled high officials of Frederick William I.

The turning point in the social career of Creutz, for example, was his marriage to the wealthy daughter of Privy Councilor von Häseler. Creutz became the owner of several large country estates, and his town residence was one of the most sumptuous and exclusive society centers of Berlin. Through similar devices Marschall, a merchant's son and a former cabinet councilor, forced open the social gates. He was treated by the court circles as one of their own after having married, first, a von Schwerin and, then, a von Münchow. His son entered the diplomatic service and fortified his position by becoming the son-in-law of his chief, Minister von Podewils.

Seldom did the representatives of this novel type of bureaucratic neo-Junker landowner meet with the persistent social boycott of the old nobles. And when they did, the next generation was usually more successful in balancing its ancestral shortcomings by mingling with the highborn as equals and by living more cavalierly than the courtly gentlemen. Thus von Boden, a former agronomist and thriving business man, after having served in the cabinet of Frederick William I, was appointed minister in the General Directory in 1739. In this capacity he performed the functions of a minister of finance, detached from, and distrusted by, the fashionable society, until 1762. A wanderer between two social worlds, he was one of the few top officials who never felt at home in the highest circles. His colleagues and subordinates thoroughly disliked him because of his plebeian assiduousness and rigorous insistence upon order, thrift, promptitude, and hard work. Even Boden's sovereign who, on the whole, supported him against adversaries, nevertheless treated him to the very end with reservations. After von Boden had completed half a century of distinguished work in the service of the crown and attained the age of seventy-six, his irascible employer did not hesitate to make a blistering attack upon Boden's personal loyalty and professional integrity. But the royal taskmaster was gracious enough to soften his snarling criticism by advising his "servant" to "deport himself better in the future, to be more diligent and exact in My service, and to think of nothing else, failing which I shall be forced, at long last, to get mad (*rappelköpfisch*)."[13] Boden's son however, although a professional failure, was socially accepted as he himself never was.

The complete merger of the two originally distinct subgroups of

[13] *A.B.B.*, XII, 63ff.

the bureaucratic nobility and its interfusion with the squirearchy reinforced the leadership position of the well-to-do nobility in state and society. The dilution of the traditional political status of the large landowners and the growth of a class of debased nobles notwithstanding, the functional restratification of the titled aristocracy and the personnel changes within the superior class counterbalanced the trend which otherwise might have lowered the general position of the First Estate. Beyond doubt, the consolidation of monarchical absolutism had inflicted considerable damage upon the old landed elite as a governing class in the literal sense. Not only had the rulers of the *Ständestaat* lost political initiative, but they had been stripped of almost all independent rights of government above the local level. The sharp decline of the corporate political power of the squirearchy was one thing; the aggrandizement of individual noblemen, at first at the expense of their order, was another. By functioning on an increasingly large scale as a bureaucracy in the absolute state, as army officers and administrative dignitaries, the Junkers recovered in new forms and on a different legal foundation many of their old powers. Moreover, they vastly extended their influence by taking possession, under the leadership of the bureaucratic nobility, of the newly built halls of central government. The crux of the matter, then, was that, indirectly, the nobility at large received a most formidable new center of gravity in the professional service elites of the absolute monarchy and that, by the mid-eighteenth century, this bureaucratic hierarchy of political power holders was no longer troubled by a serious confusion of faces at the top. In alliance with the state machine the privileged classes grew stronger than they had been in the days of opposition.

In this way, through the process of regrouping and reorientation within the upper class, the propertied nobility enlarged and intensified its grip as the politically and economically dominant group and perpetuated its social preëminence. It derived great benefit from the ambition and adaptiveness of native and foreign born nobles who succeeded in capturing high places in the monarchical state. At the same time, however, it was impelled to replace its sinking members with superior *roturiers*. Accordingly, the First Estate as a truly distinguished body of men was refreshed and sustained not by the exclusion, but the infiltration and absorption of alien elements who were the most successful and professionally most influential exponents of social competition in dynastic employment.

The bureaucratic upstart nobles and many of the satellite seminobles who furnished the bulk of the civil state aristocracy had much to give. They were, to varying degrees, in possession of trained minds, disciplined working ability, and a vast range of tested practical experience, ingenious in the amassing of riches, and proud of their accomplishments and social usefulness. By sheer weight of numbers and because of the effectiveness of their competition, they stirred some of the nobly born to greater exertions. The time had come when descendants of the old *jus indigenatus* profiteers, capable of reading the handwriting on the wall, tardily set out to learn to justify their inherited privileged status by serviceability to the common weal.

Yet, the subtle process of transformation from within which converted the bureaucratic nobility into a rather monolithic group heralded, first of all, the dawn of a noble reaction against competition in government service and against royal autocracy. Toward the middle of the eighteenth century, the system of administrative centralization by coercion, which had resulted in the gradual concentration of Prussia's "nationalized" community activities in bureaucratic channels, was firmly established. The executive personnel of the new political order had come of age. Under Frederick II and thereafter until 1806, when the Prussian state was smitten with disaster, it ceased to exercise an aggressive reform influence. Arrival was accompanied by the adoption of more relaxed attitudes. The civil state managers, as a body, developed into an essentially conservative force. Aside from handling day-to-day routine administration, they were now primarily concerned with perpetuating their position in the body politic and in upper class society. The tone was set by the official leaders, the bureaucratic nobility. Already by the end of the 1730's, they had acquired some of the earmarks of an exclusive social and political caste. Hence they were getting ready to close ranks against undesirables and trespassers and to band together against their master under the banner: *Und der König absolut, wenn er uns den Willen tut.*

Frederick II heeded both these tendencies. But this he did in his own peculiar way.

III

The "commissar class" had been instituted to emasculate the old *Ständestaat* and to enforce the political will of the dynastic usurper of sovereign authority. Indeed, it was this group that made possible the growth of effective monarchical power. At the same time, however, it was the class that came to be subservient to the old system of privilege, patronage, and nepotism. Hidden behind the façade of dynastic omnipotence, there had taken place a ceaseless, intense, and often bitter struggle for domination.

In Prussia, five contesting power elites had claimed the right and the duty to govern. First was the royal autocrat and his small cabinet. Second was the long established, self-governing squirearchy, reconfirmed after long strife as the socio-economic "foundation and the pillars of the state." The third decisive force was the dependent military service aristocracy—the very incarnation of the centralized garrison state. In accord with their glorification of the military way of life, both Frederick William I and Frederick II acclaimed the professional military estate as "the foremost and the most brilliant estate of the state." The fourth hierarchy was the dependent administrative bureaucracy, functionally indeed "l'élite de la nation" in the area of civil government. Finally, there were the persistent "fence sitters," the semi-independent functionaries of the *Regierungen.* Torn by conflicting loyalties, interests, and passions, by playing both sides, they had gradually disintegrated to the point of losing separate political identity. Through its absorption of the judiciary, civil officialdom had evolved into a huge, single, centralized organization and immeasurably enhanced its chances of throwing off the fetters of royal autocracy.

In the neighboring Habsburg monarchy, the administrative career officials of the central government had already gained the upper hand during Maria Theresa's reign. Institutionally, this found expression in the Austrian Council of State which functioned as a policy-planning bureaucratic parliament. Centralized bureaucratic absolutism rather than dynastic autocracy had effected the partial expropriation of the ancient corporate political and administrative powers of the landed nobility throughout the German-Slav provinces. Yet, the new bureaucrats remained under the control of members of the high nobility. In the absolutely-governed part of the Habsburg empire, unlike France under Louis XIV, Petrine Russia, or Prussia under Frederick William I, the high policy-making posts and the chief influence over appointments and promotions continued to be monopolized by landed noble grandees of old lineage. Maria Theresa's top-level politician-bureaucrats, the counts Cotek, Hatzfeld, Haugwitz, Kaunitz, Kolowrat, Zinzendorf, bear witness to this phase of the social redistribution of political power. As individuals they attained political preëminence under absolutism, while the landed nobility to which they belonged lost much of its former significance as an active and powerful political force.

Concomitantly, and as in all the major absolute monarchies, in Habsburg lands, too, bureaucratic state service as such was a springboard to higher social rank. Newly ennobled career bureaucrats developed, like their Prussian colleagues, into nobles of descent; but unlike the latter they had to rest content with forming what came to be called a "second society," distinguished yet second in both social and official rank. Until the reform of 1774, which liberalized the buying and selling of landed estates, the bureaucratic neonobles were, as a rule, denied admission to the landed nobility. Moreover, they were, with only a few exceptions, shut off from the strategic top positions in the service hierarchy which formed a little oasis reserved to highborn landed magnates.[14]

---

[14] See O. Hintze, *Staat und Verfassung*, 335ff.; Otto Brunner, *Adeliges Landleben und Europäischer Geist* (Salzburg, 1949), 183, 234, 309, 325–26, 336–37; Ignaz Beidtel, *Geschichte der österreichischen Staatsverwaltung, 1740–1848* (Innsbruck, 1898), I, 455; II, 41–50; Josef Redlich, *Das österreichische Staats- und Reichsproblem*, I, part 1 (Leipzig, 1920), 22–23, 39, 474–483; Heinrich Ritter von Srbik, *Metternich*, I (Munich, 1925), 438–39; Jerome Blum, *Noble Landowners and Agriculture in Austria 1815–1848* (Baltimore, 1947), 21–33.

Conversely, in France the mounting influence of the high judiciary ensured the reimposition of corporate-aristocratic checks upon the absolute authority of the crown and thus upon the centralized bureaucratic empire, built by the upstart *noblesse des hautes fonctions publiques*. The high *noblesse de robe*, being the owners of the *parlements*, were the oligarchical masters of a powerful political machine which was only temporarily forced into retreat in the age of Louis XIV. This proud group of *officiers*, established, highly experienced, wealthy, and often well educated, from 1715 onwards gradually regained political initiative and managed to assume the leadership of the *noblesse* in the formation of a common front for the defense of privilege against fiscal reform and against bourgeois competition in civil and military state service. This obstinate political and social elite enforced the dismantling rather than the consolidation of the centralized absolutism of the administrative bureaucracy. The long-persistent assault from without, combined with sedition from within, brought about the crumbling of the power of the service class of *commissaires*.

In the Hohenzollern states, throughout the eighteenth century, there was less need for concerted action in defense of noble privilege because of the lack of a liberal opposition from below and because royal pressure upon the titled aristocracy at no time was as strong as it had been in either France or Russia. The dynastic-bureaucratic-noble symbiosis which made "Prussia" possible was kept intact by means of a continuing patching of the dual political structure.

Unlike in Petrine Russia, in Prussia there had never been a time when, in principle, no respect was paid to noble birth as such and when dynastic service rank alone tended to determine noble status and access to landed wealth and thus to obliterate the value of blood and of inherited landed property. "The emancipation of the nobility" in the Russian sense was not a problem in the Hohenzollern monarchy. The Prussian nobility of all grades and of all antecedents did not have to be liberated from "servitude." Although restricted in its freedom of movement by the crown, hemmed in by occupational taboos, harassed by royal prodding and, under Frederick William I, even the occasional kidnapping of youngsters for the military cadet schools, only the lower orders of "the nonnoble riff-raff," not "the elite of the nation," were liable by law to compulsory personal conscription for state service.

IV

Frederick II succeeded in retarding the rise of aristocratic-bureaucratic absolutism in Prussia, but he was unable to prevent it. Indeed, paradoxically enough, he also did much to further it. He labored hard to tighten up the working alliance between the autocracy and the nobility. For this alliance he paid a heavy price: limitation of class competition in dynastic employment; the stiffening of the noble monopoly of the purchase and sale of *Rittergüter*; the extension of noble privileges in law and in fact; the broadening of differences in the treatment of nobles and nonnobles inside and outside government service; the reaffirmation of the superiority of inherited social rank over specialized knowledge, practical experience, and professional achievement; and the adoption of a narrow policy of ennoblement.

The concomitant transformation of the bureaucratic nobility was but another phase of the new course. Its personnel now became more fully representative of the rival subgroups of the Prussian nobility. Frederick II effected a very significant reshuffling of the bureaucratic top stratum by replenishing its membership with men from entrenched family dynasties of noble career bureaucrats, and also with "outsiders." The latter were noble army officers and *Landrat*-squires who were chosen because they were military service nobles and particularly distinguished landed nobles.

An extraordinarily astute, vigilant, and increasingly cynical statesman like *Fredericus rex* had considered reasons for detaching himself from his father's social policy. It was not simply personal fancy that induced him to threaten his own *Fiskale* with death on the gallows, if they continued to inconvenience noble estate owners by reclaiming crown lands once "alienated" to them.[15] Nor did Frederick drift thoughtlessly, when he made it almost impossible

[15] *A.B.B.*, VII, 617, 635.

for a "gentilhomme" to be responsible to a "bourgeois" where positions of consequence in the state were concerned. In a system of personalized autocracy, the social prejudices, beliefs, and illusions of the supreme leader were quite important, especially when they were in harmony with the cardinal wishes and primary interests of the dominant social forces.

Whatever the significance of his celebrated literary devotion to some of the ideals of the Enlightenment, in his early years as Prussian king Frederick II acted like a recklessly ambitious political gambler. Bent on the pursuit of a foreign policy of strength with provocation, aggressive war, conquest by force, and personal glory, he firmly resolved to lift up his state to the rank of an admired and feared Great Power.

In order to become "the Great," Frederick needed a unified, socially cohesive, and pacified home front. To his way of thinking, the task of tightening his grip on men through guile and management, of making the Prussian people serve his ends, and of fostering both the fact and the sense of common statehood called for closer bonds of union between the autocrat and the "active citizens," that is, the First Estate. Frederick, keenly sensitive to his historic, aristocratic heritage, was inclined to use the words "nobility" and "nation" synonymously for most practical purposes, for he regarded "la fleur de la noblesse" as "l'élite de la nation."

His policy of keeping down "the nonnoble riff-raff" and of sustaining the nobility was the cornerstone of an all-pervasive socio-political pattern. His social policy widened the gulf between the governing classes and the governed masses. The political order was to be stabilized by freezing the old social system with its inequality of rights and opportunities and its castelike division of labor between nobles, burghers, and peasants.

Frederick's domestic policy retarded the interclass mobility so typical of the regime of his father and deliberately reverted to the ancient equation of gentle birth with "merit." Frederick preferred to assign an exalted political function to the nobility. He protected its class monopoly over large-scale private landownership and agricultural credit, and he fortified its exclusive social position. He intensified the interaction and interpenetration of the military-bureaucratic institutions of the absolute monarchy and of the no less despotic "home rule" institutions, which sustained the traditional way of life of the squirearchy. He did his utmost to indoctrinate "the foremost and most brilliant estate of the state" with what he termed *esprit de corps et de nation.*

Through the dual policy of promoting the coöperation and interfusion of the governing elites on the one hand and of cunningly exploiting their rivalries on the other, he sought to overcome the most vulnerable feature of the Prussian polity: its inherent, long-standing dualism. He did much for the nobility, because he expected it to do a great deal for him. And he attached such high hopes to the wellborn as "the foundation and the pillars of the state," because, in his estimation, the simple "von," if acquired by birth and underpinned by the ownership of land and inherited mastery over men, made all the difference in the world.

Frederick's whole conception of the state was rooted in the aristocratic way of thinking, which took for granted a society made up of groups of men of intrinsically different value. Hence he assumed that the middle classes could be animated only by base motives. To appoint men of such background, immutable endowment, and moral defectiveness to positions of trust in the government services was "the first step toward the decline and fall of the army" and thus of the authoritarian state itself.[16] At best, their employment was a necessary evil. Hence, for instance, the promotion of numerous commoners to commissioned rank in the Prussian army during the Seven Years' War and the dismissal or demotion to inferior service functions of most of them after the return to peace.[17]

To Frederick it was self-evident that only the wellborn and particularly the scions of old landed families could be ideal servants of his state. For he attributed to this category of men certain superior, ingrained qualities which justified their privileges and made them

---

[16] *Oeuvres de Frédéric le Grand,* IX, 186.

[17] Max Lehmann, *Scharnhorst,* II (Leipzig, 1887), 59; Curt Jany, *Geschichte der Kgl. Preussischen Armee,* III (Berlin, 1929), 35–36; Karl Demeter, *Das deutsche Offizierkorps* (Berlin, 1930), 7–8.

singularly fit to function as efficient and reliable manufacturers of obedience from below. They alone were capable of cultivating loyalties and ambitions of a lofty kind, of developing a *point d'honneur*, a longing for glory and the martial virtues and ideals, a disciplined passion for service as conveyors of despotic power from above to below, thus linking the majestic autocrat at the top to the shapeless rabble at the bottom. They alone were born to lead a "heroic" life, to act with valor, fortitude, and inner zeal, ready, if not eager to make the supreme sacrifice for the sake of victory in battle. They alone, through education and indoctrination, through soft words and harsh threats, through rewards and punishment, could be induced to embrace "the Prussian Spirit" and to identify themselves as a matter of self-interest with the monarchical state and its expansion. They alone had the moral stamina needed for the development of an habitual sense of obligation and an active sentiment of attachment to an idea. They alone were justified in adhering to an exalted conception of their dignity, rank, and mission. They alone had a natural claim to social superiority and political precedence in the dynastic state, for only they could be expected to equate class honor with national honor.[18]

These few, then, had come into the world to command and to lead the many under the watchful eye of "the first servant of my state." The power of the state had to be restricted caste power. This was the essence of Frederick's aristocratic-militarist ideology of *esprit de corps et de nation*. In his state even the sentiments of "Prussian nationalism" were to be a social function of special privilege, fit for noblemen only. Consequently, in exchange for their political submission, the higher public dignities should be the exclusive domain of honorific noble class employment. In this vital matter, a royal drill sergeant like Frederick William I revealed more liberality of outlook and freedom from prejudice than his brilliantly gifted, enlightened son, the captive of class bias and aristocratic superstitions.

Montesquieu's fundamental maxim "no monarch, no nobility; no

---

[18] *Politische Korrespondenz Friedrichs des Grossen. Ergänzungsband* (Berlin, 1920), 26–33, 80; *Polit. Testamente*, 18, 29–34, 82, 84, 138, 169, 189ff.

nobility, no monarch" was destined to have quite a career in Prussia under Frederick II, who did much to stabilize the absolute monarchy by converting it into an aristocratic oligarchy headed by the heirs of noble privilege, thus shaping the pattern of the personnel administration of the Great Frederick.[19]

V

Frederick II could not halt, let alone reverse the trend which under his predecessor had given the lion's share of the administrative councilorships to commoners.[20] To be sure, there were repeated royal directives requesting that "vacancies in the provincial boards should be filled with noblemen to a larger extent than heretofore."[21] Implementation, however, was difficult, especially before the end of the Seven Years' War.

Professionally qualified noble candidates were in short supply. Frederick cordially welcomed nobles of foreign extraction in his army, but he regarded them as "undesirable" in the civil state service. He was afraid that for most of these gentlemen *travailler pour le Roi de Prusse* would be nothing but a steppingstone; later they might sell their acquired "Prussian skills" to foreign governments.[22] Besides, Frederick had learned through hard experience that technical experts taken from the middle classes were "used to work more assiduously and to go more fully into details" than their noble colleagues.[23] But he also believed that noblemen, especially if they were "tall and had brains," would do better in the army.[24] Finally, the logic of growing "bureaucratization" and the continued drive for the improvement of efficiency, combined with the unplanned,

[19] See Wilhelm Dilthey, *Gesammelte Schriften*, III (Leipzig, 1927), 183; Otto Heinrich von der Gablentz, *Die Tragik des Preussentums* (Munich, 1948), 46–47.

[20] See Elsbeth Schwenke, *Friedrich der Grosse und der Adel* (Berlin, 1911), 39; Henri Brunschwig, *La crise de l'état prussien à la fin du XVIIIe siècle* (Paris, 1947), 153ff. and appendices; *A.B.B.*, XIV, 433ff.; XV, 488–499.

[21] *A.B.B.*, XIII, 349.

[22] *Ibid.*, VII, 183–84.

[23] *Ibid.*, XV, 588.

[24] *Ibid.*, XV, 81.

stubborn facts of social mobility, proved strong enough in real life to prevent the hierarchy of hereditary estates and royal wishful thinking from blocking the social ascent of commoners and the downgrading of a sizable section of the nobility. Many of the nominating top officials, increasingly concerned with raising the standards of admission and promotion, recommended commoners rather than titled aristocrats for appointment in the higher grades.

In consequence, the numerical ratio between the two elements did not significantly change in the administrative bureaucracy during the reign of Frederick II. As a matter of fact, the preponderance of *roturiers* in the upper brackets grew. After Cocceji's personnel reforms, the vast majority of the councilorships in the judicial bureaucracy, too, was gradually captured by nonnobles.[25] The imposition of more exacting entrance requirements and working standards crowded out many noble job candidates, actual and potential. Furthermore, army service had grown in popularity in noble circles, and the *Regierungen* had lost much of their original attractiveness as exclusive bastions of Junker strength.

Oddly enough, it was only after Frederick's death that the numerical balance between nobles and commoners began to change seriously to the detriment of the "nonnoble riff-raff."[26] This innovation gained some momentum in the age of the French Revolution, when the sponsors of the Prussian Legal Code of 1794 "improved" the merit system by setting aside, as a matter of right, all state dignities of significance for members of the nobility. However, this belated legal victory of "the noble reaction" was, in part, offset by liberalizing the royal policy of ennoblement. Illegitimate sons of wellborn army officers and distinguished members of the upper civil bureaucracy, held down by Frederick II, now entered the ranks of the nobility. They were joined by wealthy merchants and manufacturers like Treskow and Eckardstein, heralding the feeble beginning of the social recognition of a new pioneering business elite.[27]

[25] E. Schwenke, *Friedrich der Grosse,* 39; H. Brunschwig, *La crise de l'état prussien,* 153–54.

[26] H. Brunschwig, *La crise de l'état prussien,* 154ff.

[27] F. Martiny, *Die Adelsfrage,* 67, 73–78; H. Rachel and P. Wallich, *Berliner Grosskauflaute,* II, 282–83.

Nevertheless, the recently ennobled Minister von Struensee, a former high school teacher, exaggerated when he told the French *chargé d'affaires* in 1799: "The salutary revolution which you have made from below will come about gradually in Prussia from above. The King is a democrat in his own way. He works unceasingly on plans for the limitation of the privileges of the nobility and will follow the scheme of Joseph II but with slower methods. In a few years there will be no longer any privileged class in Prussia."[28]

Frederick II concentrated his efforts at reform in personnel selection upon the crucial group, the bureaucratic nobility. He proceeded with caution and with moderation. Handicapped by the great scarcity of "good noblemen," who were intelligent, skilled, and experienced enough to replace, without causing administrative anarchy, the nonnoble councilors, Frederick, of necessity, had to content himself with sifting the "very important persons" only.

The remaking of the bureaucratic nobility entailed restaffing and internal regrouping. Royal intervention fostered, by design, the resurrection of the old landed nobility of birth, largely reoriented through army service, as the possessor of executive top power, though now under the crown and, therefore, surrounded by a capricious and hazardous network of checks and balances.

Frederick did not disrupt administrative power by dismissing the nobles of ascent from the service. He kept the newly ennobled in office until they died or grew very old and lost their usefulness. He actively supported the outstanding representatives of this group, Cocceji and Boden, against the machinations of their highborn colleagues. In grudging recognition of the fact that "unfortunately at the present time really capable noblemen for such a position" were not forthcoming, Frederick even promoted a handful of nonnoble career men to leading posts in the service.[29] But such was the rigidity of his policy of social discrimination that he denied these

[28] P. Bailleu, *Preussen und Frankreich von 1795 bis 1807*, I (Berlin, 1881), 505.

[29] *A.B.B.*, XIV, 493. See also M. Hass, "Friedrich der Grosse und seine Kammerpräsidenten," in *Beiträge zur brandenburgischen und preussischen Geschichte* (Leipzig, 1908), 201–202; W. Naudé, in *Forschungen*, XVIII (1905), 369ff.

men elevation to noble rank. In official status, as recognized by Frederick, they were the professional, but not the social equals of the members of the purified bureaucratic nobility.

A few isolated members of the "illborn" found a little backdoor of hope. Thus Domhardt after endless waiting and tireless campaigning gained admission.[30] Domhardt was an administrator of eminent quality, who had been a large farmer and laid the foundation of his fortune as a horse trader. He achieved the signal triumph of being appointed to the unique position of president of the two provinces East and West Prussia, of becoming one of the largest and most enterprising landowners in the kingdom, and even of wheedling a patent of nobility out of his royal master. As a rule, Frederick II reserved this rare honor for men who had distinguished themselves in military service.[31] Among the twenty ministers whom he appointed to the General Directory from 1740 to 1786, there was only a single commoner, the lonely Friedrich Gottlieb Michaelis, a pharmacist's son, who reached the pinnacle of his bureaucratic career by being employed, though for two years only, as postmaster general, in professional and social prestige the least distinguished ministerial position in the service.[32] The very rarity of these appointments merely confirmed the governing principle of cutting off administrative experts of defective social origin from the chance of competing for the highest dignities and most lucrative emoluments.

From the beginning of his political stewardship Frederick II left the old guard bureaucrats a little breathless and perturbed by filling important vacancies and newly created top posts almost exclusively with landed nobles of old lineage or with noble army officers on the active list, who were complete newcomers to the game and who

---

[30] *A.B.B.*, X, 174–75; XIV, 167–68, 173, 562; XV, 554.

[31] *Ibid.*, XIII, 27–28; J. D. E. Preuss, *Friedrich der Grosse*, I (Berlin, 1832), 453–457; II (1833), 447–453; III (1833), 550–553; M. Lehmann, *Scharnhorst*, II, 647.

[32] As the career bureaucrat Georg Michaelis happened to be the sole nonnoble chancellor of imperial Germany, by coincidence his great-great-granduncle F. C. Michaelis was the only lowborn Prussian minister of the eighteenth century who failed to acquire noble status.

assumed high service rank at one bound. With the aid of the considerate sovereign, the Junkers moved back to their ancient position of assured predominance in public administration. Thus the partially dispossessed began to dispossess their parvenu-dispossessors.

The nobility's continued decline in relative numbers within the administrative and judicial bureaucracies as a whole was more than counterbalanced by the fact that after 1740 almost all places of real profit, distinction, and decisive influence were reserved to members of the old nobility of descent. Under royal auspices they were reconstituted as a particularly privileged group. These select men were entrusted with the responsibility of presiding over the hierarchy of service officers and of managing through them the vast centralized domain of civil affairs. They were vested with the power to recommend appointments, promotions, bonuses, penalties, and dismissals, and to enforce the disciplinary codes. Not only did they have a firm grip on the execution of policy, as consultants they shared in its preparation. They were given a limited opportunity for making managerial decisions and for thinking out policy. The inferior task of transforming royal orders and directives into red tape, of conducting minor investigations, and of supervising the clerical workers and petty field agents was left, in the main, to the councilors.

The nobility's job and power monopolies in the civil state included the diplomatic posts and the positions at the royal court and, consequently, a substantial portion of public income and dignities. Of far greater weight, in view of its political impact and its consequences for the rural and urban classes, was the fact that until 1806, save for a very few social climbers, all the newly appointed ministers forming the central executive authority, all the presidents of the provincial administrative and judicial boards, and all the *Landräte* came from well-established, though not necessarily old, noble families—as was demonstrated by the Danckelmanns and by von Jariges, Cocceji's successor. Noble birth, especially with wealth and influence to back it, was sufficient to dispense with the plebeian norm of examinations, "mandatory" since 1770, and with seniority. Von Münchow, for instance, was made minister for Silesia at the age of thirty-three; the able von Schlabrendorff at thirty-five; the unscrupulous Count von Hoym at thirty. Count von Finckenstein was twenty-one years of age when he became ambassador in Stockholm. Fourteen years later he was a minister of state.

Frederick's policy proved particularly profitable to those fierce and ungovernable families who hitherto had resisted active collaboration with "Hohenzollern despotism" and "Prussian collectivism." Frederick William I had felt greatly annoyed by these "spiteful and disobedient people" and resentfully singled out the Alvenslebens, Bismarcks, Schulenburgs as "the most prominent and the most adamant families" of the Old Mark.[33]

Many English cavaliers who had supported the Stuart dynasty suddenly found themselves, after the "Glorious Revolution," on the side of "civil and religious liberty"; conversely, in Prussia, a score of Junker clans, encouraged by the reascendancy of the old nobility, discovered on which side their bread was buttered. At long last they fell into line, shed the spirit of rugged local independence and individual liberty and made their ancestral sense of social superiority serviceable to the cause of "noble reaction." By mending their fences, they found fat livings, although sometimes they had to be educated in their unfamiliar new duties by former *roturiers*. Thus, Cocceji, for example, received instructions from Frederick II to "break in" President Levin Friedrich von Bismarck, whose ideas His Majesty had found "at times very stupid."[34]

A brilliantly successful representative of this group of belated proselytes was Schulenburg-Kehnert, for thirty-two years a Prussian minister and only twenty-nine when he attained that lofty rank. His vanity and greed were not satiated until he had snatched up the largest number of high-rating offices and sinecures in the civil administration ever held by a Prussian bureaucrat of the eighteenth century. At the same time, his thirst for the external paraphernalia of power and prestige also carried him far in the military hierarchy. "Because he had once served as a lieutenant," he deemed himself good enough, as Hermann von Boyen put it, to get himself gradually

---

[33] *A.B.B.*, III, 452.
[34] *Ibid* , VIII, 44.

promoted to the rank of full general of the cavalry.[35] Professionally, a dull though diligent man of routine and, personally, a pompous character, Schulenburg managed to keep alive, for his own benefit as well as for the sake of some of his fellows, the essentials of the old spoils system.

Other ministers like von Heinitz, von Schrötter, von Stein, well-born and equipped with the necessary connections, also had not been asked to put themselves to the trouble of taking an examination when they entered the administrative aristocracy. But unlike Schulenburg, they were not only imaginative and forceful organizers, but also high-spirited men. Happily enough, a conceited mercenary like Schulenburg was but one among several distinctive types of noble top bureaucrats. As such, he made it crystal clear that not even the most generous material awards and social honors accorded for "meritorious service" were always sufficient to produce real loyalty to "Prussia" and to buy "patriotism." During the cataclysm of 1806 Schulenburg proved a dismal failure, disgracing his class and his profession by leaving the sinking ship in a hurry and by seeking refuge in the service of Napoleon's brother, the King of Westphalia.

VI

The major steps in the professional advancement of Schulenburg-Kehnert epitomized the "ideal" sequence within the transformed pattern of bureaucratic career making, a progression which Frederick II came to love: noble squire of old family; army officer; *Landrat*; board president and, then, perhaps minister. Preferentially, appointment to top service rank was at an age not higher than thirty-five.[36] By entrusting relatively numerous men of such background with directing positions, Frederick built, in the course of time, a junto of former *Landräte* and wellborn army officers within the

---

[35] Generalfeldmarschall Hermann von Boyen, *Denkwürdigkeiten und Erinnerungen 1771–1813*, I (Stuttgart, 1899), 206; see also *Forschungen*, XV (1902), 385–86.

[36] *A.B.B.*, IX, 726–27; XV, 113; M. Hass, "Friedrich der Grosse," 206.

bureaucratic nobility. Thus he brought about an internal regrouping of the leadership personnel, and he attempted to capitalize on this change by playing off the newcomers and the old-line regulars against each other. The professional and political upgrading of the squire-*Landräte* went back to the late years of Frederick William I.[37] The new course really got under way after "the soldiers' king" had made peace with the Junkers, primarily through his army reforms. The increased importance of the *Landräte*, as a group, found expression in their promotion to a higher grade in the service rank order and in the extension of their functional prerogatives.

The *Landrat*, in the age of Frederick II, was a part-time official who was charged with manifold public responsibilities. He represented the central state authority as a police chief, as a judicial keeper of public peace and order, and as a fiscal and military administrator. Part of his job was to publicize royal edicts in his district. He supervised the allocation and transfer of direct taxes and the distribution of the heavy, service-extracting military burdens imposed upon the populace. Accordingly, he took a hand, in coöperation with the regular military authorities, in billeting troops, in exacting military *corvées* such as transport services, and in personnel conscription for the armed forces. He also was a surveyor of the roads and the public utilities of his county, and he interfered, through police ordinances, in economic life.

As a rule, the *Landrat* was a particularly prominent, economically independent resident landowner and, very often, also a former army officer, who came from an old local family and received his appointment upon the nomination of the squires of his county. There were exceptions to this pattern, especially in the newly acquired provinces of Silesia and West Prussia, largely Catholic, where the landed nobility was reluctant to part with its *Ständestaat* liberties through integration into the stern Prussian police and garrison state. In these territories it was customary to appoint the *Landrat* at will: in Upper Silesia because of distrust in the loyalty of the "Austrian-minded" squires and in West Prussia for the sake of getting the "Polish

---

[37] *A.B.B.*, V, part 1, 269, 832; V, part 2, 463, 926; VI, part 2, 278–286, 651; XIV, 105ff.

rabble" under control. In rare instances a freshly installed *Landrat*, if he was a retired army officer and utterly unprepared for his new job, hired a substitute who did the work for him and in return got part of his employer's salary.[38]

In theory, the *Landrat*'s official task was to harmonize the objectives and activities of the central government with those of the local Junker landowners. In action, he usually was loyal to his class and acted as the trustee of the landed aristocracy, without neglecting, however, his personal affairs and self-interests.[39] In many ways the Prussian *Landrat* closely resembled the English justice of the peace under the Old Regime.[40] The heavy influx of these formidable guardians of the landed interest into the presidencies of the provincial centers of bureaucratic public administration and into the central executive bodies in Berlin meant that the dynastic instruments of civil government came to be operated largely by representatives of the squirearchy. Although "representatives," in their new capacity they changed, of necessity, their customary style of life and absorbed fresh ideas. By becoming career bureaucrats and top agents of absolute government they were apt to develop, individually and collectively, professional interests, loyalties, and political ambitions which were distinct from, though not necessarily hostile to, those of their noble constituents.

In Frederick's Prussia, the "purified" bureaucratic nobility was surrounded by a number of checks designed to prevent it from acting independently. In order to keep the bureaucracy in a state of political bondage, Frederick put primary emphasis on his own vigilance. He reserved to himself the supreme leadership and control of the

[38] See *Unter der Fahne des Herzogs von Bevern. Jugenderinnerungen des Christian Wilhelm von Prittwitz und Gaffron* (Breslau, 1935), 330–31.

[39] With regard to the *Landrat* and the Prussian pattern of county government, see Hans Delbrück, *Historische und politische Aufsätze* (Berlin, 1887), 166–184; O. Hintze, *Geist und Epochen*, 172–237; Ernst von Meier, *Die Reform der Verwaltungsorganisation unter Stein und Hardenberg*, 2nd ed. (Munich, 1912), 84–91; E. Schwenke, *Friedrich der Grosse*, 8–12.

[40] See Sidney and Beatrice Webb, *English Local Government: The Parish and the County* (London, 1924), 40–41, 280, 309–385; W. S. Holdsworth, in F. G. Dowdell, *A Hundred Years of Quarter Sessions* (Cambridge, England, 1932), IX–LXX.

administrative machine by pushing to the extreme autocratic direction from the cabinet, and by extending the employment of spies and informers. He introduced seasonal intimidation by means of his annual tours of inspection. But he clearly realized that personal safeguards of this kind were not enough to hold in subjection the royal servants who, he correctly assumed, "want to govern despotically, while their master is expected to be satisfied with the empty prerogative of issuing orders in his name."[41] Hence Frederick also tried to curb the bureaucracy by a policy of making public administration by a single, unified group impossible. This he sought to accomplish by strengthening the position of established competing authorities; by breaking the central administration into many units; and by creating, through the medium of the *Régie*, a new rival authority.

Although almost all the newly appointed top bureaucrats now came from the old Junker ranks, Frederick also called upon the class of large landed proprietors, as such, to contain his own administrative service class. The landowning bureaucratic nobility and the nonbureaucratic landed nobility were similar and yet divergent groups. Contrary to the dominant political trend under Frederick William I, the administrative influence and political power of the squirearchy expanded in Frederickian Prussia.

Nowhere was dynastic absolutism as an operating political order a fixed and immovable system. Under the mighty impact of the immobilizing social forces of the pre-absolutist past, the rulers of the modernized dynastic state brought about, at the utmost, a limited broadening of the social base for recruiting governmental personnel and a rather superficial rationalization of state management by means of imperfectly centralized administrative and military *étatisme* and by shifting the foundation of public affairs from "private" to "public" law. This is the contribution which monarchical absolutism made to the transition from the medieval to the modern state. Nowhere did the evolution of the absolute system involve a steady growth of governmental centralism and of bureaucratization.

[41] *Polit. Testamente*, 107. See also *A.B.B.*, IX, 726–27.

Frederick II encouraged the recrudescence of decentralizing tendencies, because he was deeply concerned about his political position as autocratic head of the state and because he came to fear the power of the royal servants. Therefore he sanctioned the reëmergence of nonbureaucratic agencies of corporate self-government and a limited revival of the political influence of the noble landowners, as a group, in the affairs of the dynastic state.[42] By supporting the natural foes of bureaucratic centralization and by promoting the reintroduction of elements of representative government, representative of the landed Junker interest, he sponsored, in effect, a partial restoration, though in altered forms, of the old territorial *Ständestaat*.

The political resurgence of the squirearchy led to several institutional adjustments and innovations. It began with the reconstruction of the *Regierungen* by Cocceji in coöperation with the provincial delegates of the landed aristocracy. Young Frederick supported the Lord Chancellor in his drive to put new life into the old official hierarchy to prevent thereby the new bureaucratic elite from becoming all-dominant in the manipulation of "nationalized" civil affairs. The concomitant upgrading of the *Landräte* was another phase of the royal policy of restraining the power of the regular bureaucracy.

A particularly noteworthy feature of Frederickian Prussia was the substantial regrowth of corporate-aristocratic home rule, functioning through the district assemblies of the noble landowners and through the committees which they elected. Through their activities in county government and administration the incoherent mass of privileged landholders was organized into cohesive local pressure groups. Through the *Landrat* and the memoranda which he submitted to the bureaucratic provincial boards, to individual ministers, to the General Directory, or to the King directly, the county associations of squires brought their reactions and thoughts to the attention of the central administration and obtained an indirect share in determining the direction and content of government policy and legislation.

Even on the provincial level, the squirearchy recovered some of its former vigor. It made its voice heard, especially after 1770 when it

[42] See O. Hintze, in *Forschungen*, IX (1897), 595–96; *A.B.B.*, XIV, vff.

gained, with the aid of Frederick, a rallying center in the newly established *Landschaften*. These institutions which did so much to foster the growth of agricultural production and the improvement of farming methods and estate management under the leadership of daring Junker entrepreneurs were not vested, in the formal sense, with any political function, let alone authority. Technically, they were merely provincial mortgage credit societies created for the purpose of ensuring a common economic advantage to their members through collective self-help and compulsory joint liability.[43] In practice, however, the directors and members of these incorporated bodies of large landowners and capital investors did not hold "politics" in contempt. The meetings of the elected board of directors (*Landschaftsräte*) lent themselves to the free exchange of information, opinions, and ideas and to the formulation of petitions, requests, and complaints, "respectfully submitted" to the central government. In matters of state legislation, the *Landschaften* frequently functioned as consultative agencies. Through formal and informal channels, they also brought pressure to bear upon ranking officials of their province who administered the government's economic, social, and fiscal policies.

The landed aristocracy of the two provinces of West and East Prussia, however, had to wait for Frederick's death to be blessed with a *Landschaft*. In West Prussia, most of the land belonged to Polish noblemen and, as it were, the king held a poor opinion of the "dissolute Polish trash." And as for East Prussia, Frederick never forgot and never forgave his noble "vassals" for the fact that many of them, during the ordeal of the Seven Years' War, had shown a kind of "esprit de corps et de nation" which made them "Russian- rather than Prussian-minded and, moreover, capable of all those infamies of which one accuses the Poles."[44]

[43] See H. Mauer, *Das landschaftliche Kreditwesen Preussens* (Strassburg, 1907), 2, 8–11, 21; Wilhelm von Brünneck, *Die Pfandbriefsysteme der preussischen Landschaften* (Berlin, 1910), 4–6, 107; J. Ziekursch, *Hundert Jahre schlesischer Agrargeschichte* (Breslau, 1927), 8ff., and *passim*; F. Martiny, *Die Adelsfrage*, 52ff.

[44] See E. Schwenke, *Friedrich der Grosse*, 6; *Polit. Korrespondenz*, 178; Robert Stein, *Die Umwandlung der Agrarverfassung Ostpreussens*, I (Jena, 1918), 524ff.

In his search for effective methods of keeping the royal servants in their allotted place, Frederick ventured to underpin administrative and political "deconcentration" by dismantling, in part, the service apparatus of the central government itself. He curtailed the managerial jurisdictions of the collegiate General Directory, weakened its unity, and dissolved its joint responsibility and collective solidarity by means of organizational manipulations.[45] He created new functional ministries, only nominally connected with the Directory which hitherto had been the supreme body of central administration. Thus between 1741 and 1770, he established special central departments for trade and industry, for the army, for mining and smelting, and for forestry, under single ministers directly responsible to him. He also instituted a separate administration for Silesia under a special minister who, residing in Breslau, was completely independent from the General Directory. Frequently, Frederick bypassed the Directory and also the other central agencies by giving orders directly to prominent members of the provincial and local administration or by appointing special commissars for special tasks. By founding the *Régie*, in 1766, he dealt a heavy blow to the permanent civil bureaucracy as a whole. This reorganization meant that the direction of the entire administration of the indirect taxes and of the customs duties and, for a few years, also of the postal service was turned over to a small group of French fiscal experts who at first were given a free hand in building up their own central, provincial, and local staff. These immigrants formed a privileged category of special royal servants. They received exceptionally high salaries, and they functioned as "public entrepreneurs," entitled to engage in private profiteering by appropriating 5 per cent of all revenues collected in excess of the stipulated minimum.

The "newest of the new bureaucrats" were headed by de Launay who, next to Frederick himself, was the most powerful man in the civil administration of Prussia during the two decades from 1766 to

---

[45] See Walter Dorn, in *Political Science Quarterly*, XLVII (1932), 75–83; Hans Haussherr, *Verwaltungseinheit und Ressorttrennung vom Ende des 17. bis zum Beginn des 19. Jahrhunderts* (Berlin, 1953), 121–148.

1786. The royal leader had meant to go even further. Frederick had intended to entrust the French reformers also with the management of the crown's timber resources and of the tobacco and salt monopolies. Moreover, he had wanted to "debureaucratize" this whole bundle of "nationalized" fiscal prerogatives by farming them out on a strictly commercial basis. Aware of the risks, de Launay declined this generous offer.[46] Thus he won a noteworthy battle for the regular Prussian bureaucracy which nonetheless regarded him as a most undesirable enemy alien.

By the introduction of the *Régie*, the traditional bureaucrats temporarily lost a large part of their managerial dominion and a major source of their perquisites. Through the rival authority of the *Régie*, the whole civil state bureaucracy was split wide open and converted into two implacably hostile organizations. Thus, just after the century-old conflict between the old and the new official hierarchies had been reconciled, a far more bitter service dualism developed which could not be resolved by compromise. Thereafter, the administrative manager class was an unforgiving and remorseless opponent of the new fiscal bureaucrats. In consequence, it was prepared, more than ever before, to close ranks with the high judiciary against the common enemy: the officials of the *Régie* and the trouble maker behind them, the bullying "royal master."

"Power controlled or abridged," as Alexander Hamilton once remarked, "is almost always the rival and enemy of that power by which it is controlled or abridged."[47] Distrustful political competition and increasing antagonism rather than harmonious coöperation marked the relations between personal autocracy and collective bureaucracy in Frederickian Prussia. The royal servants refused to function as obedient, spineless human instruments in the hands of the obstinate monarch. The tortuous policy of containing the bureaucracy sprang from the inane, false, and frightening idea which Frederick II had throughout harbored in his mind, the idea that all

[46] See Walther Schultze, *Geschichte der Preussischen Regieverwaltung von 1766 bis 1786* (Leipzig, 1888), 20, 28–60, 93, 96.
[47] *The Federalist or the New Constitution* (Everyman's Library), 72.

Prussian subjects, including "l'élite de la nation," could be kept in motion like machines by the royal chief engineer.

Frederick continued to play the central role as the initiator and maker of state policy and as the chief supervisor of the enforcement of laws and policy, but most of the checks and balances with which he surrounded his administrators boomeranged. As a matter of fact, the bureaucratic elite managed to gain a high degree of liberty from royal restraints and to exact retribution for being treated contemptuously and, as a rule, disrespectfully. Its members did not rest content with the routine job of executing official directives, cabinet orders, and predetermined policies. They effectively contrived to usurp if not the right then at least the practice of codetermining government policy and of blocking the enforcement of royal regulations and decisions if they saw fit to do so. Like the French *noblesse de robe*, the Prussian bureaucratic nobility, in moving against the absolute monarch, acted in accordance with the thought "that it could successfully overcome all the opposition he could put in action, and in due time make his authority secondary to its own."[48]

The real power of the Prussian Crown gradually declined during the second half of the eighteenth century. The formal transformation of monarchical autocracy into a system of bureaucratic-aristocratic authoritarianism, as effected in 1807 and 1808, legalized and reinforced this political development. In the reconstructed Old Regime, as it emerged from the increasingly enlightened late eighteenth century, political leadership and the responsibility for high level policy making were concentrated in the ministerial chiefs of the civil bureaucracy which preserved the tradition of paternal government by dictation. The Junker historian Theodor von der Goltz, writing at a much later time and arguing in terms of *"Realpolitik,"* understated his case when he proudly noted that the Hohenzollerns in the age of absolutism, though nominally equipped with "unlimited power," had, in reality, to rely "chiefly on their noble companions as advisers and executive organs and were

[48] *The Memoirs of the Duke of Saint-Simon*, II (New York, 1936), part IV, 9.

compelled to take into account their opinions, desires, and frame of mind."[49]

Diverse forces brought about the transmutation of the "royal servants" into a self-governing professional corporation and a policy and law making political oligarchy.

[49] Theodor Freiherr von der Goltz, *Geschichte der deutschen Landwirtschaft*, II (Stuttgart, 1903), 165–66.

Chapter Eight

The Emancipation from Monarchical Autocracy

I

In the Hohenzollern state, as in all absolutist polities sustained by large-scale, hierarchical organization of executive functions, government acquired a certain impersonal quality. Only to a limited extent, therefore, was the socio-political order molded by the character, policies, and ideas of the holder of legal sovereignty. The royal commander-in-chief, by becoming "the first servant" of "his" state, was caught in the wheels of his own bureaucratic apparatus. Whatever the monocrat might do about the managerial personnel of "the Administration," it was beyond his power to change the direction of the bureaucracy's collective drive for more freedom and independence.

In this unremitting struggle for replacing arbitrary royal powers and whimsical interference with general legal rules, the servants of the crown, organized as a continuous hierarchy on a vast territorial scale, enjoyed the enormous advantage of growing size. The tripling of the Prussian state territory and the quadrupling of both the state population and of the royal treasury's revenues from 1740 to 1806; the noteworthy advance in the governmental exploitation of economic resources; the expansion and consolidation of the service-extracting and service-rendering activities of the administrative state —all these long-term trends played into the hands of the constantly growing army of professional government functionaries.[1] Almost automatically, the bureaucracy derived great advantage from the impersonal basis of its strength; from its huge size as an organization; from its permanence, functional indispensability, and monopoly of expert knowledge; from its self-consciousness as an aristocratic status group and power elite; and from its patient and oblique obstructiveness.

Thus, without conspiring to do so, the commissioned agents of the crown, free from accountability to the governed, came to enjoy a high degree of hierarchical self-government. Sheer force of numbers ruled out effective concentration of patronage and supervisory power over the body of public administrators by direct one-man control. Even Frederick II, in matters of personnel administration, had to content himself with spasmodic fits of energetic intervention in person.

With regard to the replenishment of its membership, the bureaucracy was an essentially coöptative corporation with a strong liking for the ancient practice of hereditary transmission of status and power. The king had reserved to himself the ultimate selection of the higher officials and the power to dismiss or punish any "servant" by means of tyrannical methods. Yet, save for some army officers, mostly ill-chosen and ill-fated individuals, whom Frederick II transferred to ranking posts in the civil bureaucracy on his own initiative, the "outsiders" whom he appointed to key positions were in reality almost invariably the nominees of ministers.[2]

The *Landräte*, deemed worthy enough to be elevated to a board presidency, were selected by Frederick, as a matter of standard practice, from among a very few candidates who had the endorsement of minister bureaucrats. Cocceji and his successors as well as de Launay exercised discretionary authority in staffing their departments up to the very top, although, in the nationalized judicial service, appointments of significance remained formally subject to

---

[1] For a more detailed statistical measurement of material progress in Prussia, see G. Schmoller, *Umrisse und Untersuchungen*, 138, 166, 171, 180.

[2] *A.B.B.*, VII, 763; X, viii–ix; XIII, 122ff.

royal approval.³ After 1786, the absolute king, as a matter of routine, simply confirmed the recommendations for appointments and promotions made by the most influential courtiers and by the leading bureaucratic patronage dispensers, the ministers of the central administrative departments and the Lord Chancellor presiding over the justice department.⁴

Obscure and discreet wirepullers who belonged to the tiny, nonnoble band of chuckling cabinet councilors were also effective in helping the monarch make up his mind. Cabinet Councilor Eichel, the son of a military noncommissioned officer, made von Jariges, and not only by leaving to this intimate friend his own huge estate which evidently had not been built up solely by means of saving part of his salary, impressive though that was. It was largely through Eichel's influence that Jariges, the son of a noble French army officer, secured his appointment as Lord Chancellor.⁵ Eichel's colleague Galster, who had been bribed by Christoph von Görne—destined to establish an extraordinary record as a forger and embezzler—paid off his moral debts by suggesting to the king that Görne was ministerial timber.⁶

In the field of personnel administration, the Frederickian bureaucracy was eminently successful in diverting devices of royal control to its own ends. In the course of time, it managed to transform them into instruments of organizational autonomy and of hierarchic home rule.

In the enforcement of the stern service codes the absolute regulatory authority of the crown was diluted, in fact, by the inertia, sabotage, or willful deception of the administrative departments. The royal servants, while continuing to quarrel among themselves,

³ W. Schultze, *Geschichte der Preussischen Regieverwaltung*, 37; *A.B.B.*, XIII, 69ff., 384–85.
⁴ See Schulenburg-Kehnert's comments, in *Forschungen*, XV (1902), 415–16; and Karl Immermann's "Memorabilien," in Harry Maync, ed., *Immermanns Werke*, V, 312.
⁵ A. Stölzel, *Brandenburg-Preussens Rechtsverwaltung*, II, 239; *A.B.B.*, VI, part 1, 63–64; XIV, 450.
⁶ *A.B. Seidenindustrie*, III, 285–288; *A.B. Handels-, Zoll, und Akzisepolitik*, III, part 2, 450ff., 522; Heinrich von Friedberg, "Friedrich der Grosse und der Prozess Görne," *Historische Zeitschrift*, LXV (1890), 1–43.

learned through grim experience that life became unbearable unless they protected themselves against excessive regimentation.

No clean-cut line separated coöperation from passive resistance. How things worked out in daily life was typified by Minister von Münchow's response to a royal "order," requesting him to stir his subordinates to greater efforts. Münchow presented this directive to his staff in Breslau, but added a soothing interpretation. He advised his councilors that, in view of the fact that they "work quite differently than other boards, they should not get in the least alarmed. For this order is, no doubt, a general circular which was obviously by mistake transmitted to this board."[7]

Aside from usurping a considerable amount of authority in managing intradepartmental affairs, the top administrators imposed a very effective check upon the real power of the autocrat by jealously guarding the principal avenues to admission and promotion. The introduction of compulsory entrance examinations and the simultaneous establishment of a civil service commission (*Oberexaminationskommission*), in 1770, was a landmark in the process of growing corporate independence and of group exclusiveness. These reforms caught up with the stiffened educational and vocational requirements which Cocceji and Jariges had introduced in the judicial service.[8] With the aid of this screening method the judicial bureaucracy was rejuvenated in personnel, professional vitality, and public influence. Ironically enough, the drive to raise the caliber and qualifications of the administrative class was led by Minister von Hagen, a man who boasted that he never read a printed line.

Hagen and his associates pretended to be solely concerned with the improvement of integrity and efficiency to serve better "the aim and well-founded interest of the state ruler as well as the conservation of all classes." The reformers complained that "diligent work ceases to be fashionable nowadays" and that people had "sneaked"

[7] *A.B.B.*, VII, 12ff.
[8] *Ibid.*, XV, VII, 240–254. See also C. J. Friedrich, "The Continental Tradition of Training Administrators in Law and Jurisprudence," *The Journal of Modern History*, XI (1939), 133–142.

into dynastic employment "who did not possess the necessary ability, knowledge, and sound judgment."[9]

Acute pressures precipitated the introduction of examinations. The nerve-racking strain of the Seven Years' War was followed by economic depression and inconclusive attempts at healing the wounds of war. During this "time of troubles" which Frederick had brought upon himself and his bleeding people, the relations between the stubborn autocrat and his bureaucracy became particularly tense. The newly appointed gentlemen in charge of the central administration—almost all the old ministers had died during the war—had good reasons to search for effective means to tighten their grip over their subordinates.

Under war conditions, widespread graft, "collaboration" with the occupation authorities, professional laxity, and unauthorized exercise of powers had spread to all levels of the service.[10] The ministers fought their personal as well as the king's battle when they censured severely the numerous board councilors, _Steuerräte_ and _Landräte_, who had come "to criticize the orders which they receive and attempt to make themselves independent" by engaging in "arbitrary action, opposition, insubordination."[11]

The sharp decline of discipline, loyalty, efficiency, and service morale had seriously weakened the authority and prestige of the self-righteous and quarrelsome top executives at a time when they clashed bitterly with their employer. For Frederick put the blame on them. He taunted his principal aides for their "vile disposition," "criminal indolence," "obdurate trickery," and "infamous interests." He "complimented" them for being "no longer of any use whatsoever either to the country or to the state," and he put them at their ease by threatening them with imprisonment for life.[12] Royal distrust and vengefulness also found expression in the establishment

---

[9] _A.B.B._, XIV, 333; XV, 243, 260. See also G. A. H. Baron von Lamotte, _Practische Beyträge zur Cameralwissenschaft für die Cameralisten in den preussischen Staaten_, III (Halle, 1785), 53–72.

[10] _A.B.B._, XI, 443ff., 475ff., 523–24, 621ff., 631; XII, 128ff.; XIII, 122ff., 265; XIV, 167–68, and _passim_.

[11] _Ibid._, XIV, 351.

[12] _Ibid._, XII, 261ff.; XIII, 762ff.; XIV, 335.

of the *Régie* which further impaired the official standing and the reputation of the regular administrative bureaucracy as a whole. A little resurrection from within was essential to recover some of the lost ground. Something had to be done to make a good impression and to ensure a gradual improvement of the professional quality and reliability of officialdom.

The raising of standardized prerequisites for admission had a profound effect upon the bureaucracy as a social elite and as a political group. Whatever the motives and ostensible objectives of the ministerial sponsors of the reformed merit system, the new service tests turned out to be, in the hands of the bureaucratic nobility, a wonderful device for consolidating its control over personnel recruitment and for gaining greater freedom from royal molestations in this crucial area.

In a novel guise strong barriers were erected against the infiltration of undesirable newcomers. The examinations were competitive in name rather than in fact. In effect, the reformed admission techniques gave a new lease on life to the established pattern of inequality of opportunity by refining the traditional practices of nepotism and favoritism. Instead of encouraging free competition, the revised merit system further restricted limited competition.

The amended version of the selective system, as it actually functioned for a long time, gave preference to university-trained candidates who could meet both the social respectability and the means tests. Automatically shut off from competition was the sizable group of university students who had neither the necessary connections nor the financial resources for becoming in-service trainees and for paying the high examination fees charged to prospective councilors. Those who suffered from pecuniary undernourishment could make "careers" as teachers or preachers, not as public administrators.

Nevertheless, the door to the upper service was not yet entirely closed to *Regimentsquartiermeister, Auditeure,* and officials in the lower grades, provided they were nominated as examination candidates by high ranking superiors. The latter were vested with the delicate responsibility of carefully surveying these socially defective applicants with regard to their character, personal fitness, habits, and style of life.[13] As in the past, well-educated subalterns were not always frozen in their positions as clerical workers. Even in the age of the noble reaction one could not, as President von Schön put it, "dispense with people of this kind, because the work for which highborn councilors were unqualified simply had to be done."[14] But as seen from the vantage point of a defender of the noble claims to inborn superiority: "Middle class people know only how to work, not how to govern. . . . It is not unusual, therefore, to appoint bourgeois councilors with the prudent intent to make work easier for the noble councilors so that the latter will have time for more important matters."[15]

After the 1770's, the higher administrative service formed more than ever a self-recruiting and increasingly "streamlined" hierarchy which identified itself with aristocratic valuations and interests. Its leaders tended to admit only "congenial persons" and to recommend for promotions only those who could be trusted to play the game in accordance with the rules of the directing personnel. Unpaid in-service training, preceded by costly higher education, both general and vocational and with major emphasis on the study of *Kameralwissenschaft*, was a powerful aid in fortifying the cohesion and the prestige of the service as a socially exclusive status group.[16]

Thus a fresh impetus was given to the spirit of inbreeding and of caste. To be sure, in Frederickian Prussia the conflict arising from the inequality of opportunity between nobles and nonnobles in public life remained unresolved. This perennial source of friction, discontent, and frustration continued to retard the growth of the political striking power of the bureaucracy as a whole. Yet, even this extremely important intraservice cleavage was reduced under the conditions of the closing decades of the eighteenth century.

[13] *Ibid.*, XV., 250.

[14] Quoted in R. Grabower, *Preussens Steuern*, 112.

[15] Hans Albert Freiherr von S..., *Apologie des Adels* (Berlin, 1807), 52–53.

[16] With respect to the professional training requirements for the upper service, see *Annalen der Preussischen Staatswirthschaft und Statistik*, II (1805), 405ff.

Decisive in this respect was the revolutionizing social and political role which higher education, new concepts, and powerful ideas came to play in this age of the great flowering of German literature and philosophy.

II

In spite of the reaffirmation of noble privilege and of the premium put on the accident of exalted birth, noble status, as such, lost much of its ancient prestige in the latter part of the eighteenth century. This was not merely the consequence of the growth of a sizable group of noble paupers, illiterates, and *déclassés*. The lowering of noble rank in the social scale was, above all, due to the appearance of a new standard of grading the worth of man and of gauging merit, dignity, and social position. Personal eminence, based on notable intellectual or artistic efforts and creative attainments, challenged the primacy of the centuries-old division of society into hereditary, castelike estates—a pattern of class stratification which had been thrown into confusion by the rise of the royal table of ranks.

Together with birth and office, inherited social rank and acquired service title, higher education in the sense of *Bildung* became an important attribute of social repute. *Bildung*, as conceived by the German neohumanists in the age of Lessing, Herder, Winckelmann, Goethe, Schiller, Kant, Fichte, and Humboldt, meant much more than advanced school training, general and vocational. *Bildung*, no doubt, called for trained minds and for more and better knowledge, but no less for character and personality development. *Bildung* implied supreme emphasis on inwardness and tenderness of the heart. It invited man to seek happiness within himself by orienting his total life toward the harmonious blending of spiritual elevation, emotional refinement, and individualized mental and moral perfection.

But *Bildung* also was a channel of class mobility. In the age of the noble reaction, it was the battle cry of rising intellectual and artistic elites struggling for social recognition. *Bildung*, as a social movement in the realm of ideas, was a brilliantly constructive response against the pretensions of the nobility to ingrained human and social superiority. The new intelligentsia, meeting the approbation of professional men, patrician merchants, and educated Jewish *nouveaux arrivés*, was conscious of constituting a novel aristocracy of merit. As such, it brought literature, philosophy, learning, and the fine arts into the place of honor. It formed an elite in the normative sense, "a class of the people who have the highest indices in their branch of activity."[17] Being a community of men with fertile minds, lofty ideals, often empty pockets and mostly humble ancestors, the aristocrats of intellect and artistic talent, imbued with missionary fervor, advanced the claim to equality, if not superiority of social worth with the traditionally esteemed.[18]

Under Frederick II, by culture a Frenchman, the radiating influence of the centers of German *Kultur* in Dresden, Leipzig, Göttingen, Jena, Weimar, and Hamburg had spread to the Prussian university towns of Halle and Königsberg. Around 1790, Berlin, too, became a flourishing metropolis for the recognition of *Bildung* as a source of social distinction.[19] The time had come when high position no longer was readily taken for personal excellence; when, in the words of a contemporary, *Bildung* was a decisive yardstick for "gauging the degree of social esteem which formerly rank and external glitter alone determined."[20] "Formerly, self-assurance was coupled with comforting, somewhat overbearing, and ignorant

[17] Vilfredo Pareto, *The Mind and Society*, III (New York, 1935), 1423.

[18] See Max Scheler, *Versuche zu einer Soziologie des Wissens* (Munich, 1924), 44, 55, 72, 76ff.; Hans Weil, *Die Entwicklung des deutschen Bildungsprinzips* (Bonn, 1930), 223ff., 236; Norbert Elias, *Ueber den Prozess der Zivilisation*, I, 21ff.; Levin Schücking, *The Sociology of Literary Taste* (London, 1944), 18.

[19] Wilhelm Dilthey, *Leben Schleiermachers*, 2d ed., I (Berlin, 1922), 223–229; Josef Nadler, *Literaturgeschichte der deutschen Stämme und Landschaften*, 2d ed., III (Regensburg, 1924), 215; Hannah Arendt, *The Origins of Totalitarianism* (New York, 1951), 57–62.

[20] Knoblauch, *Ueber die sittliche und wissenschaftliche Bildung der jungen Edelleute*, as quoted in Friedrich Meinecke, *Das Leben des Generalfeldmarschalls Hermann von Boyen*, I (Stuttgart, 1896), 111.

naïveté. There was no need to prove to anybody who one was, provided that one belonged to 'society'!"[21]

Now strange new voices could be heard, uttering self-assertive provocations and revealing an attitude of arrogance rather than deference toward the titled aristocracy. For example, Fichte, the cofounder of the philosophy of German Idealism, by reviving the memory of the base arts of the forebears of the nobility, questioned the validity of its matter-of-course insistence on "superiority." The preëminence of noble social status, Fichte suggested, had its roots in "flattery, crawling, lying, and in robbing the defenseless" and in the privilege of "having lived in relative prosperity for a great number of successive generations." In our era, he triumphantly noted in 1793, "it has come about that the nobleman who is nothing else than that will be tolerated in the circles of the reputable burgher estate, the scholars, the merchants, and the artists, only by making an effort to display extraordinary humility."[22]

Inadvertently, yet constructively, the initiators of the reformed pattern of government personnel training accepted the novel standard of excellence and social respectability engendered by the ascendancy of *Bildung*. By switching over to a higher plane of general education and vocational training, the rising generation of bureaucrats managed to keep in touch with "the good life" and to substantiate its self-seeking and high-minded aristocratic longing for supreme leadership in public life.

No doubt, for many who entered Prussian government service after 1770, the edifying ideal of *Bildung* had little or no intrinsic value. These men were drawn to it out of sheer vanity. "Culture" occupied but a decorative place in their lives. It was a social fashion. It served as "an engine of social and class distinction, separating the

---

[21] Adolf von Grolman, in the introduction to *Eichendorffs Werke*, I (Leipzig, 1928), 53.

[22] J. H. Fichte, ed., *Johann Gottlieb Fichte's Sämtliche Werke*, VI (1845), 218, 221–225. A similar characterization in August Hennings, *Vorurtheilsfreie Gedanken über Adelsgeist und Aristokratismus* (1792), 24–25. See also Franz Rühl, ed., *Briefe und Aktenstücke zur Geschichte Preussens unter Friedrich Wilhelm III*, I (Leipzig, 1899), 18.

holder like a badge or title from other people who have not got it."[23] For those who could afford it, the conspicuous exhibition of ornaments of cultural refinement, such as the beautifying of residences and the collecting of art treasures, became a sophisticated means of reëmphasizing social exclusiveness.

But alongside the superficial and pretentious, there also was the much smaller number of the sincere and enthusiastic. For the latter, who frequently were on intimate terms with prominent members of the creative cultural elite, the call for *Bildung* gave focal direction to their lives. Self-disciplined dedication to an idea in the place of subservience to a personal master vitalized their political loyalties and their zeal to render public service. Among these heretics and rebels were the admirable few who meant by *Bildung* "the desire for removing human error, clearing human confusion, and diminishing human misery, the noble aspiration to leave the world better and happier than we found it; the moral and social passion for doing good."[24]

The traffic of ideas produced subtle changes in mentality and in interclass relations. In time, it exercised an attenuating as well as an inflammatory influence upon the age-old antagonism between noble and nonnoble officials. This division had been accentuated by the noble reaction which gave rise to a malcontent body of frustrated nonnoble councilors. "Common" bureaucrats, who elevated themselves to the status of truly educated persons (*Gebildete*), of "inner aristocrats," gained in self-esteem and confidence and deepened their understanding of the idea of "the career open to talent." And even if they did not feel like *beati possedentes* in the world of sublime ideas, they might find some consolation in the general depreciation of the value of noble prestige and, more particularly, in the stepping down of numerous titled aristocrats on the social ladder.

In many instances, the contrast between nonnoble "superiors," although "commoners," and noble "inferiors" who were "riff-raff," a distinction which was sustained by the facts of occupational status,

[23] Matthew Arnold, *Culture and Anarchy* (New York, 1924), 5.
[24] *Ibid.*, 7.

186 Bureaucracy, Aristocracy, and Autocracy

of service rank, and of way of life, was brought into bolder relief by
a further widening of social distance stemming from educational
inequalities between the two elements. As active holders of *Bildung*,
lowborn bureaucrats, though for the time being held back by discrimination in professional life, acquired a heightened sense of social
worth, independent of, or in opposition to, the traditional valuations
of the nobility.

In consequence of this inner liberation from old-style concepts
of aristocracy and of the increasingly critical detachment from the
official social rank scale of Frederickian Prussia, climbers now
were less inclined to demonstrate their social ambitions by aping the
timeworn ways of the wellborn. Conversely, alert, sensitive, and
imaginative nobles responded to the lowering of the value of "blue
blood," as such, by developing a desire to conform to the new standards of personal aristocracy. They actively participated in the drive
for *Bildung* by mingling with the nonnoble *Gebildete* on the footing
of social intimacy and open competition and by emulating their
pursuits.

Bildung undermined the traditional separation of the classes, but
also the ancient practice of equating the aristocracy with the nobility.
Inside and outside government service, *Bildung* became the new
bond that tied well-educated nobles and commoners together and
established them as a proud and self-reliant aristocratic fraternity,
transcending the boundaries of birth, status, profession, rank, and
wealth. This mobile group formed "a sort of freemasonry, of which
all the members continue to recognize one another through certain
invisible signs, whatever may be the opinions which make them
strangers to one another or even adversaries."[25]

By joining the intellectual and artistic elites as leaders or followers, a small section of the titled aristocracy emancipated itself
from the complacent beliefs of its class and broke away from the
idea of a separate noble education. Acting as individuals, they sought
to affirm their social superiority without putting primary emphasis
on the privileges of birth and on titled position. Instead, they aimed
at the preservation of leadership status by new means, by developing

[25] *The Recollections of Alexis de Tocqueville* (New York, 1896), 305–306.

the faculties inherent in themselves and by excelling as upholders of intellectual culture and, in professional and public life, as superior performers.

Thus, the regrouping of the governing class of Prussia entered into a fresh phase. As in France during the latter part of the Old Regime, so now in Prussia the old socio-political caste system faced a new challenge. Despite its militarist excesses, its dictatorial process of law making, the peculiar pattern of monarchical "cabinet government," and the singular character and functional role of the landed Junker aristocracy, the Frederickian state, "belonging" to the nobility, was not unlike the polity of pre-Revolutionary France. What stood out in the Bourbon monarchy was "the reign of privilege. All power, all distinction, and, as far as it was possible, all pleasure was reserved for one caste. The people paid the taxes, the *noblesse* spent them. The people furnished the soldiers, the *noblesse* the officers; the people had nothing to do with the laws but to obey them; the *noblesse* made them and administered them. The *noblesse* alone were good company; if a *roturier* penetrated into their salons it was through their condescension."[26]

The reorientation of minds, habits, and aspirations, in response to the ideals proclaimed by Germany's cultural aristocracy, affected the struggle between autocracy and bureaucracy for domination in the Prussian monarchy. The group mentality of the administrative class, a composite mentality of various levels, was deeply influenced by the influx of a new generation of young *Gebildete*. Their rise in the government services did not make it easier for Frederick II to extract from his employees unquestioning obedience and faithful devotion to temperamental personal leadership by dictation. The spread of *Bildung* in bureaucratic circles powerfully reinforced the yearning for greater individual and corporate freedom in professional life; for more authority and responsibility; for protection against arbitrary injury by those in supreme power; for guaranteed lifetime security; for the consolidation of "well-earned rights."

Above all, *Bildung* gave higher sanction to the claim to the right

[26] *Correspondence and Conversations of A. de Tocqueville with Nassau William Senior*, 2d ed., I (London, 1872), 93.

to live decently and with self-respect, that is, the right to be treated as a human being. It aided many Prussian officials to "rationalize" their defiance of the commands of harsh and sometimes vicious royal despotism. To those with delicate souls and to men with serious intellectual interests, the neohumanistic conception of man and the new individualistic philosophy of the freedom of the moral will as the answer to the unqualified demand to duty proved an inexhaustible spring of energy and fortitude in effecting their mental and moral emancipation from the tutelage of royal omniscience. With replenished inner resources, they stood ready to shunt "impossible" demands, not because of spite and obstinacy or for the sake of personal advantage or material class interests, but on ethical and humanitarian grounds.

To resistance fighters and "inner emigrants" of this kind, few in numbers, the appeal to individual conscience and judgment and to freedom anchored in self-control, in the place of unthinking compliance with detailed administrative orders and external constraints, was extremely attractive. To those who felt the urge and had the will to build their lives not merely on utility and opportunism, but also on principles and convictions; to the men who were destined to contribute much to the political leadership of the Prussian Reform Era after 1806, it was short of unbearable to be called upon by the "master" to rest content with functioning like cogs in a machine. Of necessity, they found themselves at odds with the police and garrison state which had no room for the liberal view that the individual must be regarded as an end and not a means.

The young mining official Friedrich von Hardenberg, better known under his pen name Novalis, summed up this detestation of the powers that be: "No state has been governed more like a factory than Prussia since Frederick William I."[27] Nowhere else, he added, have the spiritual and moral qualities of the subjects been stifled and injured as much as in the artificial state of Prussia sustained, as it was, by a privileged class which Stein's close friend Ludwig von Vincke, in 1800, characterized as follows: "The greater part of our

---

[27] Paul Kluckhohn, ed., *Deutsche Literatur. Reihe Romantik*, X (Leipzig, 1935), 176. See also Erich Schmidt, ed., *H. v. Kleists Werke*, V, 24–39.

nobility still live under the illusion that the state cannot exist without their unconditional exemption from all essential contributions and without the oppression and subservience of the other social classes, and that the slightest modification and concession inevitably must result in the collapse of the whole order."[28]

Displaying an abstract radicalism of thought, the speculative philosophical and literary-aesthetic movement of the German intelligentsia was essentially nonpolitical, if not antipolitical in nature. Before 1800, the doctrines of German Idealism acquired political significance only in the Prussian bureaucracy. Not only did the administrative apparatus of the state provide an institutional setting for constructive action; the rigor, rudeness, intolerance, and soullessness of Frederick's rulership affected the bureaucrats directly and stiffened their will to resist royal oppression with the aid of liberal principles. "Servants" of the crown learned to embrace "seditious ideas" and the enlightened conception of reason, as defined by Kant: "Enlightenment is the emancipation of man from his self-inflicted tutelage. Tutelage is the incapacity to make use of one's mind without the guidance of another person." To the bureaucratic disciples of Kant, individual freedom to think was the gateway to professional happiness, to self-disciplined discretionary action, to their own political liberation, and to the replacement of erratic dynastic autocracy by a more magnanimous and more efficient form of despotic government, by humanized bureaucratic absolutism, "which will find it advantageous to itself to treat man, who thenceforth is more than a machine, in accord with his dignity."[29]

Frederick's death brought relief to the Prussian bureaucracy which had been condemned to underhanded plotting and dishonest living. There was nothing great about Frederick William II (1786–1797) and Frederick William III (1797–1840); and unlike Frederick II, they did not overestimate their own wisdom. Because they were more malleable, less clever, less ambitious, and more humane, upper

---

[28] Heinrich Kochendörffer, ed., *Westfälische Briefwechsel*, I (Münster, 1930), 13.
[29] *Immanuel Kant's Sämtliche Werke* (Grossherzog Wilhelm Ernst edition), I, 163, 171.

and middle class life in Prussia and the bureaucratic ways of living in particular tended to become less militaristic and much more human. The Sparta of the North softened up from within, before it bit the dust on the battlefields of 1806. Now the enlightened, *gebildeter* bureaucrat came into his own. He differed as much from the "ideal commissar" of the "soldiers' king," as the better intendants, intelligent, well-educated, public-spirited, of Louis XVI were distinguished from their predatory and brutal predecessors in the age of Richelieu or as most of the English justices of the peace, as of 1800, differed from the squire tyrants of an earlier era.

The Prussian bureaucracy, as a whole, in its fight for job security, hierarchical self-government, and a dignified mode of professional living, scored a resounding victory during the twilight regime that lasted from 1786 to 1806.

The General Legal Code of 1794, the work of learned members of the judicial bureaucracy, reasserted, in the days of the French Revolution, the exclusive prerogatives of the First Estate and thus "the natural, inalienable, and sacred rights of noblemen." At the same time, however, the authors and sponsors of this code were keenly aware of the nonsaturated interests of their own corps. With its members, whether noble or nonnoble, they shared the passionate desire for removing once and for all the most repugnant restraints shackling their professional freedom and political aspirations. The codifiers of public, private, and criminal law succeeded in buttressing the privileges of the civil state bureaucracy which came to be labeled "well-earned rights" (*wohlerworbene Rechte*). By subjecting the crown, in matters of personnel administration, to certain binding rules, they curbed the powers of the absolute king, placed him under the law, reduced the personal element in government, and spurred the evolution of the official hierarchy into a self-centred political oligarchy.

Thereafter, career officials no longer faced the threat of arbitrary recall or punishment by the monarch. The Code of 1794 conferred upon the civil state executives the qualified legal right to permanent tenure and the unqualified right to due process of law in case of questionable conduct.[30] Only the "political" ministers, the chiefs of the managerial power machine, could be ousted without legal protection.

Simultaneously, and rather unobtrusively, in their self-assertive drive for personal independence in the exercise of powers inherent in their offices, the "royal servants" now called themselves "servants of the state" (*"Diener des Staates"*) and "professional officials of the state" (*"Beamte des Staats"*). The change of name signified the change of status and of loyalties. No longer permanent probationers and the monarch's private employees serviceable to the dynastic interest, the Prussian bureaucrats, by promoting themselves to the impersonal rank of professional state executives, did not become thereby public servants governing with the consent of, and in responsibility to, the public or even a small fraction of the governed. As political competitors of the royal sovereign, the "servants of the state" identified themselves with their hierarchical organization, that is, with the authoritarian administrative apparatus which, together with the military machine, was the Prussian state. But in contesting the autocratic position of the king as a person, the renamed Prussian bureaucracy came to favor a liberalized pattern of absolutist government. The change of name mirrored the impact of fresh ideas, of novel concepts of public welfare and of allegiance in government service, and of more voluntaristic and, therefore, more exacting standards of public ethics.

Frederick II's mental image of "the state" as a singular social entity, his written assurances to the contrary notwithstanding, still came very close to the old patrimonial formula *"l'état c'est moi."* As a matter of course, therefore, he regarded and treated the governmental executives like personal underlings charged with the management of his estate. As early as the latter years of his reign, the impersonal conception of the state in the abstract began to migrate

<hr />

[30] See *Allgemeines Landrecht für die Preussischen Staaten*, IV, Zehnter Teil: Von den Rechten und Pflichten der Diener des Staates. See also *Jahrbücher der preussischen Monarchie unter der Regierung Friedrich Wilhelms des Dritten*, I (Berlin, 1798), 20–21; Clemens Theodor Perthes, *Der Staatsdienst in Preussen* (Hamburg, 1838), 144–173.

in Prussian lands and to exercise a significant influence.[31] But as for the liberty and power-hungry civil state bureaucrats, the why is not elusive at all. In harmony with their own peculiar interpretation of *"esprit de corps et de nation,"* inner attachment to an objectified rational order, to the idea of "the" sovereign state, was infinitely more rewarding, uplifting, assuring, and promising than submission to an eccentric monocrat, even if he was a part-time bureaucrat and a personality who emanated epic glow.

III

Long before 1794, the Prussian bureaucracy, as a body, gained a considerable amount of executive discretion and irresponsible political influence in detachment from, and veiled opposition to, personalized monarchical autocracy. Undoubtedly, the self-willed power wielded by the administrative class was essentially negative in character. As long as Frederick II stood at the helm of the state, he had the last word in all matters of importance. So effective were his tactics of division and his ways of delegating power that he was the only person in the kingdom who had a comprehensive picture of the workings of the Prussian government in its entirety.

De jure, the bureaucracy remained the subservient managerial transmitter of the royal will, although the leaders were, at the pleasure of the king, frequently consulted, individually or collectively, in the execution of policy and in its preparation. But as for the determination of high policy, the initiation of laws, the planning of the state budget as a whole, and the allocation of funds, Frederick denied his top aides the status of active shareholders. And because of the ever present threat of punitive action and of the paucity of men like President Domhardt willing "to gladly risk a black eye," open opposition to Frederick's leadership was almost nonexistent.[32] Nevertheless, the royal servants were not merely administrative technicians and executive assistants. They also were the active political copartners of Frederick, who limited his powers, for they

---

[31] See A. Stölzel, *Brandenburg-Preussens Rechtsverwaltung*, I, 301ff.
[32] *A.B. Handels-, Zoll- und Akzisepolitik*, III, part 1, 161.

possessed, in fact, a tacit veto over royal legislation and executive decrees.

The check which the bureaucracy imposed upon the ruler usually took the form of negative action, reflecting an attitude of confidence, mingled with fear. By using mainly indirect methods, the managers of the administrative and judicial apparatus were able to circumvent and counteract royal decisions and orders and to paralyze the execution of policy. They were equipped with the very real power to obstruct and to divert. They practiced passive resistance through inertia, chicanery, and sophistry. They influenced policy making and steered policy enforcement into channels more desirable to themselves by withholding facts or by supplying colored information to their employer. They resorted, if "necessary," to cunning subterfuges, outright deception, and willful sabotage. In the midst of an odious atmosphere of mutual suspicion, distrust, and perpetual alertness, they exploited their powers of investigation and carried out unauthorized policies of their own by amending, undermining, or altogether emasculating royal directives.

Prussian bureaucrats, in numerous instances, simply refused to acquiesce to commands against their own judgment. Such, for instance, was the growing boldness of the directing band of Junker ministers, that they did not refrain from formally reprimanding a board president for having submitted to Frederick accurate instead of manipulated statistical data.[33] More often, however, the top officials defended the interests of their corps by shielding colleagues, even unworthy ones, against royal reprisals.

For example, during the Seven Years' War which adversely affected "the moral purification of the administration," some of the highest state dignitaries coming from "the best families," such as the Herren von Wallenrodt, von Rohd, von Gröben, and von Tettau in East Prussia, deserted their posts under flimsy pretexts. The ministerial bureaucracy in Berlin, however, was obliging enough to supply a moral alibi by hitting at the brilliant idea that these distinguished "runaway vassals" had rendered particularly "meritorious service" by leaving their "fatherland because of special devotion and

[33] *A.B. Getreidehandelspolitik*, IV, 117–18, 227–28.

loyalty to His Royal Majesty."[34] Whatever the means employed, the executive hierarchy succeeded, in the course of time, in taking the sting out of the practice of fitful monocratic rule from the cabinet.

Unlike English parliamentary "cabinet government," from the Whig supremacy under Walpole until the middle of the nineteenth century, the bulwark of the aristocratic landed oligarchy in office, Prussian "cabinet government" was the chief organ of monarchic autocracy. It was the principal instrument for controlling the bureaucrats in accordance with Frederick's maxim: "You must let yourselves be governed obediently and not govern!"[35]

Parliamentary cabinet government, largely sustained by corruption in the form of borough mongering, was peculiar to the political ways of life of the English upper class under the Old Regime. It was "a mark of English freedom and independence, for no one bribes where he can bully."[36] In despotic Prussia, the cabinet's cardinal function was to furnish one-man leadership by dictation to all the dynastic services and to the community at large. Frederick II, even more vigorously than his predecessor, exposed his top officials to a veritable barrage of cabinet orders. Intervention by rude and sarcastic executive directives and contemptuous rebukes, spiced with sardonic humor, was all the more exasperating to members of the bureaucratic nobility as nonnoble subalterns, working in the guarded seclusion of the cabinet and hiding behind the veil of complete secrecy, drew up or even initiated these tokens of royal affection and trust.

In spite of Frederick's indomitable efforts, the effectiveness of cabinet government was seriously challenged by his subordinates. In a political system of highly concentrated personalized authoritarianism, a well established bureaucracy could accomplish a great deal by obstructiveness and trained mediocrity. The royal servants of Prussia ultimately made the king's power inferior to their own. A fleeting glance at two important historic episodes will illustrate

[34] *A.B.B.*, XI, 314ff.; XII, 269; XIV, 167–68.

[35] *Ibid.*, XII, 261ff.; XIII, 762ff.; XIV, 335; *A.B. Handels-, Zoll- und Akzisepolitik*, III, part 1, 375.

[36] L. B. Namier, *England in the Age of the American Revolution* (London, 1930), 4–5.

the protracted duel between bureaucracy and autocracy for political domination.

In Prussia, essentially an agricultural state, the crown's agrarian policy was a pivotal test of the real strength of the monarch and his bureaucratic rival. In this crucial matter, from the late days of Cocceji until the eve of the Stein-Hardenberg reforms, the bureaucratic nobility functioned as the political ally of the squirearchy. With the use of forged evidence and deliberate falsehood and trickery, the leaders of the administrative service, now strongly supported by the *Regierungen*, also worked hand in hand with the local politicians, mostly wealthy landowners.[37] They succeeded in thwarting completely Frederick's modest efforts to pave the way for the transformation of flexible leaseholds into hereditary tenures and for a reduction, let alone the abolition, of servile labor obligations on private estates. By standing together on this vexing issue which profoundly affected the whole social order, the regrouped governing class of Prussia reduced to nought the absolute power of the monarch.

After the precedent set by Cocceji, the model for the "right attitude" was fixed by another neo-Junker, von Brenckenhoff. He had been commissioned to perform, in coöperation with the War and Domains Board of Pomerania, the preliminary spadework for the liquidation of hereditary personal servitude as an institution. Upon completion of their investigations, these gentlemen spoke with the air of authoritative expertness in advising Frederick guardedly, politely, but firmly, that this thorny problem could be "solved" only by keeping intact the *status quo*: "For the use of servile labor is indispensable to the noble estates. Besides, each estate owner, as he is responsible for the conservation of his peasants, hardly will burden them with unnecessary services. Furthermore, the commutation of these labor dues into limited services would encounter such difficulties that it would be short of impossible to carry it out on the noble

---

[37] *A.B.B.*, XIII, 93, 283ff.; XV, 54–55, 88–89, 220–21, 378; O. Hintze, in *Forschungen*, X (1897), 275–309; J. Ziekursch, *Hundert Jahre*, 184–221, and *passim*; *Die Neumark. Jahrbuch des Vereins für die Geschichte der Neumark*, IV (1927), 4–8.

estates."[38] Small wonder that, prior to 1807, the official policy of promoting partial emancipation of the private serfs got nowhere, except in those instances when it was executed by progressive squires, thinking and acting on their own initiative.

Thus Frederick was entrapped by the very forces which he had sought to hold in leash. The royal policy of playing off the landed nobility and the bureaucracy against each other resulted, in fact, in the formation of a united front against the arbitrary power of the crown. From the 1730's until the agrarian reforms of the early nineteenth century, the interrelations between the nonbureaucratic landed aristocracy and the landed bureaucratic nobility were marked by coöperation and harmony rather than by mutual suspicion and conflict. Only after 1806 did a deep chasm develop between these two groups.

It was in alignment with the squirearchy that the bureaucracy usurped the function of codetermining agrarian policy. But even when standing alone, the official hierarchy proved strong enough to fortify its position as a self-willed political power group. From the twenty-year struggle over the *Régie* it was the regular bureaucracy, not the autocrat or the new rival authority of the *Régie*, which emerged as the ultimate victor.

The establishment of the *Régie* was precipitated, in part, by the General Directory's courteous refusal to coöperate with Frederick's plan for starting postwar reconstruction in the midst of deep economic depression by increasing taxes. In turning down this ill-conceived program of fiscal reform, the Directory, by implication, ventured to treat His Royal Majesty like an amateur; and one of the members of this board, Privy Councilor Ursinus, was soon thereafter given the opportunity by the supreme commander of reconsidering his "impertinent report" during a lengthy sojourn in prison.[39] With the aid of the *Régie*, Frederick hoped to break once and for all the "royal servants," for "otherwise I shall never bring the *canailles* into subordination."[40]

[38] *A.B.B.*, XIII, 283ff.

[39] W. Schultze, *Geschichte der Preussischen Regieverwaltung*, 27ff.; *A.B.B.* XIV, 174ff.; *A.B. Handels-, Zoll- und Akzisepolitik*, III, part 1, 361, 374ff.

[40] *A.B. Handelspolitik*, III, part 1, 375.

Confronted with this new danger, the administrative and judicial councilors and their superiors closed ranks against the hated competitors. The counteroffensive of the regulars passed through several phases. It began, by means of passive and active resistance, with the methodical sabotage of the work of the *Régie* officials who at once were accused of resorting to "despotic and arbitrary methods" in the fashion of "a Spanish inquisition."[41] The opposition ended, in 1786, with the dissolution of the *Régie* and the formal reappropriation of its powers and emoluments by the old hierarchy.

In the meantime, a prolonged campaign, directed toward discrediting the *Régie* executives by gradually destroying Frederick's confidence in the competence, personal integrity, and professional loyalty of the newcomers, had yielded handsome results. For the regulars who, from the outset, had acted as self-appointed spies, informers, and vilifiers derived no little satisfaction from the fact that Frederick, in the course of his zigzag policy of intimidation, called upon them to keep a sharp eye, but now as commissioned secret agents or supervisors, upon their rivals. Moreover, the powers of the enemy were trimmed by the more direct method of infiltration. In other words, French *Régie* functionaries were gradually replaced by "Prussian" bureaucrats, that is, in the opinion of Minister von Werder, by "honest Germans."[42]

Obviously, then, even in Frederickian Prussia cabinet government did not rule supreme. During the two decades from 1786 to 1806, the cabinet as the chief tool of monarchical autocracy not only lost much of its original effectiveness, its whole political structure changed.[43] Under Frederick William II, the military courtier von Bischoffwerder and the newly ennobled Minister von Wöllner, "a scheming and roguish blackcoat," as Frederick II had characterized

---

[41] *Ibid.*, III, part 1, 181; *A.B.B.*, XIV, 186–87.

[42] For more detailed illustrations of these various techniques, see *A.B. Handelspolitik*, III, part 1, 156–57, 160ff., 166ff., 180–81, 221ff., 229ff., 253, 256, 276ff., 284ff., 287, 290–326; *A.B.B.*, XIV, 186–87, 195–96; *Preussische Jahrbücher*, CXXX (1907), 283. See also Edith Ruppel-Kuhfuss, *Das Generaldirektorium unter der Regierung Friedrich Wilhelms II.* (Würzburg, 1937), 38, 98ff.

[43] See O. Hintze, *Staat und Verfassung*, 290–91; *idem, Geist und Epochen*, 558ff.

him, were the real holders of royal power. Under Frederick William III, however, his cabinet councilors Mencken, Beyme, and Lombard exercised, in the name of the absolute king, unaccountable, yet increasingly ineffective authority. The royal monocrat as active top bureaucrat ruling in person, by means of written instructions from the cabinet, his bureau, was replaced by the rulership of the bureau itself. The monarch who did not want to depend on his ministers became, in fact, even more dependent on his bureaucratic cabinet councilors, who attempted to direct and to supervise the work of the executive elite. Under these conditions there developed an unavoidable struggle for supreme political leadership between the nonnoble, subaltern cabinet officers on the one hand and the noble ministers and the ranking officials of the central administration on the other hand.

After the death of Frederick II, the ministers as well as the various departments became freer, bolder and more independent in their fields of activity. Their actual power as partners in the control of public affairs sharply increased at the expense of royal absolutism. As early as 1788, it was, in the light of the hard facts, unrealistic to try to force the will of the cabinet upon a man of such caliber as Minister von Heinitz by admonishing him: "In the civil service I demand from ministers the same compliance and unflinching obedience which I demand from My generals in the army. . . . I take charge of the business of government Myself and hence will permit no one in the departments to issue unauthorized orders, for I wish to be informed of everything in advance and demand that one waits for My orders."[44]

Royal cabinet orders and pious declamations of this kind obscured the changes in real life. Such was the widening discrepancy between political fiction and political fact that a new balance of power was struck during the interim regime from 1786 to 1806. What still needed to be done was to legalize this transformation of the absolute

[44] *Forschungen*, VII (1894), 429-30; XXXVIII (1926), 321; XXXXI (1928), 333. See also Wilhelm Dilthey, *Gesammelte Schriften*, XII (Leipzig, 1936), 149.

system and to consolidate the gains made by the politician-bureaucrats. Although they had come to call themselves "servants of the state," they wanted to be the masters of the state. Accordingly, the exercise of negative political power, which after the death of Frederick II was followed by the illicit assumption of *de facto* power, had to be cemented by concentrating the official responsibility for centralized authoritarian leadership in the hands of the most highly placed members of the administrative bureaucracy.

This was what Baron von Stein, leading the "revolt" of the ambitious top group of official executives against Frederick William III and his cabinet, sought to accomplish on the eve of war in 1806. In this first and preliminary contest Stein, the great warrior, lost out. A cabinet order scolded him for being "an obstinate, perverse, stubborn, and disobedient servant of the state, who, flaunting his genius and talent, is far from having the best interests of the state at heart, is led by caprice and acts from passion and personal hatred and bitterness. Such state functionaries are just the ones whose manner of working is most disadvantageous and dangerous for holding together the state."[45]

Yet, by 1806, such was the professional, social, and political status of the executive bureaucracy among the governing elites of Prussian society that the operators of the powerful civil state machine were best prepared to function as the dominant leadership group in the body politic.

Subject to the leveling influence of a standardized service code which made no distinction between nobles and commoners, the members of the official hierarchy were bound together by the similarity of their professional functions and the possession of corporate privileges, fortified by the recent acquisition of permanent tenure and by their liberation from effective cabinet control. They had a common interest in enhancing the influence and the reputation of their corps. By habit and by taste they were inclined to identify themselves with a system of centralized political authoritarianism

[45] Georg Winter, ed., *Die Reorganisation des Preussischen Staates unter Stein und Hardenberg*, I (Leipzig, 1931), 114.

which gave them a particularly notable share in its power, emoluments, honors, and distinctions. They had developed a similar mode of life, a common tradition, embodying common experiences and various common standards of value.

Function, interest, education, and corporate self-esteem had combined to promote a spirit of clannishness and a feeling of solidarity toward the rivaling groups of the governing class. Although the civil bureaucracy was disrupted by internal competition, intrigues, and treachery, its members were united in the consciousness of belonging to an aristocratic service estate of superior, if not infallible, experts.

And indeed, as a social prestige group, along with the army officers' corps, higher officialdom stood at the summit of the urban class hierarchy of Prussia. Furthermore, in view of its impressive income level, its display of conspicuous consumption, and the high degree of financial independence which many of its members enjoyed on account of their diversified property holdings, the piling up of interlocking economic positions, and the interpenetration of urban and rural wealth, the bureaucratic elite also occupied an assured upper class position in Prussian economic society. The top bureaucrats either came from the rich segment of the landed nobility or in the course of their careers entered it and were absorbed by it. Thus, the civil state managers, as a group, derived strength not merely from their official authority and status but, in a roundabout way, also from other sources of political and economic power and of social eminence.

Dissatisfied with the modest role of carrying out predetermined dynastic policies, the university-trained hierarchy of professional administrators, led by Junkers and neo-Junkers, had evolved into a well-organized, self-recruiting and self-governing corporation, with a political will and political influence of its own. Some of these *de facto* commanders of the administrative apparatus of the absolute monarchy had gained active status in the new intellectual aristocracy, while numerous others had become fellow travelers of this cultural elite. The bureaucrats claimed the dignity of an exclusive political intelligentsia and hence the moral right as well as the paternal duty to determine policy and thereby the standards of social welfare and the content of public utility.[46]

Long and arduous preparations had resulted in the gradual merger of administrative, economic, political, and intellectual leadership functions. The "servants of the state" had arrived at the considered group opinion that once and for all they knew best what was best for "the State" and that their omnipotence was the quintessence of a monarchical system of rulership. In short, the bureaucratic elite was ready to assume political mastership.

As Professor Kraus, Kant's distinguished colleague in Königsberg, summed up the situation in 1799: "The Prussian state, far from being an unlimited monarchy," actually is "but a thinly veiled aristocracy," a state moreover in which "this aristocracy rules the country in undisguised form as a bureaucracy."[47]

[46] In the words of Councilor von Lamotte, *Practische Beyträge*, I (Berlin, 1789), xiii–xiv: "Only irresponsible and presumptuous people who habitually judge matters which they do not understand can find fault with our system of public administration. Their approval should be as irrelevant to us as their praise. Only those can be expected to appraise properly the quality of this system who have been active insiders and distinguished themselves as experts." Prussian bureaucrats are justified in taking for granted that "the solid pillars of the administrative order of their fatherland . . . will remain a model for other states until remote times, when the idle chatter of iniquitous critics and rash manufacturers of blueprints will long be forgotten."

Reflecting, in more impersonal terms, the same spirit of professional self-esteem, Georg Heinrich Borowski, *Abriss des praktischen Cameral- und Finanz-Wesens . . . in den Königlich Preussischen Staaten*, 3d ed., I (Berlin, 1805), xxxvii–xxxviii: "The Prussian system of government administration and finance is undoubtedly the best of all; it is a model for other countries. Since this is certain and recognized, it is thus endowed with high value and dignity. Manifestly, therefore, it is based on perfectly valid and unquestionable principles; it rests on reproachless and infallible maxims; it is the most beneficial for the State, that is, it must be able to foster, as it actually does, the felicity and power of the ruler and his state as well as the happiness and prosperity of the subjects."

[47] Christian Jacob Kraus, *Vermischte Schriften*, II (Königsberg, 1808), 247.

Chapter Nine

The Emergence of Bureaucratic Absolutism

I

A strange political bedfellow gave the Prussian bureaucracy the opportunity for bringing to its climax the struggle to abridge royal prerogatives and to acquire the powers of "cabinet government." Napoleon Bonaparte, Emperor of France *"par la grâce de Dieu et les constitutions de la République,"* was consolidator of the most effective type of bureaucratized absolutism theretofore known. The military conquest of Prussia by the master of the mighty new police state, organized as a plebiscitary dictatorship, had been preceded by the less spectacular yet potent invasion by the doctrines of the French Revolution. This ideological intrusion had helped to bring into relief the social fermentation which had already taken place in eighteenth-century Prussia: "the accumulation of superior elements in the lower classes and, conversely, of inferior elements in the higher classes."[1]

But it was neither the disturbance of the domestic social equilibrium nor the dawn of novel concepts of public welfare, civic rights, and communal responsibilities which furnished the impetus to the sudden concentration of the political leadership in the ministerial bureaucracy under the deceptive banner unfolded, in 1807, by Hardenberg: "Democratic principles in a monarchical govern-

[1] V. Pareto, *The Mind and Society*, III, 1431. See also the penetrating concrete comments in Albrecht Thaer, *Einleitung zur Kenntniss der englischen Landwirthschaft*, 2d ed., I (Hannover, 1801), 679-80.

ment: This appears to me the formula fitting the spirit of the age."[2] Clearly, without the battles of Jena and Auerstedt in 1806, precipitating the greatest disaster that had ever smitten the Hohenzollern state, it would not have come to what Hardenberg termed a "revolution from above" and Altenstein a "revolution from within."

This "revolution" is identical with the short-lived Prussian Reform Era. Beginning in 1807, it had virtually run its course by 1812. During these few years the worst cracks on the surface of the social and political order were patched up and a few narrow but solid bridges were built over the old caste barriers. The War of "Liberation" from 1813 to 1815 brought liberation from the yoke of Napoleon I, but it also freed the rulers of Prussia from the practical necessity of making further concessions of a serious nature to the middle, let alone the lower classes.

The Reformers were men of practical affairs though, during the crucial year of decision, they frittered away valuable time with the preparation and discussion of abstract blueprints. Their melodramatic talk about "revolution from above," "revolution from within," and "democratic principles in a monarchical government" confused the issues. There was no revolution against either absolute government or privilege as such. A streamlined system of political absolutism; a modified pattern of aristocratic privilege and social inequality; a redistribution of oligarchical authority among the revitalized segments of the traditional master class; a promotion of personal liberty and freedom of occupation and economic enterprise —these were the principal results of the work of the bureaucratic saviors of Prussia.

As in France, in 1787 and 1788, so in Prussia, in 1807, the initiative came from above in effecting a regrouping of the political forces and in assailing the most obsolescent claims of the titled aristocracy. It was supplied by the ministerial bureaucracy, faced with an acute crisis situation. In France and Prussia alike the reformers at the center met resistance. But there the similarity ended. In France, "noble resistance to oppression," the opposition of the *noblesse de robe*, of the landed, the army service, and the ecclesiastical nobility

[2] G. Winter, *Die Reorganisation des Preussischen Staates*, I, 306.

to the curtailment of their privileges and the recasting of the governmental structure, was broken by the political emancipation of the
Third Estate. In Prussia, however, throughout the confused and
confusing years of Reform, the struggle for predominance remained
almost altogether the internal affair of the upper ten thousand.

Popular excitement and direct action from below—the widespread
desertion of peasant-serf soldiers and isolated local peasant revolts,
had practically exhausted themselves by the end of 1807. Only the
unfamiliar war of words, as waged by middle class intellectuals and
noble dissenters, continued. But this outburst of verbose revulsion
against the discredited Old Regime did not imply a serious bid for
power on the part of the governed classes. After 1807, French occupation troops and French levies had a profound effect upon the alignment of social forces. They diverted the discontent of the lower
classes. Although awakening from their stupor in regard to civic
life, the perplexed Prussian people were still divided into myriads
of unconnected social and regional groups and, politically, an
amorphous, inarticulate mass.

Resting on a narrow social base, the "revolution from within"
was, in substance, a factional struggle within the governing class.
The active fight for and against social and political rejuvenation
was confined to men who were members of the traditional rulership
elites and experienced in the exercise of leadership. It merely brought
to its culmination the old triangular contest for supremacy among
royal autocracy, the ambitious bureaucracy, and the self-governing
landed aristocracy.

Thus the social groups engaged in the battle for control of Prussia
and her people were the very elements who had sustained the Old
Regime. In social complexion, the Prussian revolution never went
beyond 1787–1788, the incipient, the aristocratic phase of the French
Revolution. Only in the realm of political ideas, social theories, and
institutional experiment did Prussia reflect a more advanced stage
of development. Her revolution was instigated, directed, and carried
out by imaginative bureaucrats and army officers who had become
government employees in the old days.

Such was the vitality of the traditional social hierarchy of estates (*ständische Gesellschaft*) and the unbroken continuity of the authoritarian structure of the body politic (*Obrigkeitsstaat*) that active participation in political life even now remained the exclusive business of the superiors, bits of popular window-dressing notwithstanding. What gains there were in reducing the sum of human unhappiness and social injustice came as a benevolent gift from above and by autocratic methods. Until 1848, only through the civil bureaucracy, the army, the diplomatic service, or by influence as a courtier or member of the squirearchy was it possible to play a significant role in practical politics.

Into the gap created by the collapse of cabinet government and the ignoble failure of the old military and civil top authorities, in 1806 and 1807, stepped a tiny but determined clique of critically thinking servants of the state who emerged from these chaotic years and from the clash of ideas and of power seeking personalities as victors. Their ascent heralded not only the bolstering of the political position of the executive government bureaucracy but also the growing influence of *Gebildete* of personal distinction within the hierarchy.

These men of good will and superior intelligence, with reputations to keep or still to be made, were drawn to the tasks of reconstruction because it was a unique opportunity to project some of their ideas into the outer world. But it was also, in an atmosphere of general disintegration and insecurity, an opportunity for extraordinary personal advancement.[3] Consumed by will to power and sense of destiny, the new leaders were not afraid of assuming the responsibility for holding the tottering state together and for attempting to give a democratic touch to *esprit de corps et de nation*. They obtained control of the machinery of the central government by

---

[3] Regarding this latter aspect as a motivating factor, see Adolf Ernst, ed., *Denkwürdigkeiten von Heinrich und Amalie von Beguelin aus den Jahren 1807–1813* (Berlin, 1892), 23–26, 74; Franz Rühl, ed., *Aus der Franzosenzeit ... vorzugsweise aus dem Nachlass von F.A. von Stägemann* (Leipzig, 1904), xi–xxv, 10; Wilhelm Steffens, *Briefwechsel Sacks mit Stein und Gneisenau 1807–17* (Stettin, 1931), 49; Dietrich Gerhard and William Norvin, eds., *Die Briefe Barthold Georg Niebuhrs*, II (Berlin, 1929), 48, 64–65, 81, 92, 95, 102ff., and *passim*.

successfully undermining the position of their competitors or, as Niebuhr, the banker, historian, and bureaucrat, saw the situation in 1806, by managing "to drive out the originators of the downfall."[4] These courageous politician-administrators, led by Hardenberg and Stein, formed a faction which "for the time being could expect for themselves only advantages and no disadvantages from the democratizing Enlightenment" and which "by swimming with the stream thought to escape the pressure of that stream."[5]

Thus the process, long in the making, of replacing the absolute monarch and his cabinet by the ministerial bureaucracy as the chief holder of positive political power entered its decisive phase in 1807 and 1808. After the "dress rehearsal," staged by Hardenberg and his associates in the spring of 1807, Stein, who then became the central figure in the bureaucracy's struggle for political "empire building," called for "bigger and better" centralization rather than for a diffusion of power.

Ironically, it was Stein who won for the administrative hierarchy its greatest victory. By theoretical conviction and, while out of office, also by personal predilection, Stein was equally opposed to monarchical "cabinet government," authoritarian rule by professional administrators, democratic government, and Bonapartist Caesarism. His "Germanic" political ideal favored a system which was roughly similar to the aristocratic model of the contemporaneous English constitutional monarchy, with its medley of inheritable privileges, franchises, and liberties, rendering impossible centralized despotism. Lofty-minded and strong-willed, but muddled in his political thinking, as a man of action Stein sought to combine the best of the absolutism of Frederickian Prussia with the efficiency of a Napoleonic police regime, and to blend both with the partial revival

---

[4] Bernhard Vobian, *B. G. Niebuhr und der Freiherr von Stein* (Bischofswerda, 1935), 24; *Die Briefe B. G. Niebuhrs*, II, 51–52.

[5] Carl von Clausewitz, "Nachrichten über Preussen in seiner grossen Katastrophe," *Kriegsgeschichtliche Einzelschriften*, ed., Grosser Generalstab, X (1888), 424. See also Eckart Kehr, "Zur Genesis der Preussischen Bürokratie und des Rechtsstaats," *Die Gesellschaft* (1932), 105ff.

of the archaic *Ständestaat* and with more up-to-date forms of constitutional representative government.[6]

While in office, Stein's libertarian political creed proved incompatible with his executive tasks as Prussia's bureaucratic top autocrat. The ideas of Hardenberg, empirical realist and smooth diplomat, were not quite as "beautiful" as Stein's. Hardenberg learned much from Napoleon Bonaparte, as later Bismarck did from Louis Napoleon. Hardenberg's "democratic principles in a monarchical government," when put to the practical test, left room for the imprisonment of political opposition leaders without legal process. But even Stein, the "liberal," when he encountered criticism and sabotage of his dictatorial orders, did not flinch, in good Old Prussian fashion, from recommending repressive and punitive measures. He favored the "managing" of public opinion; strict surveillance of, and spying on, the more prominent members of both the bureaucracy and the squirearchy; and the punishment of officials, "who distinguish themselves by loose talk, fault-finding with the government, incapacity to grasp and to will the new."[7]

After the shake-up in governmental top personnel, civil liberty was to rest, even for the privileged classes, on administrative discretion. A public discussion of its policies was a novel experience for the Prussian bureaucracy. The impatient new commanders of the civil state machine, in threatening reactionary and radical critics, political competitors, and dissenting officials with reprisals, simply stepped into the shoes of the royal autocrats of the eighteenth

[6] In the early nineteenth century, German political theory drew a sharp distinction between *"landständische Verfassung"* and *"Repräsentativverfassung."* As defined by Friedrich von Gentz: *"Landständische Verfassungen* are those in which members and delegates of independent corporations exercise a right of participation in state legislation on the whole or in certain branches of it by means of codeliberation, assent, counterproposals, or other constitutionally legitimate forms. *Repräsentativverfassungen*, on the other hand, are those in which the persons entitled to direct participation in the most important tasks of the Administration are deemed to represent not only the privileges and the interest of particular estates but the whole mass of the people." Quoted in Ernst Kern, *Moderner Staat und Staatsbegriff* (Hamburg, 1949), 34.

[7] Erich Botzenhart, ed., *Freiherr von Stein. Briefwechsel, Denkschriften und Aufzeichnungen*, III (Berlin, 1932), 328–29.

century. The military reformers moved in the same direction. In the attempt to tighten their grip and to bridle the freedom to criticize the newly appointed authorities, in 1808, they assigned to the senior officers "the obligation and the right" to restrain "the younger or uneducated members of the officers' corps, engaging in irresponsible talk and passing improper judgment on public affairs or matters of state."[8]

Whatever their original hopes, professed intentions, or ultimate objectives, the reformers functioned as the builders and superintendents of a liberalized police state in which the bureaucracy formed the core of the ruling class. The real political meaning of "democratic principles in a monarchical government," as consolidated under Hardenberg when he became Prussia's state chancellor from 1810 to 1823, was the replacement of capricious royal rule by a more impersonal system of bureaucratic absolutism, culminating in enlightened ministerial despotism tempered by the will of the privileged classes. The formal abolition of cabinet government and of the cabinet itself as a political institution, in 1808, gave belated legal expression to this shift in the political center of gravity.

As characterized by a liberal Prussian government official of the Restoration period, the transformed Old Regime was "a system of rulership by career bureaucrats peculiar to the Prussian state, in which the king appears to be the top functionary who invariably selects his aides from the intellectual elite of the nation, recognized as such by means of truly or allegedly rigorous examinations. He allows them great independence, acknowledges thereby their co-rulership and, consequently, sanctions a sort of aristocracy of experts who purport to be the true representatives of the general interest."[9]

In the reformed absolute monarchy, that is, the oligarchical *Beamtenstaat*, government was a matter of issues rather than personalities. Prior to the great international social crisis that began with the French Revolution, the determination of the content of policy had

[8] Rudolf Vaupel, ed., *Das Preussische Heer vom Tilsiter Frieden bis zur Befreiung 1807–1814*, I (Leipzig, 1938), 472.

[9] Otto Camphausen to Ludolf Camphausen, November 10, 1843, in Joseph Hansen, ed., *Rheinische Briefe und Akten zur Geschichte der politischen Bewegung 1830–1850*, I (Essen, 1919), 609.

caused friction between the king and his executives. But by and large, they had agreed on fundamentals and central purposes. A far more important source of disharmony and conflict had been the struggle over the method of making and implementing policy. The bureaucrats had turned against their master because they had come to regard the whole pattern of employer-employee relations in the upper brackets of the government services as degrading, harmful, and intolerable, as detrimental to their own as well as to the public interest.

After 1806, even the survival of the Prussian state was in doubt, and the conscientious but slow-witted occupant of the throne was unqualified to think out daring new policies. In these circumstances, the ruling group became identical with the removable heads of ministries recruited from the bureaucratic career service. In their hands was concentrated the *de facto* power to make the basic political decisions, to determine policy by taking the initiative and managing the king, to plan legislation, to issue decrees having the force of law, to control policy enforcement, and to direct the routine work of the administrative class. Technically, they were responsible to the absolute monarch who remained the legitimate sovereign and an active power not subject to judgment. But his political role was limited by the ministers who through their countersignatures assumed responsibility for royal ordinances and gave legal sanction to them. Moreover, all personal intervention of the monarch in the operation of the administrative machine was eliminated. Actually, absolute government by public law now meant the legally regulated collective autocracy of the bureaucratic aristocracy, headed by the small elite of ministers and ministerial councilors responsible to their conscience and to such strong "prime ministers" as Stein and Hardenberg.[10] But the tenure of the highest political officeholders was precarious, for it was threatened by irresponsible court influences and by rivaling intraservice factions.

The reorganized central government remained free from all popular control. The servants of the state, having freed themselves

[10] See Hans Schneider, *Der Preussische Staatsrat 1817–1918* (Munich, 1952), 22, 62, 117.

from arbitrary interference by the king and the accident of the monarch's personal leadership, subordinated the dynastic interest to the good of their state and to the aspirations of a wider public. With the transition to bureaucratic authoritarianism, and in accentuation of the late eighteenth-century trend toward enlightened progress, the government acted as a benefactor rather than an exploiter and oppressor. While adhering to a strictly oligarchic conception of political liberty and preventing the imposition of constitutional checks upon its authority, the new masters made the subjects, elevated to the status of passive citizens, an object of humane paternalism. They sought to gain confidence, not to inspire awe and fear.

The reformed bureaucrats governed by persuasion as well as by coercion. The conversion of problems of administration into problems of politics and of ranking administrators into political leaders; the identification of politics with executive government; and the spectacular role now played by ideas and emotions as political weapons required modernized techniques of political management. Without the appeal to ideals and sentiments and the use of propaganda on a high intellectual plane, the new political bureaucrats—the bureaucrats in political key posts—could not discharge their functions properly. Hence the growing importance and enhanced prestige of *Gebildete* in the governmental hierarchy. Prompted by expediency, a sharpened sense of public service, and growing sensitivity to criticism coming from the articulate groups, the landed aristocracy, the professional classes and the commercial bourgeoisie, the reformers used a different language than their predecessors in the effort to impress a larger audience than before.

II

The remaking of the Prussian system also involved an attempt to transform the governing elites from "artificial" into "natural" aristocracies. Thus the founding of bureaucratic absolutism had its social corollary in revulsion against "the noble reaction" of the second half of the eighteenth century. Competition, merit, privilege, and equality, as reinterpreted by the bureaucratic revolutionists linked to *Bildung*, had indeed an important long-range effect upon the social composition and the caliber of the civil state hierarchy, the army officers' corps, and the Junker squirearchy.

As a matter of principle as well as of good politics, the time-honored system of hereditary social estates was smashed by the October Edict of 1807. The exclusive legal privileges of the nobility, having become untenable, were abrogated. In law, the status and the opportunities of common and inferior people were improved. *De jure*, the mere possession of a noble title distinguished nobles from commoners after 1807. Thus the way was cleared for the slow growth of a more competitive and freer society. But the removal of legal obstacles to individual advancement and, eventually, to the development of open classes was largely offset by the perpetuation of privileged professional status groups (*Berufsstände*) of high social rank which preserved or even fortified many of the persistent traditions and exclusive rights of the abolished First Estate. The aristocratic order, built on inequality of rights and the cult of social hierarchy, was kept intact by allowing greater individual freedom of access to the superior classes, by sharing special privileges and advantages with a growing number of nonnoble intruders.

During the initial years of Prussia's great calamity the prestige of "the foremost and most brilliant estate of the state" reached an extremely low ebb. Intellectual aristocrats of "inferior" social origin like Fichte found that the vast majority of noblemen were "the first estate of the nation only in the sense that they were the first who ran away where there was danger and tried to gain the mercy of the common enemy by depraved crawling and treacheries."[11] Forthright, public-spirited bureaucrats of old noble lineage like Stein scorned "the gentlemen of Prussia" for being a class of "wily, heartless, wooden, half-educated men who, after all, are only fit to be corporals or bookkeepers" and "deserve to be whipped with scorpions," although they "push themselves to all positions from minister of state and field marshal down to municipal inspector."[12]

[11] J. G. Fichte, *Sämtliche Werke*, VII (1846), 523, 530.
[12] *Freiherr von Stein*, II, 209; III, 9, 296, 328–29.

No less blunt was the judgment of educated Junker squires with exacting standards, of men like Arnim-Boytzenburg and Fincken-stein. They decried "the spirit of narrow-minded usury and cabal prevalent in our circles," made up mainly of "turbulent, unpatriotic, self-interested men" who "without merit of their own merely want to profit from the results of the merit of their ancestors."[13]

In the face of this situation, the civil bureaucracy, led by neo-Prussian noble immigrants and Old Prussian landed aristocrats, managed to strengthen its position in the community, not only as an authoritarian political group but also as a social status elite. The reformers moved not against privilege as such, but merely against privilege as a preserve of the nobility and against the dusty idea that birth furnished a monopoly to merit.

In the realm of public personnel policy and in resumption of certain tendencies under Frederick William I, the builders of bureaucratic absolutism committed themselves to "the career open to talent." Thus they hoped to knit the government services together in a somewhat novel way. Something had to be done to mobilize extraordinary energy and zest for work; to improve efficiency, discipline, and morale; to fortify the *esprit de corps* of the bureaucracy; and to command the respect and loyalty of the disquieted public.

As a matter of principle, differential treatment between the high and lowborn was replaced by equality of opportunity. As defined by Hardenberg in 1807, henceforth "every position in the state, without exception, shall be open not to this or that castelike group but to all social elements possessing merit and capacity."[14]

In the short run, "the career open to talent," as implemented in practice, merely meant that, except for the lonely "outsider" Niebuhr, established higher grade career bureaucrats of some personal distinction were advanced to influential positions. But this was only if they had the necessary connections and were willing to function as staunch political supporters of the ministers. As for the more distant future, nepotism and favoritism retained much of their

---

[13] Friedrich Meusel, ed., *Friedrich August Ludwig von der Marwitz*, II, part one (Berlin, 1913), 191.

[14] G. Winter, *Die Reorganisation des Preussischen Staates*, I, 314.

traditional effectiveness in the regular bureaucracy of the reorganized administrative and judicial boards. However, these appointment and promotion practices were mitigated by the broadening of opportunities for men of superior ability and enterprise and by the more highly selective form of patronage which developed with the stiffening of competitive examinations on the basis of costly higher education and long in-service training.

The method of staffing the ministerial bureaucracy was more modern. Here family appointments and personal considerations often had to give way to political patronage, especially since ideologies had gained such an importance in the struggle for power that they tended to tear families apart and break up friendships and intraservice cliques and factions.[15] "The career open to talent" came to mean the career open not to the vocationally most competent, if politically neutral or lukewarm, but to the politically talented with the "right opinions." The standards of selection, as applied to the ministerial bureaucracy of Reform Prussia, reflected this trend. More decisive than professional qualifications were the political leanings, views, and convictions of the candidates, if convictions they had. As put with refreshing frankness by Eichhorn, a "reformed bureaucrat" and the Prussian minister of education from 1840 to 1848: The government or, in other words, the bureaucracy "is by no means neutral; on the contrary, it is biased, totally biased."[16]

The new alliance between merit and politics, as mirrored in the changing pattern of personnel administration from 1807 to 1815, worked out, on the whole, to the advantage of nonnobles and the recently ennobled. To be sure, in tacit recognition of the continuance of noble descent as a special asset in state service, almost all the top officials in Reform Prussia (Stein, Hardenberg, Auerswald, Altenstein, Dohna, Bülow) were nobles of old lineage. But most of their chief advisers and executives were men of more humble social

[15] For those familiar with the political role played by specific individuals, it will be meaningful to ponder the fact that, for instance, Scharnhorst and Councilor Schmalz, Clausewitz and Marwitz, Raumer and the Gerlach brothers were relatives.

[16] Quoted in Max Lenz, *Geschichte der Universität Berlin*, II, 2 (Halle, 1918), 39.

antecedents. The highborn ministers surrounded themselves with a picked staff of assistants who combined professional excellence with the proper political attitude and, in many instances, with a high level of general education. Their services were essential to the consolidation of positions, to effective action and to a good impression upon the educated who formed public opinion and wished to be governed by their own kind. In these delicate matters Hardenberg took the greatest care and scored the greatest success.

Several types of bureaucrats were represented in the purged personnel of the ministerial bureaucracy, functioning as the new ruling intelligentsia. One of these was made up of experienced and well-informed administrative technicians like Klewiz and Sack. Klewiz in particular, throughout his long professional life, epitomized the kind of adaptable career specialist who always found himself on the side of what seemed to be the strongest political current and the most fashionable social faction. Among the first-rate experts were some, however, with deep convictions and a real passion for constructive work and generous deeds. To this element belonged, for instance, Friese and Councilor Scharnweber, Hardenberg's right-hand man in matters of agrarian legislation. Another type of new political bureaucrat was symbolized by sensitive, young, enthusiastic intellectuals like Schön, Stägemann, and Hardenberg's private secretary, von Raumer, called by his enemies "little state chancellor." But there also were among the ranking members of the Prussian official hierarchy, in this unique age of intimate association with Germany's cultural elite, brilliant and less easily manageable savants like Niebuhr and Wilhelm von Humboldt.

Slower and harder to implement was the recasting of privilege and the opening of career opportunities to "nonnoble talent" in the Prussian officers' corps. As late as 1805, long after he had become a pungent critic of the government's foreign policy of armed neutrality, Scharnhorst, the central leader of the military reform movement, had found the army "animated by the best spirit, courage, and skill; nothing is lacking."[17] But altered circumstances produced new views. "Democratic principles in a monarchical government," as defined

[17] Karl Linnebach, ed., *Scharnhorsts Briefe*, I (Munich, 1914), 266.

by Scharnhorst and his colleagues in the Fundamental Order of 1808, meant that *Bildung* and personal stamina, in place of the accident of birth, constituted a claim to the position of officer: "In times of peace, knowledge and education only, and in times of war, exceptional bravery and quickness of perception. From the whole nation, therefore, all individuals who possess these qualities can lay title to the highest positions of honor in the military establishment. All social preference which has hitherto existed is herewith terminated in the military establishment, and every one, without regard for his background, has the same duties and the same rights."[18]

This new principle blasted a trail for enduring modifications of old-style noble privilege. But much of what was abolished by law lived on, for generations to come, by custom. Until the war of 1813–1815, the novel standards of selection had hardly any effect on the social composition of the officers' corps. It remained an almost exclusively noble group. What changed was the total number, the age level, and the physical, mental, and moral caliber of the officers retained in active service.[19] For the practical tasks in hand, "merit" had to be defined largely in negative terms. This meant, for instance, denial of promotion, at least in principle, to any officer, "who is addicted to drinking, or enters into indecent relations with debauched and vulgar females, or has social intercourse with people

[18] R. Vaupel, *Das Preussische Heer*, I, 533. See also Reinhard Höhn, *Revolution Heer Kriegsbild* (Darmstadt, 1944), 92–93, 435–36.

[19] Of the 7121 active officers, as of 1806, only 1638 survived the scrutiny of their records and retained a place on the regular payroll, as of September 1808. As for the rest, 398 had died in battle or passed away, 1421 had been retired or dishonorably discharged, while 3664 were put on the inactive list with half pay. Rejuvenation, in terms of age, meant the elimination of the overaged and of the noble "children" who, according to the custom, at the age of twelve or thirteen had become officer candidates with the rank and the responsibilities of noncommissioned officers. By 1806, the age of the top ranking Prussian generals had ranged from seventy to eighty-two. The average age of the chiefs of the 33 cavalry regiments had been sixty-four, while more than half of the battalion commanders in the infantry had been above fifty-five. See Curt Jany, *Geschichte der Königlich Preussischen Armee*, IV (1933), 14–17; Colmar Frhr von der Goltz, *Von Rossbach bis Jena und Auerstedt*, 2d ed. (Berlin, 1906), 125ff.; General Frhr von Freytag-Loringhoven, *Was danken wir unserem Offizierkorps?* (Berlin, 1919), 19.

of bad repute, or frequents disorderly houses, or makes a profession out of gambling, or does not know how to honor the relations of subordination by failing to show respect due to officers of higher rank, or who in any other way reveals a base way of thinking."[20] For, Scharnhorst explained, without the expunction of the most glaring abuses of noble class privilege the army will further deteriorate, "never earn the esteem of the nation and remain the laughing stock of the educated classes."[21]

The legal removal of special noble privilege in the military service led, eventually, to the qualified sharing of professional status prerogatives by a rising number of nonnobles. But more important than the broadening of the social base of personnel recruitment was the strengthening of the officers' corps as a self-governing bureaucratic corporation perpetuating itself through the method of cooptation. The military service estate profited greatly from reform. For the establishment of bureaucratic absolutism buttressed its position as a highly favored professional status group and privileged social elite. Besides, the military bureaucracy filled, in part, the power vacuum created by shipwrecked cabinet government. "The Army," under the leadership of "political officers" sharing in policy making, developed into a more active political force than it had been previously.

The civil bureaucracy had been transformed into a powerful, independent political oligarchy at the expense of the crown. Similarly, Scharnhorst and Gneisenau liberated, to a very considerable extent, the military bureaucracy from the whims of personal interference by the monarch. They moved toward standardization of the regulations governing tenure, promotions, remuneration, and pension rights. And the dismissal of many half-wits and sinecure holders laid the foundation for the gradual transmutation of the military service aristocracy into a better educated and more dedicated hierarchy of salaried professional experts.

"Democratic principles in a monarchical government," in the

----

[20] R. Vaupel, *Das Preussische Heer*, I, 472.
[21] Rudolf Vaupel, ed., *Stimmen aus der Zeit der Erniedrigung* (Munich, 1923), 204.

officers' corps, fostered a process of internal democratization which, in fact, resulted in the tightening up of aristocratic *esprit de corps*. The new regulations of 1808 contained the fateful provision that an officer candidate who had passed the required examination could obtain a commission only upon subsequent election by a regimental group of officers. From this liberty to keep out undesirables stemmed a novel set of social group prerogatives. They entailed the transformation of the officer class into democratically organized units of decentralized self-administration. These were invested with the privilege to manage their personnel affairs with a considerable degree of independence and to exercise collective self-control in safeguarding high standards of conduct, comradeship, and gentlemanly honor. The nobility, for a long time to come the all-dominant group of officers, was not slow in turning these corporate rights to good account by preserving the social structure and mentality of the professional military class as an exclusive caste of cavaliers in uniform. The replacement of traditional methods of disciplinary action by military courts of honor had a similar effect. Reform turned out to be a blessing for the military nobility, for the outcome was the retention of Junker control over the officer class, through the officers over the new, free citizen soldiers and thus over the bulk of civil society.

In neither the civil nor the military service elites did the legal repeal of exclusive noble rights signify the destruction of privilege. Instead, it meant the "democratization" of aristocratic privileges. What formerly had been the special preserve of noblemen now was made accessible, on the footing of legal equality of rights and opportunities, to *nouveaux arrivés* with the required degree of education, now the official mainspring of privilege. For the time being, this meant the improvement of career chances for some bureaucratic commoners who had been held back on account of their low ancestry. As for the future, eminent service rank in itself assured a high place in the social and political hierarchies. Social arrival did not have to be supported any more by the conferment of a title of nobility, although this continued to be a widespread practice.

The continuance of an aristocratic pattern of status, class, and political opportunity was also clearly reflected in the impact which "liberty" and "equality" were to have upon the composition and attributes of the squirearchy. Bureaucratic authoritarianism cleared the way for the conversion of landed Junkerdom from a noble caste into a socially mixed aristocracy. Thenceforth, it formed an open economic class of large landowners and capitalist entrepreneurs, without losing its traditional position as a legally privileged social and political group.

Prussia's revolution from above was the work of many minds and divergent factions. From the beginning, compromise was the keynote of the attempt to establish a workable equilibrium. The Edict of 1807, as well as Hardenberg's economic and social legislation of 1811, 1812, and 1816, were not designed to hurt the landed upper class but to gain it a new lease of life by means of timely concessions and innovations. "Noble riff-raff" elements were to be replaced by "natural aristocrats," by men with uncommon skills, education, personal achievement, and ample material resources, worthy of being the holders of special rights and high social rank and of giving orders to "inferiors." Behind reform was the idea of a reformed elite which would justify its privileges by superior work.

As the nobility's rights of priority to the better government jobs, reconfirmed by the General Legal Code of 1794, were repealed, so also its legal monopoly in the ownership of large private estates was liquidated to make "the career open to talent." After the collapse of land speculation in 1806 and the severe agricultural slump that followed, the old caste barriers on the land market had, in the words of the Edict of 1807, "a very unfavorable influence on the value of landed property and on the credit of the landed proprietor." Or, as Altenstein, in 1807, stated the issue: Not only the general interest is adversely affected by these rigidities, "but also the nobility itself as landowners. The exclusion of competition diminishes the value of the estates."[22]

The reforms gave a new legal foundation to large-scale landowner-ship by combining the principle of liberty from noble caste privilege with the principle of equality of landed upper class privilege. After

[22] G. Winter, *Die Reorganisation des Preussischen Staates*, I, 400.

1807, it was possible, simply by buying a *Rittergut*, for any "vagabond who had the purchase price," to become a Junker by status. For the destruction, by dictatorial decree, of the system of landed castes transformed the *Rittergut* into an object of open competition and free trade by removing all legal shackles which had restricted the buying and selling of certain "social types of land" to particular classes of people. Small wonder that defenders of the old order, then and later, were upset by the prospect that noble estates could now be acquired by "merchants, Jews, petty storekeepers, tailors, bankers, tenant farmers, peasants or others who in a different capacity had come into possession of the necessary amount of money."[23]

The revolution from above perpetuated in law, and not merely in fact, the distinction between privileged and nonprivileged classes. But the revolution did away with all legal distinctions within the estate-owning class and gave uniform legal rights to all its present and future members, not by abrogating the traditional fiscal, civic, political, and most of the economic privileges attached to the noble ownership of *Rittergüter*, but by extending these prerogatives to all nonnoble buyers of noble estates. Thus reform, by changing the rules of the game, created the necessary legal prerequisites for broadening the social base of aristocratic landownership and privileged business entrepreneurship.

On such a foundation patrimonial justice and special hunting rights were retained until the Revolution of 1848. The exemption of *Rittergüter* from the land tax, wherever that was the historic inheritance in the Prussian provinces, remained in effect until 1861. Curtailment of the squire's independent local police power did not come before 1872. Squirely church patronage lingered on even longer. County self-government and county administration remained directly under the clutches of the owners of *Rittergüter* until 1891. And as for newly created political privileges, enacted after the Reform Era, the law gave to the small landed aristocracy, as such, the absolute majority in the provincial diets, as they were revived

---

[23] Friedr. Wilh. von Geisler, *Ueber den Adel als einen zur Vermittlung zwischen Monarchie und Demokratie nothwendigen Volksbestandtheil* (Minden, 1835), 56.

after 1823.[24] And in addition, from 1850 to 1918, the big agrarians (*Grossagrarier*) also occupied, *de facto*, a highly privileged place in the lower house and, in law as well as in fact, an even more eminent position in the upper house of the Prussian parliament (*Landtag*).

Thus after 1807, not noble birth or acquired noble rank *per se* but the ownership of a *Rittergut*, a peculiar kind of transferable landed property, became, apart from the government services, the chief spring of "well-earned rights" and of special civic and political prerogative. Put differently, because economic liberalism gained the upper hand on the land market, the Prussian landed aristocracy, as a class, became increasingly demarcated by economic factors. Noble squires continued to enjoy an exclusive legal status in their economic capacity as large landowners, but no longer in their social capacity as noble proprietors of estates. But the landed aristocracy as a whole ceased to be identical with the Junker nobility in possession of *Rittergüter*. Modernized Junkerdom was a peculiar class of business-men, composed of all legally privileged large landowners, whether noble or nonnoble.

This development of the noble estate of squires into an open aristocracy, recruited from varied social strata, had started with the economic aftermath of the Seven Years' War, when a small number of commoners secured royal permission to replace noble bankrupts as owners of *Rittergüter*. During the subsequent decades of feverish land speculation and agricultural improvement, infiltration by the lowly born, often under cover of hired noble straw men, had received a fresh impetus.[25] The work of the reformers was, in part, but a

---

[24] In the provincial diets of the six central and eastern provinces of the Prussian state, the owners of *Rittergüter* were represented by 221 deputies, the corporate towns and the peasant proprietors together by only 216. In the provincial diet of Brandenburg, the *Rittergutsbesitzer* who paid the trifling total amount of 26.472 tlr in land taxes had 34 representatives; the peasantry, paying 734.068 tlr, had but 12 representatives. See L. Bühl, *Die Herrschaft des Geburts- und Bodenprivilegiums in Preussen* (Mannheim, 1844), 238–39, 243; Joseph Hansen, *Gustav von Mevissen*, II (Berlin, 1906), 211.

[25] As for statistical details and some of the legal aspects, see Leopold Krug, *Geschichte der staatswirtschaftlichen Gesetzgebung im preussischen Staate*, I (Berlin, 1808), 22–35; Friedrich Benedikt Weber, *Handbuch der staatswirtschaftlichen Statistik* (Breslau, 1840), 351.

belated move to legalize this change of economic and social reality. During the nineteenth century the democratization of the landed aristocracy was speeded up, above all, by economic fluctuations, by the ups and downs in the movement of prices, rents, costs, output, sales, and profit margins. The heavy influx of nonnoble buyers of estates was most striking in times of prolonged agricultural depression.[26] The change in ownership personnel did not seriously impair the cohesion of the Junker squirearchy, since, as a rule, social mobility was accompanied by rapid assimilation between the newcomers and the old established elements. But as to political leadership, social mores, and ideological outlook, it was the old landed nobility which continued to set the standards that governed the life of the landed aristocracy as a whole.[27]

And what this meant was brought home, at the outset, to the overambitious new rulers of the Prussian monarchy, the makers of bureaucratic absolutism.

III

The triumph of the civil and the military bureaucracies was not undisputed. They had won the battle for intraservice home rule and, so it seemed at first, also for political supremacy in the community at large. In 1806 and 1807, the collective power of the landed nobility was sapped by calamitous economic recession, by the fear of peasant uprisings, and by the lack of coördinated organization or a constructive program for action. But as later in 1848, so now the Junker masters of rural Prussia speedily regained self-confidence. Bursting forth from their seclusion in the counties and stigmatizing the reformers as "Prussian Jacobins," they advanced their claim to political parity.

[26] As early as 1856, of the total of 12339 *Rittergüter*, only 7023 were owned by noblemen. See K. Fr. Rauer, *Hand-Matrikel der in sämmtlichen Kreisen des Preussischen Staates auf Kreis- und Landtagen vertretenen Rittergüter* (Berlin, 1857), 451; Georg von Viebahn, *Statistik des zollvereinten und nördlichen Deutschlands*, II (Berlin, 1862), 309.

[27] See Rudolph Meyer, "Adelstand und Junkerklasse," *Neue Deutsche Rundschau*, X (1899), 1078–1090.

On the verge of establishing themselves through the concentration of political controls in the top bureaucrats as the ruling class, the state service hierarchies, though headed by landed aristocrats, were contained by the squirearchy's "counterrevolution from below." After a brief period of extremely strained relations, the memorable showdown between these contenders for mastery resulted in an arrangement based on live and let live. The "servants of the state" were most reluctant to share political liberty with other groups, even if they were upper class groups. But since they adhered to essentially aristocratic concepts of freedom and authority, they could stabilize their position only by sharing real power in the determination of policy with men of their kind, with the squires. The strengthening of the authoritarian rule of both the bureaucratic elite and the landed aristocracy turned out to be the outstanding result of the substitution of bureaucratic absolutism for monarchical autocracy in the pre-industrial society of Prussia.

The "counterrevolution" involved more than the resurrection of the noble estate owners as a force in politics, in sharp acceleration of a trend which went back to the antibureaucratic tactics of Frederick II and to the resurgence of *Ständestaat* tendencies in the latter part of his reign. The struggle to limit the power of the bureaucracy also transformed the landed Junker class into a self-conscious, ideologically fortified political group. Judged by their deeds and the consequences of their deeds, the reformers fought a battle not against, but for the landed aristocracy by removing deterrents to the further growth of large agricultural enterprise, by emphasizing "the career open to talent," and by invoking the spirit of *noblesse oblige* in public life.

What turned amicable rivals into bitter opponents during the Reform Era was the attempt of a few "servants of the state," regarded as "foreigners," "theorists," and noble renegades, to dictate terms to the Old Prussian Junkers, to interfere in the sacrosanct sphere of *Gutsherrschaft*, and to encourage freedom of economic enterprise not only for squires, but also for common people. This, together with fear of the ultimate social and political consequences of "the ideas of 1789," stirred the wrath of the serf masters, aroused their passions, but also brought into bold relief their sense of power, class prejudice, pride, selfishness, and, through their leaders, their inner resilience. Administrative, economic, and political problems were converted into a conflict of ideas, and that made attitudes more intransigent and disrupted intergroup relations. This came about largely through the work of intellectuals who attached themselves to the competing partisan groups within the upper class.

From the Reform Era the nobility at large emerged as the social bulwark of political conservatism, although a number of prominent nobles, whether bureaucrats or landed aristocrats, played an important role in the leadership of the liberal parties until the 1870's. Directed against centralized absolutism, monarchical or bureaucratic, and against leveling democratization in any form, the "counterrevolution" of the "First Estate," the *"ständische Reaktion,"* as it came to be called, aspired not just to the restoration of the *status quo*, as of 1806. It aimed at the establishment of a limited monarchy through the partial revival of medieval constitutionalism, of the representative institutions and hoary political valuations of the preabsolutist *Ständestaat*. In consequence, the country squires, in their fight against bureaucratic rule without consent, free competition, and equality of opportunity, called for the restoration of the ancient provincial estates. Presenting themselves as "the most valuable class," they reintroduced into the political debate the idea of having a legal, historically rooted right to cogovernment and especially to a definite share in legislation. They invoked the Recesses of the Diets of 1540 and 1653 as if they were still current law. They advanced the thesis that old laws could be changed only through "contractual" agreement between the crown and the provincial estates. They questioned the legitimacy of the central government's authority and hence challenged the legality of measures passed by executive decree. They revived the old battle against administrative law.

In this reactionary struggle Old Prussian noblemen turned to theoretical reflection and doctrinal self-clarification. Their views of liberty, authority, law, justice, and morality were colored by their social status and historic inheritance. Like the French *parlements* and *noblesse*, in 1787–1788, the Junker sponsors of ideological regrouping made effective use of the most up-to-date intellectual means. Thereby they gave modern expression to political objectives which were intimately linked to antiquated historical traditions.[28]

The leaders of the "counterrevolution," men like Marwitz, Knesebeck, Prittwitz, Finckenstein, and Dohna, were incapable of producing a political theory and social philosophy of their own. They were, however, adaptable and efficient borrowers who embraced the antirevolutionary gospel of political Romanticism, including its irrational mysticism, complemented by tenets from Protestant pietism and Lutheran orthodoxy. The basic stock of their ideas they took, first, from Burke, Adam Müller, and Gentz; after 1815, also from Ludwig von Haller, the Swiss-German jurist, and, a little later, from Julius Stahl, a baptized Bavarian Jew.

Like Stein, the liberal conservative, whose basic theoretical views came close to those of the most articulate doctrinal crusaders of the "counterrevolution" and who, after 1815, joined the conservatives even in political battle, they were ardent admirers of a romanticized version of English constitutionalism. Noninterference by the bureaucratic state and the strengthening of a decentralized system of noble self-government they regarded as the quintessence of political liberty. This was the time to denounce the dangers of "bureaucratic despotism" and to assail its upholders, "the revolutionists in Prussia," for looking upon "the excellent English constitution, but with French, that is, with merely administrative eyes." Now the Junkers, deeply concerned about their liberties, thundered against the attempt of "the revolutionary administration" to "trample underfoot the

[28] See Karl Mannheim, "Das konservative Denken," *Archiv für Sozialwissenschaft und Sozialpolitik*, LVII (1927), 68–142, 470–495; *idem, Ideology and Utopia* (New York, 1936), 33, 107, 207ff., 245; Alfred von Martin, "Weltanschauliche Motive im altkonservativen Denken," in *Deutscher Staat und deutsche Parteien* (Munich, 1922), 342–384; *idem*, "Der preussische Altkonservatismus und der politische Katholizismus," *Deutsche Vierteljahrsschrift für Literaturwissenschaft und Geistesgeschichte*, VII (1929), 489–514.

most sublime form and guarantees of freedom, the corporative estates."[29]

Although the champions of "right versus tyranny and arbitrariness" purported to fight not so much for their "interests," but rather for high "principles" and lofty "ideals," they considered themselves "realists" in contrast to the "idealistic" and "utopian" reformers, with their "false" concepts of liberty, equality, and authority. Not all, however, argued their case in abstract terms. According to the mournful forebodings of some, "elegance with all its graces would perish from the earth, unless one makes sure that by far the largest part of the national wealth remains in the hands of the nobility."[30] Rank-and-file Junkers, as distinct from the well-educated few, were even more specific in spelling out the social function of the doctrinal glorification of "true liberty" and divinely ordained social inequality. As a group of clumsy Pomeranian squires summed up the situation: "Our estates will turn into a hell for us if independent peasant owners are our neighbors."[31]

In political action, the ideology of reactionary conservatism was a powerful aid, first, in the stubborn defense of accustomed prerogatives and, then, in the aggressive drive for additional privilege. To Niebuhr the principles of the "Old Prussian party" were but "the cloak of an altogether heartless selfishness."[32] Hardenberg characterized his adversaries as men who pretended "to speak as intermediaries for the people, while, in reality, they merely fight for their privileges to the detriment of the people."[33] Even Ranke who did not easily find fault with members of the Prussian ruling class eventually arrived at the conclusion that among the nobles were

[29] Quoted in Friedrich Lenz, *Agrarlehre und Agrarpolitik der deutschen Romantik* (Berlin, 1912), 37. See also Adalbert Bezzenberger, ed., *Aktenstücke des Provinzialarchivs in Königsberg aus den Jahren 1786–1820* (Königsberg, 1898), 29–52.

[30] Hans Albert Freiherr von S...., *Apologie des Adels* (Berlin, 1807), 114.

[31] G. F. Knapp, *Bauernbefreiung*, 2d ed., II, 274.

[32] Adolf Trende, ed., *Forschungen zur internationalen Finanz- und Bankgeschichte* (Berlin, 1929), 81.

[33] F. Meusel, *Friedrich August Ludwig von der Marwitz*, II, part 2, 25.

some "who identified their obligation to obey with the preservation of their privileges."[34]

The recalcitrance of the squirearchy, in its great trial of strength with the bureaucracy, paid a substantial dividend, as reflected in the course of state legislation and in the government's handling of the land problem and of servile tenure. The resistance movement was successful in enforcing significant revisions of government bills before they were enacted. This happened in the case of Hardenberg's agrarian Edict of September, 1811. But political pressure from "below" also led to frequent amendments of the laws already made. Thus, for instance, while keeping intact the abolition of hereditary personal subjection, all existing types of rent, dues, fees, and labor services incumbent in servile tenure were reconfirmed for the smaller peasants with hereditary holdings. Furthermore, the counter-revolution was potent enough to thwart legislative plans altogether, to prevent the execution of laws, and to enforce the formal revocation of others. Such, for example, was the fate of the important *Gendarmerie-Edikt* of 1812 which aimed at the transformation of the Prussian *Landrat* into a sort of French subprefect and at the "nationalization" of police administration by replacing on the rural local level the patrimonial private jurisdictions with the public state.

The Prussian bureaucracy, engaged in a two-front war against the autocratic powers of the monarch and the oligarchic powers of the squirearchy, consolidated its victory over the crown by making far-reaching concessions to the landed aristocracy. Under bureaucratic absolutism the Junkers regained, in effect, though in altered forms, the substance of the political *Ständestaat* privileges which had been expropriated from them in the age of royal dominance. This restoration of effective cogovernment, supported by influential court camarillas in the generations to come, was a most valuable addition to the civic and fiscal privileges, economic power, rights of local government, and high social status which the squires had retained throughout.

The Hohenzollerns had built dynastic absolutism on compromise

---

[34] L. von Ranke, *Denkwürdigkeiten des Staatskanzlers Fürsten von Hardenberg*, IV (Leipzig, 1877), 244.

with the Junkers. Bureaucratic absolutism, too, came to rest on a working alliance with the large landowners. The purpose of this alliance was the perpetuation of rulership by aristocratic elites. Its primary political function was to hold down and to divert liberal and democratic movements. Even Wilhelm von Humboldt came to adopt the view that privileged landed property and old style corporative political representation were particularly appropriate "safeguards against democracy."[35]

By 1815, the political hegemony of the bureaucracy, flushed with victory in the War of Liberation, was firmly established, although its wings had been clipped by the squirearchy. What followed was the process of consummation. As the holder of unaccountable government authority and as the professional governors of the modernized authoritarian state, the administrative elite reached the zenith of its historic career during the generation from 1815 to 1848. It was the chief bearer of positive political power in the community.

Like most of the landed aristocrats, most of the bureaucratic aristocrats of this period considered it a salient part of their mission to "bridle the masses," to "keep the mass of the people divided and under observation."[36] The two partners, being authoritarian power groups, had a common interest in keeping the Prussian people almost free from acquiring political experience and in preventing the state from becoming more than the expression of the conscience and will of the privileged classes. Claiming for themselves a monopoly of political wisdom, they were apt to regard as impertinent any serious criticism that came from "the lower orders." Some energy, therefore, had to be devoted to the suppression of liberal and radical "demagogues," and to the upsetting task of curbing the flow of "seditious" ideas.

Not yet seriously perturbed by the problems of a rising industrial society and not yet bothered by the restraints which the introduction

[35] Wilhelm Richter, ed., *Wilhelm von Humboldts Politische Briefe*, II (Berlin, 1936), 293.

[36] F. Meusel, *Friedrich August Ludwig von der Marwitz*, II, part 1, 196ff. See also Adolph Heller, *Preussen, der Beamtenstaat* (Mannheim, 1844), 162ff.; Joseph Hansen, *Rhein. Briefe*, I, 201, 204–05, 219; II, 34; Kurt Wolzendorf, *Der Polizeigedanke des modernen Staats* (Breslau, 1918), 101–113.

16

of constitutionally limited government was to impose upon their powers in 1848, the members of the higher civil state service as yet saw little reason for doubting their abiding preëminence in the polity. Nor did they feel tempted to question the solidity of an administrative system which, greatly improved in personnel, ethos, technical efficiency, and public utility, had remained a mirror of the aristocratic social order. In the words of a reformed reformer: "We live in the happy tranquillity of absolutism to the great disgust of the proponents of constitutional government."[37] This was the classical age of Prussian bureaucratic absolutism, strictly speaking. It calls for further description and analysis—at some other time.

[37] Stägemann to Olfers, April 9, 1832, in Franz Rühl, ed., *Briefe und Aktenstücke zur Geschichte Preussens unter Friedrich Wilhelm III*, III (Leipzig, 1902), 494.

Index

Absolutism, vii–viii, 5, 8, 11–14, 17–
20, 22–23, 27–28, 35, 37, 39, 42,
45–48, 69–71, 87, 109, 122–123, 134–
137, 150–154, 159, 168–169, 173,
175, 187, 189, 191, 194, 198–199,
201–202, 208–210, 222, 226–227
Administration, central, 3–6, 10–13,
31, 37–39, 68–69, 96, 99, 116, 126–
127, 130, 167–169, 171, 173–174, 209,
223, see also Centralization, General
Directory, Ministers; provincial, 39,
52–53, 69, 96, 98–99, 116, 131, 133,
167, 169–170, see also Boards of War
and Domains, Estates as political
bodies, Ständestaat; local, 3, 11–12,
28–31, 39, 41–43, 45, 48, 53, 60, 69,
78, 126, 130–131, 135, 166–167, 169,
195, 219, 224, 226, see also City
administration, Seignioral jurisdictions
Administrative law, see Law, public
Administrative systems, 1–3, 6, 12–14,
37–38, 47–48, 50–51, 87, 133, 151,
171
Agrarian policy and legislation, 29, 43,
131, 195–196, 214, 218, 226
Altenstein, Karl Freiherr von Stein
zum, 203, 213, 218
Alvensleben family, 164
Argentina, ix
Aristocracy, general, vii, 10, 17–19, 23–
24, 51–52, 73, 87, 102, 113, 125, 130,
137–138, 154, 156–159, 182–184, 186,
201, 211, 217–220, 222, 227–228, see
also Bureaucracy, relations to aristocratic groups; intellectual and artistic, 41–42, 123, 182–187, 200, 214;
landed, vii–viii, 10, 16, 18–19,
28–34, 48, 58, 71–72, 114, 119, 135,
153–154, see also Junkers; political,
vii–viii, 8, 10, 13–14 18–19, 23,
31–33, 54–55, 71–73, 109, 122–123,

133–139, 141–142, 150–154, 156–159,
217–218, 226–228, see also Bureaucracy, political activity, Bureaucratic nobility, Junkers, Ständestaat;
Austrian, 43–44, 119, 140, 153;
British, 31, 51–52, 164, 190, 194;
French, 16, 43–44, 134–136, 140–
142, 146, 154, 173, 187, 203–204,
224; Polish, 146, 166–167, 170; Russian, 44, 119, 141–142, 146, 154;
Swedish, 44; ennoblements, 16, 62,
81, 106–107, 119, 122, 124, 128, 139–
142, 147–148, 153, 160–162
Armies, 12, 33, 36, 47, 102; Prussian
army and officers, 35–38, 40, 51,
59–61, 63–66, 69–71, 79, 83–86,
102–104, 109, 118, 120–122, 124–
125, 129, 139, 144–146, 152, 155, 157,
159–160, 162, 164–166, 176, 200, 204,
208, 211, 214–217
Arnim-Boytzenburg, Friedrich Abraham Wilhelm Graf von, 212
Arnim-Boytzenburg, Georg Dietloff
von, 125–127, 132
Auerswald, Hans Jakob von, 213
Austria, see Habsburg monarchy
Authoritarianism, vii–viii, 11–14, 17–
20, 22–23, 25, 45–46, 48, 137, 173,
194, 205 207–210, 222, 227–228,
see also Absolutism, Dictatorships,
Law, public, Totalitarianism
Autocracy, see Absolutism, Authoritarianism

Baillis and sénéchaux, 3
Barfuss, Hans Albrecht Graf von, 62
Bavaria, 37
Berlin, 41, 69, 116, 125, 149, 183
Beyme, Karl Friedrich, 198
Bischoffwerder, Johann Rudolf von,
197